Royal Horticultural Society

GROW FOR FLAVOUR

GEEK SPEAK, TRANSLATED

For an obsessive botanist like me, delving through thousands of scientific papers and trialling all manner of cutting-edge horticultural techniques has been an epic amount of fun.

Translating these mountains of academic geek-speak into a book of simple, real-world techniques that the most novice gardener can master, however, is not without its challenges. The simple fact is that, even with quadruple-tested recipes, results will vary according to a huge number of factors. Even the very nature of what constitutes 'good' flavour is subjective, so I am the first to hold up my hands to say that there will be a certain amount of unavoidable personal bias here.

Academic journal entry this book is not, nor is it meant to be a textbook for agricultural engineers. Instead, it is an interpreted, evidence-based guide for foodie gardeners looking to score better-tasting harvests, no matter who they are or where they live.

Royal
Horticultural
Society

GROW FOR
FLAVOUR

JAMES WONG

Photography by Jason Ingram

Illustrations by Toby Leigh

MITCHELL BEAZLEY

CONTENTS

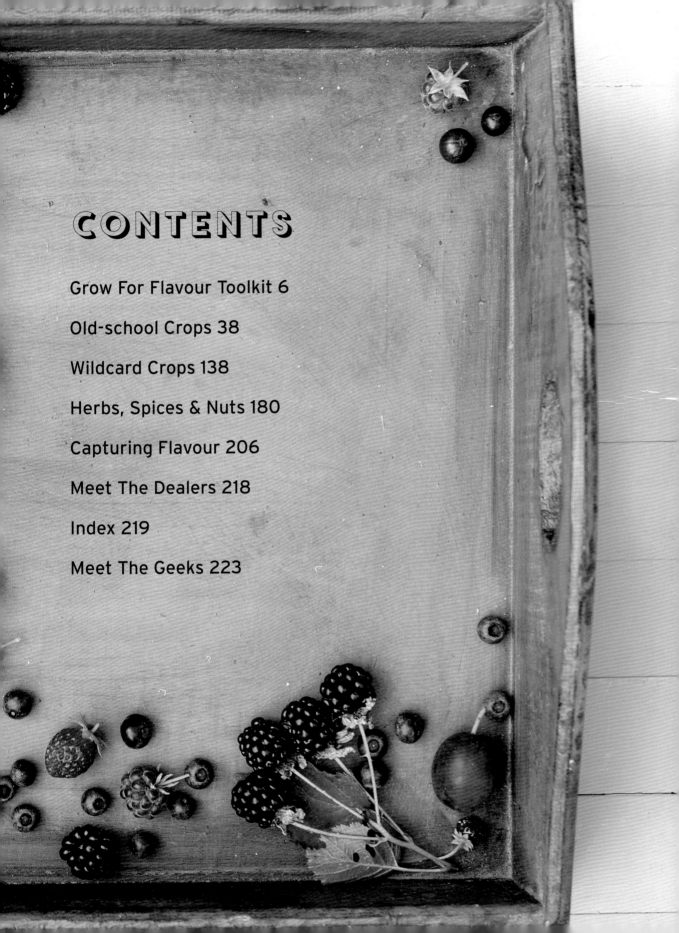

GROW FOR FLAVOUR TOOLKIT

GROWING THE WONG WAY

'Home-grown *always* tastes better than shop bought.'

Does this sound a familiar promise to you? These, or words to a similar effect, seem to be the compulsory opening line to every article on growing fruit and veg that has been written in the last 20 years. To me as a scientist, however, there's just one problem with them: they are not necessarily true.

In fact, once you take into the account the 'I grew it, therefore it must taste better' placebo, *many* home-grown crops in reality taste pretty much the same as (if not sometimes worse than) their supermarket counterparts. I'm looking at you, celery, swedes and cabbages.

To me, the shocking thing is that a lot of standard gardening advice (essentially lifted from 19th-century agricultural practices) actually conspires to water down crop flavour in the all-consuming pursuit of yield above all else. As a final blow to a foodie grower's morale, many of the horticultural rules we adhere to with slavish devotion are often either based on pure myth or have only limited scientific basis. But this does not have to be the case!

In this book I aim to turn the tables on conventional gardening advice, using the latest scientific research to allow it to live up to its No. 1 promise: delivering truly unsurpassed flavour. This unique, research-based approach ditches the traditional obsession with maximizing yield and can not only measurably improve the flavour of your crops, but could also dramatically reduce your workload, banish gluts and even boost the nutritional content of your harvest. Think of it as growing for maximum flavour and minimum labour, with some cutting-edge science to back it up. And I'll be busting some of the longest-held gardening myths along the way.

Following these principles could quite genuinely give you tomatoes that are more than 150 percent sweeter, strawberries with 100 times the aroma compounds, chillies with double the fire power and beetroots with three times less earthiness. My approach, devised after an extensive review of more than 2,000 scientific papers in journals from around the globe, aims to piece together the latest research on how variety choice and growing techniques can affect crop flavour, translating academic geek-speak into a simple set of tips and tricks that anyone can do.

I have personally tried and tasted the crops grown under this system and dozens of varieties were trialled at RHS Garden Wisley in Surrey. These crops might not give you record-breaking yields. They might not give you perfectly blemish-free, symmetrical harvests. They might not follow the rules your granddad taught you. But they will almost certainly guarantee you flavour that is second to none – plus some very funny looks from the allotment old guard. So let's get started!

GROWING MYTH NO.1
HOME-GROWN ALWAYS TASTES BETTER

WHY WHAT TASTES GOOD, DOES

Ever thought that fish and chips taste better with a wedge of lemon? Well, believe it or not, that's millions of years of evolution guiding you instinctively to add the antibacterial chemical citric acid to kill the harmful germs that produce unpleasant 'fishy' aromas. Depending on where in the world you were brought up it might not be lemons you reach for but chilli, tamarind, vinegar, wasabi, ginger or soy sauce instead. Yet all of these contain antibacterial substances that, like lemon juice, help combat 'off' flavours and in so doing render the flesh safer to eat.

Even the Inuit, who have access to very few plant-based condiments, will ferment fish until its levels of antibacterial acetic acid peak before adding it to fresh fish as a germ-fighting seasoning. Whoever you are and wherever you live, the rawer and fishier your fillet, the more antibacterial agents you are likely to add.

In fact, our entire perception of good flavour is a complex collaboration between our senses of taste, smell and touch that has developed to perform two simple functions: **keeping potentially harmful stuff out of our mouth, while allowing the good stuff in.** This elaborate chemical detector has evolved over millions of years to be capable of sensing and evaluating thousands of substances, helping filter potentially toxic or germ-filled elements out of our diets, while causing us to seek those high in energy and nutrients. **It is no coincidence that most dangerous toxins taste overwhelmingly bitter** (a flavour most humans find unpleasant), while most high-calorie, safe-to-eat foods in nature taste sugary sweet. We rarely stop to question why we select, combine, prepare or cook ingredients the way we do, but at the root of all of these activities is the instinctual drive to consume safe, nutritious food. **Far from being based on independent choice, the science of good taste is largely hard-wired into our genes.**

HANG ON, ISN'T FLAVOUR SUBJECTIVE?

While there are, of course, distinctions in flavour preferences between individuals and cultures, **the chemicals that are generally perceived as tasting pleasant actually vary very little across the globe.** For example, even the infamous durian fruit of Southeast Asia, whose fetid odour has long been cited by Westerners as the perfect example of a culturally acquired taste, derives its flavour from the same group of sulphur compounds, including antioxidants and essential amino acids, that give European food staples like Camembert cheese their aroma. A scent, ironically, that many Southeast Asians perceive as gut-wrenchingly awful.

In fact, it is not just the chemicals themselves, but also their concentrations that we seem to have a more or less universal preference for. **Taste tests, for example, show that adults around the world prefer the taste of liquids sweetened in the narrow range of 8–10 percent sugar.** This happens to be the same amount as is contained in our most popular fruit crops, suggesting an evolutionary basis for the preference. It is no coincidence that this is also the exact same concentration used by most soft drinks manufacturers. **The preference range between other major tastes is even more narrow,** for while total salt consumption in Japan, for example, may be markedly higher than in much of Western Europe, the concentration used in most recipes hovers broadly around the same point. Research by US neuroscientists has gone even further, suggesting that the perfect 50:50 ratio of fat and sugar found in many processed foods is far more appealing than any other combination of the two substances. Their tests revealed that this precise formula fired up the brain's pleasure centres in a similar way to drugs like cocaine and heroin and was equally addictive. It seems that, despite what we perceive as wide variations in flavour preference, in the context of all the possible substances we could consume and the quantities in which we consume them, **our perception of 'good' flavour is pretty universal.** This is why most people would prefer a slice of blueberry pie to a plateful of twigs, soil and pine bark - molecular gastronomists aside.

Exception 1: The Herb Of Evil!

Loving or hating coriander is genetically determined, explaining its divisive effect at dinner parties. A range of studies from around the world has suggested that sensible people like me possess a copy of the OR6A2 gene that causes us to perceive coriander not as bright and citrusy, but as soapy and bleach-like. Unfortunately, us coriander-phobics are in the minority (roughly 20 percent of the population), condemning us to a lifetime of picking it off our plates at Asian restaurants. **Believe me, you can *try* to like it, but your genes will resist.**

Exception 2: Instinctive Medicine?

Anthropological studies of some African populations have revealed that there is a genetic association between people's sensitivity to bitter flavours and the local incidence of malaria. According to researchers at the University of Pennsylvania, this trait may have evolved to encourage the consumption of bitter plants that contain antibacterial or immune-enhancing substances that confer some protection against the disease.

These are, however, exceptions to the general rule that the notion of what tastes good is pretty universal.

ANATOMY OF THE PERFECT STRAWBERRY

So, what do you need to do to make your harvests tastier? Scientists have developed a loose formula that, according to taste panels around the world, will universally up the perceived flavour of any crop. All you need to do is raise the levels of sugars, acids and aroma chemicals while simultaneously reducing the amounts of pungent or bitter flavours and fibre they contain. Need more convincing? Here's theory in action.

SUPERMARKET STAPLE

'Elsanta' strawberries dominate the supermarket shelves of Northern Europe and have frequently incurred the foodies' wrath for their poor perceived flavour.

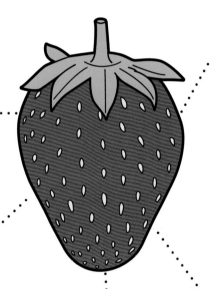

LOW SUGAR

In almost every taste test the higher a crop's sugar content, the better its tasting score. Indeed, with most fruit and veg it seems like there is no upper limit to how much added sweetness will improve their flavour ranking. No wonder 'Elsanta', with its meagre average of 6 percent sugar, is so unpopular.

LOW ACID

Lacking sugar wouldn't be so bad if the fruit was rich in acid, as tart fruit – although not great for eating raw – make excellent candidates for jam. That is why fruit varieties bred for cooking, such as Bramley apples, generally have large amounts of acid to offset the avalanche of sugar that is added to pies, jellies and jams. Sadly, lack of sugar and lack of acids simply creates what many people describe as a weak, watery flavour.

LOW AROMA CHEMICALS

'Elsanta' is known for producing only modest amounts of aromatic chemicals. To me, this is a huge demerit as these are the most important group of all to create good flavour. After all, anyone can add extra sugar or acids like lemon juice or vinegar to a dish to improve its flavour, but the complex fragrance of freshly picked strawberries or sun-ripened tomatoes is almost impossible to fake.

HIGH(ER) FIBRE

Dense fibres in the flesh create the firm texture needed to handle packing, handling and storage. But this same property gives the fruit a hard, crunchy texture. Sound familiar?

HIGH(ER) BITTER, SPICY, EARTHY OR 'OFF' FLAVOURS

When stored in a modified atmosphere, inert gases help greatly extend the shelf life of many shop-bought strawberries. But research has consistently shown that this also creates a spike in chemicals known to result in 'off' flavours, such as ethyl acetate – a substance also found in nail polish remover. Nice!

HOME-GROWN HERO

'Snow White' strawberries are a new gourmet introduction, loved by top chefs and consistently ranked as one of the best flavoured in taste panels.

70% MORE SUGAR

A sky-high sugar content of over 10 percent puts 'Snow White' near the top of the range: sweeter than Coca-Cola and containing over 70 percent more sugar than 'Elsanta' on average. Health freaks, don't panic! The best news is that growing techniques that up the amount of sugar in your crops generally have the knock-on effect of sending the aroma compounds and nutrients, including key antioxidants, soaring.

30% MORE ACID

With 30 percent more acid than 'Elsanta' on average, these have a bright spritz of tartness that balances out their high sugar content. Even given their sweetness, without this crucial acidity the fruit could be perceived as having a bland, 'flat' flavour. As your tongue detects acids, your saliva glands ramp up their production to balance out the pH of your mouth, which also makes foods appear juicier AND more refreshing.

2x THE AROMATIC COMPOUNDS

Containing up to a whopping 2x the aromatic compounds of 'Elsanta', 'Snow White' is famous for its knock-out fragrance, including hints of kiwi, pineapple and candyfloss.

Aroma chemicals are crucial as scientists estimate that only 20 percent of flavour is experienced by your sense of taste alone, with the vast majority perceived instead through smell as the aromatic compounds waft up the back of your throat and up your nose. The effect is so great that, if you close your eyes and pop a peg on your nose, slices of apples and onions are almost indistinguishable.

LOWER FIBRE

Generally speaking, the less tough and stringy fibres your crops contain, the more people will enjoy eating them. A soft, tender texture allows the flavour chemicals to be liberated more easily from the cells of the plants, making them taste more rich and intense. For most fruit crops this won't be too much of an issue, but for leaf crops this could turn almost inedible living fibreboard into sweet, succulent salad.

SHOULD WE BE MAKING CROPS SWEETER?

Sugar has had an awful lot of bad press lately. So should we really be aiming for sweeter fruit and veg? Well, yes and no (in my non-dietician's opinion).

There are two main factors that determine the sweetness of fruit and vegetables: the concentration of sugar within their cells versus the amount of pungent sour or bitter-tasting chemicals that can mask its sweetness.

UPPING SUGARS

Most horticultural practices that up sugar content do so either by directly increasing the plant's production of the sweet stuff itself, or by reducing the amount of water in crops, making the existing sweetness more concentrated. Both these practices tend to boost the concentration of pretty much all the chemicals in a plant's tissues, including aroma compounds, vitamins, minerals and antioxidants. In fact, sugar paradoxically is often the key building block plants use to create these health-promoting chemicals in the first place, making for harvests that are not just sweeter, but also more nutrient-dense. According to a number of trials, these very substances might even help offset the negative health effects of excess sugar consumption. Happy days!

LOWERING PUNGENCY

To me, the problems potentially arise when the sweetness in crops is improved not by upping sugars, but by reducing their content of sour and bitter chemicals, many of which are key nutrients, in order to bring the sensation of sweetness to the fore. Many famously sugary varieties like 'supersweet' onions and sweet cherries do not necessarily contain more sugar than their 'sour' or 'pungent' counterparts – they just have less of any other substances that may disguise this flavour. To me, this prioritization of sugar at the expense of other potential nutrients, although often offering tastier results, is worrying. However, it is worth pointing out that the total amount of sugar in these crops can remain largely unchanged from that in their 'non-sweet' alternatives.

I can't help but think, rather than fretting too much about sugars in fresh home-grown fruit and veg, that we should perhaps focus on not overindulging in chips, burgers and fizzy drinks. **Or is that too obvious?**

BETTER FLAVOUR CAN ALSO MEAN BETTER NUTRITION!

To me, the best thing about growing for flavour is that pretty much all horticultural tricks that improve crop quality also result in increased nutritional value. It's not often that greedy indulgence and health-guru virtue go hand in hand, now is it? Let me explain...

Take tomatoes as a classic example. Research by US biochemists, published in the journal *Science*, has shown that all the important flavour and aroma chemicals in this much-loved fruit are actually derived from, in their own words, 'essential nutrients and health-promoting compounds'. They are chemicals produced by plants that humans have evolved to hone in on to identify foods rich in essential nutrients, as well as substances with valuable antimicrobial, antioxidant and anti-carcinogenic activity. **Put simply, the more flavourful a tomato/strawberry/cherry/ grape is, the higher its nutritional value is likely to be.**

Some of these chemicals are obvious ones like sugar (the ultimate source of almost instant energy) and ascorbic acid (aka vitamin C), which contribute to the pleasant tartness of many foods. Others are a little more unexpected. **Some compounds, such as methyl salicylate, which gives tomatoes some of their leafy, herbal notes, work like aspirin to thin the blood and reduce inflammation.** The aromatic substances responsible for their rosy, fruity scent work in an even more indirect way. Produced from the breakdown of phytonutrients known as carotenoids, the intense fragrance of tomatoes is an excellent indicator of their concentration of these health-promoting compounds.

> Researchers at the University of Florida have shown that all the important flavour chemicals in tomatoes actually derive from key nutrients and health-promoting compounds.

There Is Always A Catch

There are, however, some notable exceptions to this rule. **Generally, people will seek out the tenderest harvests, selecting those crops that are lowest in healthful fibre.** This is a hangover from our days as hunter-gatherers, when pretty much all food was stuffed full of indigestible levels of fibre and when consuming only the youngest, softest shoots was essential to meeting our energy needs. The problem is that, through the last 20,000 years of devising ever more ingenious ways to select, breed and process fibre out of our food, we have become a little too successful at reducing our intake.

We have also become rather adept at removing bitterness from our diet, and not without good reason. **Most toxins have a bitter flavour, so we have evolved to be sensitive to this taste.** Babies and young children will universally reject bitter foods – including ones some adults love, such as broccoli and Brussels sprouts – to protect themselves instinctively from potential poisoning. The curious thing about most toxins is that they are dose-dependent, being dangerous at high levels but often having health benefits such as antibacterial, anti-inflammatory or antioxidant activity in small quantities. **It is precisely the bitter chemicals in watercress, broccoli, red wine and tea, for example, that are the phytonutrients behind their so-called 'superfood' status.**

MY GOAL

The goal of this book is not to boss you around and tell you what to eat; it is simply to advise you on how to grow crops with qualities that most people would perceive as being tasty. The way I see it, if this happens to come with improved health benefits, that is just a pretty great bonus.

Throughout, however, I will be pointing out simple tips and tricks that could improve your crops' nutritional value, even if that is at odds with mass flavour appeal. This way you can make up your own mind on how you want to grow.

WHY TOMATOES DON'T TASTE LIKE THEY USED TO

From tomatoes to strawberries, commercial crops of all sorts have attracted criticism over the years for their perceived decrease in flavour, and frankly often with good merit. The problem is not that agricultural science can't figure out how to produce a tastier tomato, but that sadly there has often been little incentive for growers to do so. Let me explain...

THE GROWERS' PARADOX

The customers of most farmers are not you and me, but powerful intermediaries such as supermarkets. As clients, they have until very recently been largely unconcerned with taste or nutrition, paying growers exclusively by the weight of crops they produce, demanding with this the longest possible shelf life, an immaculate appearance and the ability to withstand industrial washing and packing. Flavour and nutrition, if they feature at all, have historically often come right at the bottom of this long list of requirements.

In fact, **reading through hundreds of scientific trials in the research for this book, I found pages of detailed experiments and ingenious advice on how to create firmer, less blemished, shinier, more standard-shaped crops, without reading a single mention of flavour.** In the case of commercial herb growing, some papers even pointed out the ability of certain techniques to maintain the fresh appearance of herbs that had long since lost much of their flavour as a positive benefit! When I was filming on a leek farm a few years ago, a farmer proudly showed me his trial grounds of hundreds of new leek varieties – part of a breeding programme to find the perfectly uniform leek that would fit more easily into the machinery that seals 'multibuy' packets together. Shockingly, among well over 200 promising new varieties, not a single one had actually ever been tasted. But, hey, I can confirm they looked 3D-printer perfect.

Unsurprisingly, many of these developments have come at the expense of both flavour and nutrition, particularly in the arena of crop breeding. **Larger crops have often been created by pumping them with more water to swell their size and increase their firmness, diluting their flavour.** Cherries, for example, are frequently heavily irrigated before picking to swell their fruit with moisture, upping their harvest weight and extending their shelf life, while in the process watering down their flavour. In some countries, plum growers have even experimented with spraying their crops with putrecine, the chemical that gives rotting flesh its odour, to make them more resistant to damage from picking and handling. Sadly, this practice significantly reduces their sugar,

vitamin and antioxidant content. **Longer shelf life has also been achieved by picking fruit unripe before it has a chance to develop its normal levels of sugars and aroma chemicals, as well as by chilling and packing to arrest development.** Intense breeding work has been guided by desire for thicker, chewier skins and harder texture to make tomatoes that will sit happily on the shelf for weeks, not hours, before going bad.

In short, the paradox of modern commercial growing from a foodie's point of view is that the brightest minds in agricultural engineering, crop breeding and commercial horticulture have often until recently been paid to create crops of worse eating quality. Just imagine what our food would taste like if the same horticultural geniuses had been driven by flavour!

GROW LIKE A SUGAR BEET FARMER

Traditionally, one of the few crops where farmers are paid a premium for the flavour of their harvest is sugar beets. This is because sugar manufacturers are less preoccupied with the shape and size of the beets themselves, and more with the purity and concentration of the sugars within them. This has triggered up to a fivefold increase in the sugariness of beets in the last century.

IS THE NUTRITIONAL VALUE OF OUR FOOD DECLINING?

A number of scientific studies have reported a marked reduction over the past 60 years in the nutritional content of a variety of major crops, which have been attributed to the widely cited phenomenon known as the 'dilution effect'. This theory states that as crop yields increase, their content of vitamins and minerals (many of which give them their characteristic flavour) tend to decrease.

In one pioneering British study researchers compared the mineral compositions of historical collections of British wheat grain over a 160-year period. They noted that, while between 1845 and the mid-1960s the zinc, iron, copper and magnesium remained stable, since that period each of these minerals had shown a significant decrease. **The fall coincided with the introduction of new high-yielding cultivars.**

A US study published in *Journal of the Science of Food and Agriculture* also sought to compare older, low-yielding wheat cultivars with more productive modern hybrids, by growing them alongside each other. Echoing the British findings, their results concluded that the **minerals iron, zinc and selenium have seen a reduction following the introduction of high-yielding varieties**.

A similar trend has been noted in three recent studies which compared historical nutritional composition data for a wide range of fruits and vegetables, in both the UK and North America. Their findings suggest that fresh produce on both sides of the Atlantic showed a marked drop - between 5 and 40 percent - in some (but not all) of their major nutrients between the 1930s and 1980s.

According to Dr Donald Davis, a biochemist at the University of Texas at Austin, who found falls in several of the key nutrients of 43 garden crops: 'Emerging evidence suggests that when you select for yield, crops grow bigger and faster, but they don't necessarily have the ability to make or uptake nutrients at the same, faster rate.' Although quick to point out that further research was needed, he remarked: 'More worrisome would be declines in nutrients we could not study because they were not reported in 1950 - magnesium, zinc, vitamin B-6, vitamin E and dietary fibre, not to mention phytochemicals.'

THE GOOD NEWS

Fortunately, in recent years and in response to increasing consumer pressure, commercial growers have finally been given incentives to start improving not only the yield, but also the nutritional and eating quality of their crops.

Several breeding programmes have begun to create crops like broccoli, strawberries and tomatoes with higher nutritional value. **Tomato growers, traditionally the focus of much foodie rage, have made major changes in the way they grow their crops**, investing in techniques to improve fruit quality, with phenomenal results. In the words of one large tomato grower: 'People are now willing to pay that little bit extra for improved taste and quality, which means we can afford to focus on flavour like never before. It is so exciting!'

The upswing of this new scientific interest in improving flavour and nutritional value is that hundreds of trials have been carried out around the world, many of them directly applicable to even the tiniest backyard plots. Freed from the need to maximize yields, extend shelf life and produce crops out of season, **home growers armed with this information are arguably in the best position of all to create truly jaw-droppingly tasty harvests**. This book is designed to show you exactly how to do this.

0

THE NUMBER OF TIMES THE WORDS 'FLAVOUR' AND 'TASTE' WERE USED IN THE US DEPARTMENT OF AGRICULTURE'S 2014 ACTION PLAN FOR CROP BREEDING.

FLAVOUR GROWING: THE GROUND RULES

A huge array of horticultural factors can determine how tasty your harvest will be, including everything from sunlight and soil type to watering, pruning and even the presence of certain microbes. No, really!

Research into exactly how to tweak each of these factors to manipulate the hundreds of chemicals that influence crop flavour is still in its infancy. But we hort geeks have already discovered a range of super-simple techniques that have been scientifically demonstrated measurably to boost the eating quality of fruit and veg. Here's my guide to the top seven factors that influence flavour.

NURTURE
FLAVOUR FACTOR 1: VARIETY CHOICE

All Crops Are Not Born Equal

In the great nature-nurture debate, trial after trial has shown that far and away the single most important factor in determining crop flavour is genetics. This dictates everything from how much sugar a plant is capable of producing to the aromas it can conjure up and in what proportion, irrespective of its growing environment. **Think of it this way: with enough make-up, stylists and airbrushing, anyone can look OK in a photo but, let's face it, supermodels were just born beautiful.** The unique genetic make-up of some crops can result in truly spectacular differences between varieties.

SOME SWEET CORN VARIETIES CONTAIN **10x** THE SUGAR OF OTHERS

SOME TOMATO CULTIVARS HAVE **20x** THE ANTIOXIDANT LYCOPENE OF OTHERS

SOME STRAWBERRIES CONTAIN **35x** THE AROMA COMPOUNDS OF OTHERS

The Great Limiting Factor

With concentrations of some tomato aroma chemicals varying up to 3,000-fold between varieties according to researchers at the University of California, trust me when I say that if you get your variety choice right then you are three quarters of the way there. Clever growing techniques can make a good variety even better, but you simply cannot make a rubbish variety taste great.

Heirloom Varieties Don't Always Taste Better

Despite what die-hard romanticists will tell you, the age of a variety does not go hand-in-hand with its flavour. OK, many heirloom varieties do indeed taste incredible, being unencumbered by the 20th-century plant-breeders' fetish for the pursuit of disease-resistance and yield. However, **when cutting-edge techniques are directed into seeking out flavour, the results can easily trump any old-school variety.**

Take **'Sungold'** tomatoes or **'Mara de Bois'** strawberries, both famed for knock-out aroma. Their quirky looks and unique taste mean they are often referred to as 'old-fashioned' or 'heritage' types, but they were both actually bred as recently as the 1990s. If that makes them heirlooms, I suddenly feel very old!

Likewise, most heritage pea varieties taste terrible, having been bred in an age before we ate them as young and sweet petits pois and instead stewed them up for hours into the stodge-fest that is pease porridge. Likewise, lovers of sweet corn will know that modern 'supersweet' hybrids can be up to 10 times more sugary than old 'favourites'. **To say that heirlooms always taste better is nothing more than horticultural ageism.**

TRIED & TASTED

Knowing which cultivars offer the best flavour can be tricky. **Seed catalogue descriptions are notoriously biased.** The common idea that heirloom veg are always tastiest is simply untrue, and some of the worst-tasting varieties often come with the most deceptively delicious-sounding names. In fact, without physically trialling dozens of varieties for yourself it is really impossible to know.

Just as well that I have munched my way through hundreds of different varieties to shortlist only the true flavour heavyweights. These are not always the highest yielding, easiest to grow or most pest-resistant, but what I can guarantee is that **every variety in this book has been personally tried and tasted by me to offer what I consider to be truly epic eating quality.**

GROWING MYTH NO.2
HEIRLOOM VARIETIES ALWAYS TASTE BETTER

Don't Grow What You Can Buy

To my mind, by far the most convincing reason to grow your own is the simple fact that it allows you access to a whole world of otherwise 'unbuyable' varieties.

Take, for example, the anthocyanin-supercharged **'Rubel'** blueberries deemed 'too small' by supermarkets, or the deep, melting flesh of **'Morello'** cherries that is just too delicate to cope with being flown across the planet. Even **'Malwina'** strawberries, which have the most incredible fragrance, have been rejected by commercial buyers for being *ehem* 'too red'.

Sadly, however, despite offering mind-boggling choice, **many seed catalogues seem to insist on promoting the exact same varieties that are popular in the shops**, guided by the assumption that home growers want to reproduce exactly what they see on the shelves of the major supermarkets. Trust me, if you set yourself up in competition with the giants growing **'Elsanta'** strawberries and butternut squash, you are unlikely to be convinced by the flavour difference you get.

Catalogue Translator

Have you ever heard of the word 'bijou' used by anyone other than an estate agent? Everyone else says 'tiny'. Well, in much the same way and unbeknown to most newbies, **seed catalogues have their own cryptic code which requires cracking if you are to root out great flavour**. As a very rough guide, if you see the words 'exhibition variety', they translate as large and watery, as do 'huge', 'giant' and 'mammoth'. 'Novelty', 'ornamental' and 'patio' mean they have been bred for looks or small size, not taste. **If the best thing about a variety is its taste, I can assure you this will be proudly emblazoned in the top line.**

What You Won't See In This Book

While I do love fresh peas, new potatoes and sugary parsnips, I must admit I rarely grow them. To get a single serving of peas, I would need to turn over half my tiny garden to growing nothing else. Even the fanciest home-grown 'Jersey Royals' taste, to me, only marginally different to shop-bought. Growing parsnips successfully (in my experience) would require me to be endowed with some kind of superhuman horticultural ability, and do not even get me started on those 'patio aubergines' that are in all the catalogues. After three valiant attempts, I have concluded I have more chance of seeing a unicorn than a bumper crop of aubergines from a pot on my deck.

For me to grow a crop, it needs to taste so unrecognizably different from sad, shop-bought specimens that the mere promise of it makes me want to get out and dig on a cold winter's day. It also has to be practical enough for me to be able to see a harvest come the summer in spite of my unfortunate lack of green fingers.

For this reason you will not see in these pages cabbages, sprouts, everyday onions, summer radishes, aubergines, potatoes, cauliflowers, celery, parsnips, cucumbers or sweet peppers, all of which have failed the horticultural acid test that is my backyard. If you love these and have a burning desire to grow them, please be my guest. It's just that I would feel a bit of a fraud recommending them on the merits of their flavour difference alone.

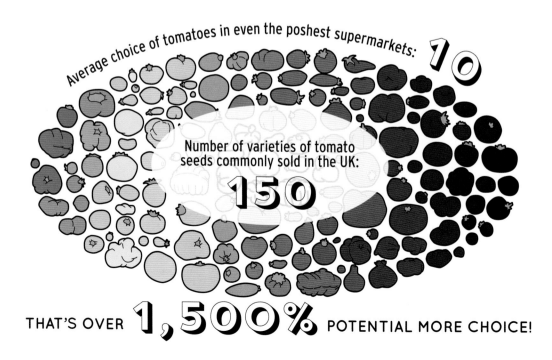

Average choice of tomatoes in even the poshest supermarkets: 10

Number of varieties of tomato seeds commonly sold in the UK: 150

THAT'S OVER 1,500% POTENTIAL MORE CHOICE!

NURTURE

The French, who know more than a little about food, have a wonderful word, *terroir*. This refers to a special set of characteristics such as geology, geography and climate that conspire with a plant's genes to produce its flavour. The same phenomenon was noted by the Chinese for its effect on tea, thousands of years ago. More recent analysis has shown that genetically identical plants grown in different conditions can differ dramatically in their internal chemistry and therefore in their taste.

STRESS IS GOOD

Key among these factors is stress. Most of the aromatic compounds, acids, bitters and spicy chemicals responsible for crop flavour are defence chemicals. Working in ingenious and often unexpected ways, these chemical weapons help plants fight against threats such as insect attack, drought and searing UV light. The more stress a plant is under, the more of these chemicals it will manufacture. Here are just a few examples.

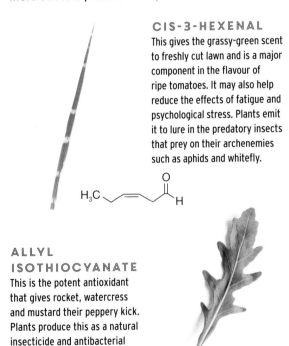

CIS-3-HEXENAL
This gives the grassy-green scent to freshly cut lawn and is a major component in the flavour of ripe tomatoes. It may also help reduce the effects of fatigue and psychological stress. Plants emit it to lure in the predatory insects that prey on their archenemies such as aphids and whitefly.

ALLYL ISOTHIOCYANATE
This is the potent antioxidant that gives rocket, watercress and mustard their peppery kick. Plants produce this as a natural insecticide and antibacterial agent to stave off attack and infections.

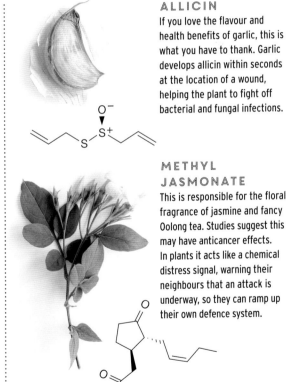

ALLICIN
If you love the flavour and health benefits of garlic, this is what you have to thank. Garlic develops allicin within seconds at the location of a wound, helping the plant to fight off bacterial and fungal infections.

METHYL JASMONATE
This is responsible for the floral fragrance of jasmine and fancy Oolong tea. Studies suggest this may have anticancer effects. In plants it acts like a chemical distress signal, warning their neighbours that an attack is underway, so they can ramp up their own defence system.

MORE STRESS = MORE FLAVOUR *AND* LESS WORK
The raising of defence chemicals means these elite botanical athletes not only taste better, but are also more resilient and easy to grow, giving you maximum flavour for minimum labour. **Plants spoiled by lashings of water and feed, by contrast, are effectively lounging by the pool, cocktail in hand.** They may be larger and lusher, but contain way less of the good stuff. The key to growing for flavour is to introduce just enough stress to maximize the production of these chemicals, without damaging their overall health.

FLAVOUR FACTOR 2: SUNLIGHT

Pretty much all fruit and vegetable crops will not only grow better, but also produce a measurable increase in flavour when grown in full sun. Plants are effectively living solar panels that capture the sun's energy and use it to make sugars, acids, fats and aromas – basically everything that tastes good. In short, with almost every plant in this book, the more light you can get them under the more intense their flavour will be.

Tricks To Catching More Rays

Scientists at the University of Nottingham in England found that doubling the light levels over strawberry plants grown in shade led to a twofold spike in their aroma compounds. Fortunately, even for those without the perfect plot basking in full sunlight unhindered by trees and buildings, there are a few simple ways of giving your plants the maximum amount of light.

Ditch The Glasshouse

Despite being totally transparent to the human eye, **glass can filter out as much as 40 percent of the light available to your plants**, particularly if it's dusty. That's potentially a 40 percent reduction in their sweetness and flavour!

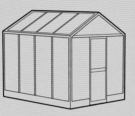

Growing hardy plants outdoors or just keeping glasshouse glass scrupulously clean can dramatically improve how much light they receive.

Reflect It In

Using a pale-coloured gravel on the paths between your beds, or painting the walls and fences of your plot white, will instantly turn them into giant reflectors. This bounces light onto your plants and can result in a noticeable growth spurt. It will also have the rather convenient side effect that your garden will appear larger and brighter even on the dullest days.

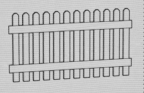

Get Scissor Happy

Ironically, one of the key factors that can block the light from fruit is the tree's own leaves. In fact, research suggests that apples at the top of the tree can be twice as sweet, deeper in colour and even richer in antioxidants as those on the bottom. As with all things in life, there are down sides to going for the low-hanging fruit.

Pruning to create an open, clear canopy will take just a few minutes, allowing more light in to where your crops need it.

Make A Trade-off

Most people will (very logically) reserve the sunniest spot in their garden for a seating area, often to then (very illogically) put up a parasol, trellis or pergola to shade it out.

For dedicated flavour growers, swapping these two features around will give you both better-tasting crops and dispense with the need for sun shelters. OK, so your tan may suffer, but your taste buds won't.

The Exception To The Rules

While higher light levels will absolutely up the flavour intensity of your fruit and veg, in certain leafy crops it will also boost the chemicals responsible for fiery or pungent tastes, which some people find unpleasant. Rocket, kale and dandelion greens, for example, will be stronger and more bitter if grown in full sun at high summer, but milder and sweeter in light shade.

Colour Therapy

Researchers have discovered that it is not just the amount of light, but also its quality that effects plant growth.
Back in the 1990s, studies at Clemson University in South Carolina revealed that the different wavelengths reflected off coloured plastic mulches are capable of both upping yield and dramatically improving flavour.

Trials at both Clemson and Cornell universities found that tomato plants grown through red plastic mulch produced higher yields, with boosts of up to 20 percent over those grown with no mulch. Strawberries echoed this yield increase, producing more aroma and tasting sweeter. Rolls of red plastic mulch can be easily bought online, so why not experiment with this yourself and see if it works for you?

Basil grown over green surfaces in the Clemson University trials produced significantly higher concentrations of aroma and phytonutrient compounds. Simply painting your glasshouse shelf green and popping pots on top of this just might improve their flavour in the same way.

RED

GREEN

Researchers concluded that the light reflected off red and green mulches works by mimicking that bounced off nearby plants. Through sensors in their leaves, crops such as tomatoes and strawberries detect this spectrum of light as evidence of potential competition and react by diverting more energy into growth and reproduction. This simple device seems effectively to 'trick' your plants into creating bigger, tastier fruit. Genius!

SILVER

BLACK

US studies in the 1970s showed that peppers grown over aluminium foil produced 85 percent more fruit, with a dramatically lower incidence of aphid damage. Researchers concluded this was due to the increase in the total amount of light the plants received, with other studies also reporting this to trigger a similar reduction in pests. To mimic this effect, line your glasshouse shelves with a layer of kitchen foil.

Growing outdoor melons through a sheet of traditional black plastic mulch helps heat their roots. Trials show this can cause their fruits to ripen 3-4 weeks earlier and produce higher yields. This is well worth a try and, in soggy summers, it could mean the difference between success and failure. I prefer to use a mulch of black biochar, a by-product of charcoal manufacture that is easier to lay and improves soil texture.

FLAVOUR FACTOR 3: WATERING

Water is necessary for all plant life. However, excessive irrigation is a sure-fire route to less tasty crops. When absorbed through the roots and pumped into the cells of leaves and fruits, water dilutes the concentrations of sugars, vitamins and aroma chemicals within the cells, quite literally watering down their flavour. A dubious reward after hours of battling with the hose.

In fact, most fruit and veg crops actually hail from semi-desert, Mediterranean climates and will tolerate dry conditions far more readily than you might imagine. **Cutting down on the water has frequently been demonstrated to improve crop flavour and nutrient content, particularly in tree fruit, without denting yield.** The sweetness of cherries, grapes, pears and peaches, as well as the sugar content, Vitamin C and antioxidant levels of apples and even the spiciness of chillies, have all been recorded as rising as watering regimes are lowered.

This reduction in irrigation also prevents rampant leaf growth, which can divert resources away from the fruit and shade out the sunlight from reaching them. Winemakers believe a restricted water supply forces the roots of vines to delve deeper into the soil, giving them access to key minerals that result in a richer, more complex flavour. **Some Californian growers of premium tomatoes will stop irrigation altogether after the plants are established.** This practice, known as 'dry farming', creates noticeably smaller plants and meagre yields, but can send the concentration of flavour chemicals within the fruit sky-rocketing. Even in root crops like beetroot and carrots, lower irrigation can cause sugar content to rise, with nutritious polyphenols increasing by up to 86 percent.

Encouraging these tougher, more resilient plants with deeper root systems does of course mean that, if watering is interrupted for whatever reason (holidays, forgetfulness, just plain laziness: delete as appropriate), the rugged specimens will often sail through unhampered. **The key is to lavish water on your plants only when they are first planted out** (a few weeks for annual crops, a few months for trees and shrubs), then progressively wean them down to an absolute minimum.

FOR FRUIT CROPS the most crucial time to cut down watering is in the days leading up to harvest: just one week of slight drought stress is capable of producing an almost magical transformation in flavour.

IN LEAF CROPS my advice would be the opposite, with greens being noticeably smaller and often containing spicier, more bitter flavours. If you like your rocket to taste really fiery, skimp on the water, but if you prefer it milder (as most people do) get out there and spoil it with the hose. This added water will also make your greens more tender and succulent, not tough and fibre-filled.

IN ROOT CROPS SUCH AS BEETROOT AND CARROT, LOWER IRRIGATION CAN BOOST SUGAR AND ANTIOXIDANT CONTENT BY UP TO **86%**

FLAVOUR FACTOR 4: SOIL & FERTILISER

Proper feeding is essential for crops to achieve their full flavour potential, yet sadly there is a lot of misinformation about it out there. Luckily for us flavour growers, the best techniques also happen to be the simplest, cheapest and easiest to do. Here's all you need to remember.

Always Grow In Soil

Despite what glossy magazine ads tell you, from a foodie's perspective **growing crops in garden soil will almost always produce better results than even the fanciest pre-mixed composts**. For starters, crops grown in the ground need far less watering and, if the soil is prepared well, minimal applications of fertiliser. They will also contain a broader range of the essential minerals and micronutrients that enable them to achieve their maximum flavour potential. Even if you only have a balcony or patio to grow on, filling your pots with a soil-based potting mix rather than a compost-based one will allow you to reap maximum benefits.

Heap On Organic Matter

The easiest way to improve the long-term natural fertility of your soil is to **add lots of organic matter such as compost or leafmould**, which not only introduces a balanced mix of nutrients, but also works to boost the populations of beneficial microbes. Suitable organic matter can either be made at home or picked up cheaply (or, depending on where you live, even for nothing) at your local recycling centre. Scatter a 5cm (2in) layer over your soil each spring, work it lightly into the surface and the worms will do the rest.

Go Easy On The Liquid Feed

Most commercial fertilisers, aimed at maximizing yield, will contain large quantities of the major nutrients essential to plant growth: nitrogen, phosphorus and potassium. For the benefit of non-plant geeks, this is kind of like being fed an exclusive diet of protein, carbs and fat. Most such fertilisers, however, contain little or no iron, copper, zinc or other minerals and micronutrients that are essential for the overall health both of plants and of the people who eat them. Raised on this horticultural equivalent of a junk-food diet, your plants will indeed grow lush and large, but research has demonstrated this can come at the expense of taste and nutrition.

Excessive amounts of these major nutrients, in particular nitrogen, have been shown to reduce not only the sugar content of your crops, but also the acids, antioxidants and essential minerals like magnesium and calcium – basically everything that gives them flavour. Tomatoes, despite often being labelled as 'gross feeders', seem particularly sensitive, with studies suggesting that they experience a significant drop of flavour and phytonutrients when fed large amounts of nitrogen. This effect is echoed across a wide range of crops from lettuce and beetroot to kale and radicchio, which can experience a reduction in vitamin C of as much as 20 percent.

The great irony is that domestic garden soils (particularly those of my native UK) are not generally deficient in the major nutrients if well maintained. In fact, **the repeated applications of concentrated liquid feeds over long periods can actually degrade the quality of your soil.** Large doses of phosphorus in particular have been shown to kill beneficial microbes, which help improve the your crops' resilience to pests and diseases. These 'friendly' symbiotic bacteria and fungi can also help improve drought-resistance and nutrient access and can even play a role in the generation of plant flavour compounds. Those are some pretty hefty benefits. Harming their populations, as you can imagine, is therefore not such a great idea.

GARDENING MYTH NO.3

GROWING IN A POT IS EASIER

MIX UP SOME TONICS

If you fancy giving your crops and the microbes that support them a helping hand, there are cheap, widely available substances that have been shown to supply much needed minerals and micronutrients and to boost soil microbes, without excessive use of nitrogen or phosphorus.

SUPER SEAWEED

Long used as a fertiliser, seaweed is a rich source of all manner of minerals and trace nutrients such as zinc, selenium and iron that are often lacking from garden soils and indeed from our diets.

Seaweed is also a source of potassium, a major plant nutrient that is linked to improving the flavour and nutrients in crops like tomatoes, strawberries, pears and melons. According to US researchers, this extra potassium can even balance out the vitamin C-lowering effect that excessive nitrogen levels can have on crops.

If you live by the coast you will have ready access to an enormous supply of seaweed. All you need to do is scatter this over your beds. In no time it will rot down to release its valuable minerals. You can also buy seaweed growth tonics, which are easy to dilute and water on.

MEGA MOLASSES

This by-product of sugar manufacture is, like seaweed, a rich source of trace minerals and potassium, but it also comes with a third secret weapon, sugar.

Just as you feed yeast with a little sugar water to spark it into action when baking, this sugar can work in your soil to boost beneficial bacteria and fungi from day one.

It can also be absorbed by roots, giving them a quick burst of energy that can prove a lifeline for ailing or stressed plants. In studies at the universities of Reading and Florida it was found that watering newly transplanted trees with a dilute sugar solution improved root vigour and establishment and could enhance the plants' tolerance to environmental stresses such as de-icing salt by over 50 percent.

Molasses is already widely marketed in the US as a general-purpose fertiliser and, although it is currently not widely recognized in Britain, I believe this will change. By far the cheapest way to get your hands on it in the UK is as a horse supplement, sold online for almost a third the price it will cost in little jars in health-food shops.

Dissolve 450g (1lb) molasses in a 9 litre (2 gallon) watering can and drench this over your crops at a rate of 1 litre (1¾ pints) per square metre (10 sq ft) once a month throughout the summer.

FLAVOUR FACTOR 5: PEST ATTACK

When crops come under attack from pests, they ramp up their production of natural defence chemicals to fend off the assault. The curious side effect is that this can cause them to become not only much tastier to humans but also potentially higher in a range of important nutrients. Garlic becomes more pungent, tomatoes sweeter and raspberries more fragrant, among many others.

Fake An Attack

Fortunately, **us hort geeks have devious ways of tricking healthy plants into 'thinking' they are under attack, churning out way more flavour and nutrition without the inevitable loss of yield that comes with genuine pest infestation.** We do it by applying substances that mimic the plant stress hormones, and you won't believe how easy it is.

GARDENING MYTH NO.4

PESTS ARE ALL BAD

ASPIRIN BOOSTER SPRAY

Aspirin was originally derived from salicylic acid – a naturally occurring plant hormone – and it works in a virtually identical way as this. When applied to some plants it can effectively 'turn on' their immune systems, causing them to enter a state that is called 'systematically acquired resistance'.

INGREDIENTS: Dissolve a quarter to a half of a 300mg soluble aspirin tablet in 1 litre (1¾ pints) water. (Sorry, paracetamol and ibuprofen do not work!)

APPLICATION: Spritzing aspirin solution over your plants has been demonstrated in some trials to be enough to cause them to perceive an attack is under way. Interestingly, in annual plants it seems that, once these are turned on, they stay on for the rest of the plants' lives, meaning that a single application could be effective for the whole season. Just to be sure, I like to apply this once a month during the summer. Anything to up my chances!

Stronger Plants: Plants become more resilient to environmental threats such as cold, heat and drought. These effects have been demonstrated in a broad range of studies from all over the world in crops as diverse as sweet corn, tomatoes, potatoes and strawberries.

Tastier Harvests: Crops can also become noticeably better flavoured *and* more nutritious. In one study, tomatoes sprayed with salicylic acid saw their sugar levels soar by over one and a half times and their vitamin C content increase by 50 percent. Similar results have been found in sage, olives, strawberries, garlic, apples and peaches.

Science Geek Anecdote: According to some trials, this effect can even provide an element of resistance to pests and diseases, including, according to one study, a 47 percent reduction in the incidence of blight on tomatoes sprayed with the solution.

JASMINE FLAVOUR SPRAY

The sweet scent of jasmine flowers is produced by methyl jasmonate, a chemical distress signal emitted by plants when they are under attack from pests. Wafting through the air, it warns neighbouring plants of the danger and causes them to ramp up their own defence systems in anticipation.

INGREDIENTS: Jasmine floral water (used to flavour cocktails and desserts, as well as in aromatherapy) contains a hefty dose of methyl jasmonate. Little 100ml (⅙ pint) bottles can be bought online for no more than the price of a decent beer. Go for 100 percent natural, edible-grade products.

APPLICATION: Spritzed onto your plants shortly before harvest, this spray can 'trick' them into perceiving a threat, zapping up the flavour and nutritional potential of your harvests.

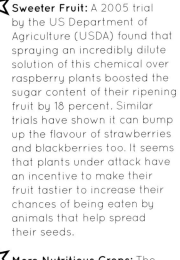

☆ **Sweeter Fruit:** A 2005 trial by the US Department of Agriculture (USDA) found that spraying an incredibly dilute solution of this chemical over raspberry plants boosted the sugar content of their ripening fruit by 18 percent. Similar trials have shown it can bump up the flavour of strawberries and blackberries too. It seems that plants under attack have an incentive to make their fruit tastier to increase their chances of being eaten by animals that help spread their seeds.

☆ **More Nutritious Crops:** The same USDA raspberry trial also showed that methyl jasmonate could almost double the fruit's anthocyanin content. This spike in antioxidant content has also been shown in apples, raspberries, blackberries, grapes and broccoli. More research is underway, but in the meantime I for one am armed with the spray gun.

☆ **Science Geek Anecdote:** Research has shown that methyl jasmonate even acts like a natural pheromone to lure in predatory insects such as ladybirds that can feed on unwanted pests in your garden. That's a pretty ingenious chemical!

KEEPIN' IT LEGAL

Applying aspirin and jasmine water as flavour-boosting sprays is a quick, fun and perfectly legal way potentially to supercharge the taste of home-grown crops. While there is some evidence that their constituents may also help naturally to boost plants' own defences against certain pests and diseases, current EU legislation means that they cannot be legally recommended for this use. My geeky anecdotes that reference these studies are therefore strictly for academic interest only.

FLAVOUR FACTOR 6: PRUNING, GRAFTING & THINNING

Of all gardening techniques, pruning seems the most likely to fill newbie flavour growers with dread. This is a huge shame, as just a few quick snips of the secateurs can dramatically improve the flavour, quality, size and even yield of fruit, while also creating more compact, resilient plants. Here's my express guide to surgically enhancing your plants to send their flavour and nutrition into overdrive.

Let In The Light

A simple technique called crown thinning can dramatically improve fruit quality, by allowing light into where it is most needed. This is normally carried out in winter or early spring when the tree is not in active growth.

Before

Up here fruit will taste great, and according to some trials can contain up to twice the sugar, and even more antioxidants.

The poor, light-starved fruit down here will be sharp and watery by comparison, and even less brightly coloured.

After

Simply removing any dead, crossing or congested branches will allow light and air to penetrate into the canopy more easily.

A more open tree shape also reduces the likelihood of pest infestations and can even boost yields by improving access to the flowers for bees.

Plants with thick, dense canopies receive optimum light levels only at the top and outer edge. The tree's own leaves act to block light from reaching the fruit, stunting their true sugar and nutrient potential.

Limited air circulation towards the centre can also cause pests and diseases to flourish. Not good at all.

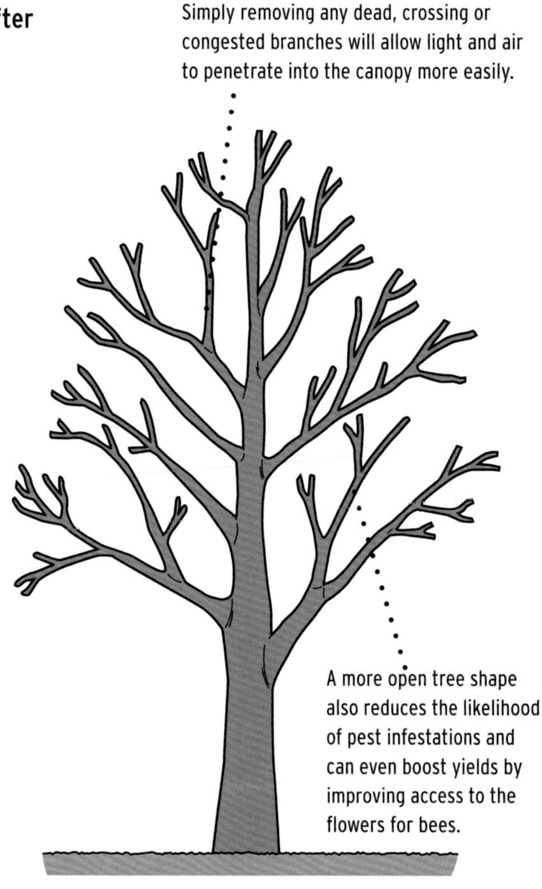

Trees with airier canopies have larger, sweeter and more nutrient-rich fruit, which are more evenly developed across the plant.

These trees will also be neat and more aesthetic to look at, and cast less shade on the garden, meaning increased light (and flavour) in the crops around them too. Not bad for 10 minutes of trimming, hey?

Go For Grafted

Research suggests that fruit trees grafted onto dwarf rootstocks may produce measurably better-tasting harvests. The reported benefits include higher sugars, more acids, more nutrients and even larger individual fruit size. The authors of these studies have suggested that this phenomenon might work by restricting the leaf growth of the trees in a similar way to pruning, creating airier canopies that use sunlight more efficiently, without the masses of leaf growth that can shade out fruit and drain the plant's resources. In short, most of the benefits of pruning without actually having to do it!

These effects have been reported in crops as diverse as cherries, apples, plums, pears and citrus all over the world. As if that wasn't enough, **dwarf fruit trees also start producing their first harvests much earlier and their small stature means they fit better into our ever-shrinking gardens.** They are also easier to prune and pick from. For impatient, urban flavour growers like me they are a godsend. Look for the word 'dwarfing rootstock' on the nursery label or catalogue entry when you buy your little tree.

Focus Their Energies

Plants fuel the growth of their leaves, roots, flowers and fruit using their sugar reserves. The more of these they are trying to produce at the same time, the more thinly their resources are stretched. It seems that plants, like guys, are terrible multitaskers.

Pruning and thinning are nifty techniques to reduce unnecessary drains on plant resources, allowing them to concentrate all their energies on one goal (i.e. tasty fruit). Light summer pruning - pinching out the sideshoots on tomatoes or removing the tips off pear tree branches once they have set fruit, for example - restricts excessive leaf growth, so energies are not diverted away from developing fruit.

Reducing the number of fruit on each plant is called 'thinning'. Snipping off some of the young fruitlets shortly after they have formed will cause the remainder to become larger, sweeter and higher in nutrients. In fact, studies show that the earlier you do this and the more you remove, the better the quality of the remaining fruit will be.

No matter how many times you have done this, snipping off fruit seems heart-breaking at the time, but believe me you will thank me come harvest season.

Still sceptical? Check out the comparison below between fruit from thinned and unthinned pear trees of the same size, age and variety from RHS Garden Wisley.

UNTHINNED FRUIT

This will give you loads of tiny, poorly formed fruit that are all skin and seeds.

What little flesh there is will be less sweet, contain fewer nutrients and have a pithy texture.

THINNED FRUIT

OK, so you will get less fruit, but each one will be massive and measurably sweeter.

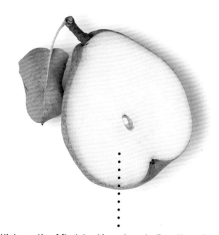

Higher ratio of flesh to skin and seeds. Even the colour and nutrient levels are improved. Virtually no core, too!

FLAVOUR FACTOR 7:
HARVESTING & STORING

This bit seems so deceptively simple that you might wonder why I have included it. Surely once you have got this far the flavour can't alter that much? Well, surprisingly, harvesting and storing can have almost as major an impact on final flavour as more obvious factors like variety choice. Fortunately, however, it is by far the easiest to get right. This is all you've gotta do.

PICK 'EM RIPE

In quick-maturing fruit such as berries, the aroma compounds experience a meteoric rise during the last few days of ripening. Pink strawberries, for example, can contain as little as 1 percent of the aroma compounds of fully red ones. That effectively translates to a massive hundredfold leap in flavour in as little as 10 days!

It's not just the aroma compounds either, as sugars and phytonutrients generally also spike in the run up to full ripeness, with an accompanying dip in acids conspiring to send their perceived sweetness charging to the fore. Although some fruit can continue to ripen once picked, research shows that they never achieve anywhere near their full flavour potential if severed from the plant too early. Suppressing the temptation to pick not quite fully ripe fruit for just a day or two could pay off in a truly monumental increase in eating quality.

DAYS

1   2   3   4   5   6   7   8   9   10

AROMA x100

The only two exceptions to this rule I can think of are pears and persimmons, which have the quirky botanical habit of tasting far better if you pick them just before they are fully mature and ripen them off the tree. What can I say? In horticulture there are always exceptions to the rules (even mine!).

Timing Is Everything

Water, sugar and aroma levels within plants can fluctuate dramatically throughout the day and, of course, with the amount of irrigation you give the plants. **Picking the right time to harvest can result in surprisingly different flavours.** For example, commercial growers of roses for the essential oil industry know that the concentration of the aroma chemicals in their produce can soar up to sixfold, peaking just before midday. Most melon farmers, by contrast, will pick their fruit at the crack of dawn after a generous watering the night before to ensure their crops have swelled to maximum weight (a treatment which, sadly, also gives them minimal flavour). **To break it down for newbies, here's my express guide to catching your crops at their very tastiest.**

GARDENING
MYTH NO.5

FRESH IS BEST

Succulent Salads

For the mildest, most tender salad leaves, **harvest in the cool of the morning**, as that is when plants' moisture levels will be at their highest. Giving your crops a soaking an hour before will boost this further, helping simultaneously to dilute any bitter or spicy chemicals and to create the juiciest, crunchiest texture possible.

Studies from around the world show that morning is also the best time to harvest herbs like lavender and basil, as the flavour-packed essential oils they have generated overnight will not yet have been evaporated by the midday sun.

Sugar-charged Fruit

For the sweetest, most intensely fragrant fruit, in contrast, **harvest in the late afternoon on a dry day.** Plants will have had all day under the sun to ramp up their sugar and flavour compounds and will have lost some of their moisture, which can dilute flavour. The water content of grapes, apples and tomatoes all dip in the heat of the afternoon - as does that of root crops like beetroots and carrots - creating a peak in sweetness across the board.

Fresh Is (Not Always) Best

We are always told that the fresher the fruit and veg, the better it tastes. But this is only partially true.

Sure, some of the old sweet corn varieties can lose up to 60 percent of their sugars within just 12 hours of picking. However, some crops like **winter squash, pears and strawberries positively increase their flavour and nutrition on storage.**

This can be just a few days in the case of strawberries. Or it can take months, with butternut squash reaching its peak sweetness a full three months after harvest.

The Fridge Can Spell Doom

Storing your harvests in the fridge might seem logical, and indeed for leafy crops like salads it is. However, with some crops it can spell doom.

It is not just that our palates are less able to detect flavours at low temperatures (this is why fizzy drinks warmed to room temperature taste jaw-achingly sweet), but that **chilly conditions can actually halt flavour production in some crops.**

Tomatoes stored below 10°C (50°F) experience a dramatic shut down in the chemical reactions responsible for their flavour. Worse still, kept at this temperature, they will lose those they have already generated. After just two days in the fridge they will taste less sweet, less aromatic and more bitter. Similar effects have been noted in strawberries, peaches, melons, onions and sweet potatoes. Store these on your kitchen counter and serve at room temperature.

PLANTING: A USER'S GUIDE

Sowing seeds and planting trees are the universal starting points for any fledgling flavour grower. However, much standard gardening advice on how to do this is hopelessly out of date, either neglecting some of the latest game-changing discoveries or insisting on doling out techniques that were disproven years ago. Sometimes both! This is my evidence-based guide on how to get off to a flying start. Old-school horts look away now!

SEED SOWING

Any reputable seed brand will supply you with detailed instructions on exactly when to sow each crop and the precise temperature and depth that will work best. What many of them neglect to mention, though, are these three simple tips, which according to a number of trials could significantly improve your chances of success.

Aspirin & Seaweed Soak

For tricky-to-germinate seeds like parsley and 'supersweet' corn, this quick-fix soak could be a godsend. Add a tiny splash (10ml/2 teaspoons) seaweed extract and a quarter of a 300mg soluble aspirin tablet to 1 litre (1¾ pints) water and soak your seeds in this overnight before sowing.

This may sound bonkers, but I assure you it is based on sound science. Seaweed extract contains a cocktail of natural plant hormones that are involved in triggering the germination process, while aspirin and its related compounds can help seedling emergence and the ongoing cold tolerance of the resultant plants in lacklustre springs. **Multiple trials have demonstrated that soaking seeds in either of these chemicals before sowing can significantly improve the germination of everything from soy beans and sweet corn to peppers, broad beans and tomatoes.** Although this may not be universally applicable, and much more research is needed, I will take any help I can get with the very trickiest seeds.

Pick Your Growing Medium

They may all look pretty similar on the shelves of the garden centre, but trust a serial seed sower like me when I say that **there can be an enormous difference between the success rates of different seed composts.** At RHS Garden Wisley, trials into peat-free composts have reported excellent germination results from coir (a finely milled coconut fibre) mixed with a natural mineral called vermiculite at a ratio of eight to one.

Both coir-based seed compost and vermiculite are widely available in any good garden centre.

Get Touchy-feely

Seed sown indoors can start to grow long and leggy in the warmth and low light levels of the average windowsill. Raised in this cosseted environment, the soft, floppy seedlings will come up against a monumental reality check when they are finally planted outdoors - collapsing in the cold and being torn up by wind. **One simple trick, however, can make your young plants up to 37 percent stockier, increase their cold tolerance by a whopping six times and even improve their establishment rate by 70 percent.** Some pretty impressive stats for a technique that will take you all of 10 seconds a day to do and cost you nothing.

When your seedlings reach about 3cm (1 in) high, slowly and gently stroke their surface backwards and forwards. A piece of card or a feather can be used on particularly small or delicate seedings. Doing this just 10 times once a day can, astonishingly - according to a trial at America's Cornell University - be enough to trigger dramatic changes in their internal chemistry. It causes vibrations which mimic that of wind or passing animals that sensors within the leaves are capable of detecting. Plants respond by churning out chemicals that cause them to become stockier and more resistant to cold, wind and even pests. **Think this sounds crazy? Well, many commercial growers actually have specially designed robots to do this job for them.** No kidding!

YOU MIGHT LOOK WEIRD DOING IT, BUT A DAILY STROKE CAN IMPROVE YOUR SEEDLINGS' ESTABLISHMENT RATE BY UP TO **70%**

THE SEEDLING WHISPERER

TREE & SHRUB PLANTING

From digging in bucketfuls of organic matter to delicately coddling the rootball and dusting it with bone meal, pretty much every aspect of standard tree-planting advice has very little scientific basis. The good news is, though, that by not doing any of the above you are likely to get far superior results. Experimenting with modern scientific principles has transformed how I plant trees.

Go For Bare-root

Bare-root plants are not just much cheaper to buy and available in a far wider range of varieties, but are also likely to establish significantly better. Make sure you order them early though, and plant them as soon as they arrive.

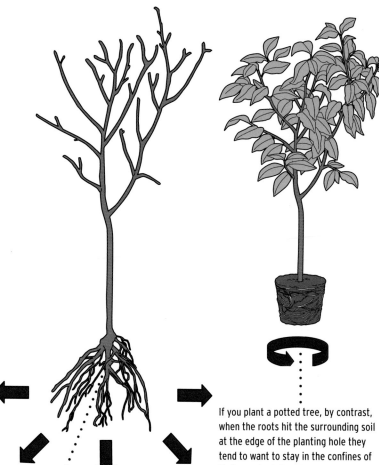

The lack of fluffy compost around their roots, encourages bare-root plants to venture out into the surrounding soil more readily. Their autumn planting season also happens to be the very best time to get new trees established.

If you plant a potted tree, by contrast, when the roots hit the surrounding soil at the edge of the planting hole they tend to want to stay in the confines of their wonderfully rich, aerated potting compost. This causes them to wrap around the perimeter of the hole, behaving as if they were still in a pot. When the roots eventually swell to their mature size they can end up strangling the tree like a woody girdle. This is nothing short of tree abuse!

GARDENING MYTH NO.6 PRETTY MUCH EVERYTHING YOU HAVE BEEN TOLD ON HOW TO PLANT TREES

IF YOU MUST PLANT A POTTED TREE

In the late autumn or winter, cut an 'X' along the bottom of the rootball about 2cm (2¾in) deep, scoring this along the edge right up to the soil surface if very root-bound. This form of pruning triggers the plant into producing lateral roots, thereby stopping spiralling in its tracks. Then lower the tree into the hole and wash off as much soil as you can from around the rootball, using a hose. Continue to plant as per a bare-root tree. Although this sounds crazy and goes against most standard advice, rigorous trials at the University of Washington have demonstrated that the technique described above produces far superior results.

Plant In A Square Hole

Planting in a square, not round, hole further prevents the roots from spiralling. When they hit the corners they flare out and into the surrounding soil - helping establish the tree much faster.

Give 'Em the Sweet Stuff

Transatlantic studies at the universities of Reading and Florida have suggested that applying a dilute sugar solution similar to my molasses mega booster on page 27 can dramatically improve the establishment rates of newly planted bare-root trees.

Scattering a thick layer of mulch around the base of your tree will help seal in moisture, reduce weed growth and improve the structure of your soil. I like to use woodchips, as they are widely available. You can even inoculate the woodchips with the spawn of edible fungi (see page 148), which will help break the woodchips down faster into rich compost.

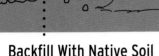

Backfill With Native Soil

Follow the standard advice of digging in loads of organic matter into a planting hole and you are effectively planting your tree in a submerged 'pot' of rich, fertile compost within the harder, poorer surroundings of your native soil.

In fact, **not a single scientific trial has ever demonstrated that amending the soil in the planting hole this way helps establish trees any better than simply doing nothing**, with several studies showing the exact opposite.

Instead, just backfill your hole with the soil you dug out in the first place, firm in with your heel to remove any air pockets. Water in well and keep well watered for the first two years to help establish your little tree. Keeping newly-planted trees well irrigated is probably the most important factor between success and failure, so it is super-important that you aren't mean with the hose.

Ditch The Bone Meal

Most old-school gardening advice will instruct you to sprinkle bone meal over the roots of newly planted trees in order to encourage their growth. **The reality is that, although this does result in trees putting out more roots, it works mainly by hampering the growth of beneficial mycorrhizal fungi.** These naturally occurring fungi act like a second root system, working symbiotically with your plants to give them enhanced access to water, nutrients and even protect them from pests and diseases. Knocking back their populations with bone meal forces the tree to grow larger roots to compensate, at a great energy cost to itself. In short, applying bone meal is a total waste of time!

Many leading horticulturists will instead recommend a dusting of mycorrhizal fungi granules, which are available at every garden centre. From a scientific point of view, however, it is still unclear whether supplementation with shop-bought mycorrhizal fungi is effective for all tree species.

OLD-SCHOOL CROPS

TOMATOES

If you can grow only one vegetable this summer, I implore you, make it a tomato. More than any other vegetable, the home-grown tomato's intense fragrance and complex flavour guarantee that, when pitted against sorry supermarket offerings, it will pass the blindfold test every time.

With tomatoes coming in a bewildering range of flavours, some so bizarre that they taste more like fruit-salad ingredients than pizza topping, it is really hard to resist collecting varieties with trainspotter-like obsession.

VARIETY GUIDE

By far the single biggest factor that influences tomato flavour is genetics. This dictates everything from the amount of sugar they produce to whether they have a rich, savoury flavour or a delicate, tropical fruit-like aroma. I have personally tested more than 400 different varieties from all over the world, to hand-pick the very best flavour.

Fortunately, the colour of tomatoes correlates quite neatly with broad flavour characteristics, giving you a rough visual guide to flavour, a bit like those giant festive tins of chocolate. So let's get started...

RED & PINK

The classic, old-fashioned tomato flavour, with higher acidity than many other colours, rounded off by warm savoury notes. Their red hue is caused by lycopene, a phytonutrient linked to a lower incidence of certain types of cancer.

'Rosella'

A unique rose-pink cherry tomato with a bold, fruity flavour. Being intensely sugary, 'Rosella' has a distinct raspberry/blackberry jamminess that is rounded off by a fresh mint-like edge. So sweet is it that it seems almost more of a dessert fruit than a vegetable. Oh no, let's not start that whole debate again...

☆ 'Tomaccio' *The Best for Drying*

Twelve years of intense breeding work in the pursuit of the ultimate sun-dried tomato have created this ingenious modern hybrid using wild species from the highlands of Peru. So well suited is it to drying that the fruit often start to shrivel while still attached to the plant, creating beautifully sun-dried cherry tomatoes on the vine. As with all the best varieties for this purpose, it has a good, balanced flavour when fresh, but develops an altogether richer, more comforting brothiness when fully dried. Yum!

'Flamingo'

When grown properly, 'Flamingo' is probably the sweetest of all tomatoes, right up there with sugar heavyweights like 'Russian Rose', 'Orange Paruche' and 'Green Envy'. In addition to its pure syrupiness, it has an incredibly fragrant, fruity flavour - more like summer berries than classic tomato - with only a fleeting hint of umami.

☆ 'San Marzano' *The Best for Sauces*

This heritage Neapolitan variety bred specifically for sauces will have you making marinara like a proper Italian mama. Its low water content gives it a spongy, almost foamy texture when raw, but which magically transforms into rich, silkiness after the briefest simmering. With its slightly spicy aroma and rich depth, it should be mandatory growing for any self-respecting pizza and pasta fans.

'Gardener's Delight' AGM

No exotic, far-flung story behind this one: just genuine, old-fashioned flavour. This seemingly universally popular cherry tomato that everyone's granddad once grew is well known for kicking out loads of high-quality fruit on unfussy plants. The only catch? There appear to be several distinct strains sold under the same variety name, not all of which have the same flavour intensity. So growing 'Gardener's Delight' has turned into a bit of horticultural gamble. Frustrating! **'Gardening Delight'** is a new variety that is said to be an improved 'restoration' of the original, a bit like a digitally remastered version of a classic film. A great solution if you (like me) have had a dud batch before.

'Corazon'

Spot-on, summer-holiday tomato flavour. Sweet and tangy in equal measure, this heritage 'oxheart' type comes with the added vigour of a modern F_1 hybrid. One of the best candidates for simmering down into soups, sauces and stews, this tomato's drier flesh and lower acid content guarantee silky smoothness without biting sourness, every time.

☆ 'Pink Brandywine' *The Best for Slicing*

Dating from 1885, this is famously one of the best-flavoured tomatoes, producing truly giant, almost seedless fruit with a gutsy, old-fashioned tomato flavour and meaty texture. It's incredibly tasty yet incredibly prone to cracking, as its sheer monster size means its thin skins often just can't contain the fragrant flesh. One bite of a thick, juicy slice in a home-made burger at your next barbecue, however, and I promise you will forgive it this one failing.

'Russian Rose'

An heirloom Russian form that sparks off what I can only describe as a flavour explosion when it hits your taste buds – and stays with you for several minutes after eating. I promise you I am not exaggerating! With waves of super sweetness, intense umami and finally rich tanginess all competing for your attention, it's almost too intense, as if someone had injected the fruit with MSG (monosodium glutamate). Small, spindly plants and poor yields meant that I was almost going to chuck this one on the compost heap early on in my trial. But I am so, so very glad I didn't. I'll be growing this guy every year.

'Belriccio'

With an intense 'classic' tomato flavour, 'Belriccio' is a permanent fixture in my tiny plot for its wall-to-wall flesh with little or no seeds. Tangy, rich and with an almighty zing, they are the key to making a truly olympic-grade BLT.

ORANGE & YELLOW

These are some of the highest sugar forms, with less acid and savoury umami chemicals than most others, resulting in an altogether more tropical fruit-like flavour. The orange colour is often provided by beta-carotene, a much-celebrated antioxidant.

'Sungold'

Widely considered the benchmark for good cherry tomato flavour, 'Sungold' has a sky-high sugar content and bright fruity taste and is perfect for salads and bruschetta. An excellent outdoor performer and early cropping too.

'Yellow Pear'

Super high-yielding plants whose history dates back over two centuries. With their fragrant, sweet 'tropical' flavour like a cross between apricot and pineapple, these tomatoes are a real show stopper on a summer party vegetable platter.

'Tangerine'

A meaty slicing variety with a sweet, complex flavour. It contains an unusual form of lycopene, which some trials have suggested is more easily absorbed by the body and therefore makes 'Tangerine' a richer source of antioxidants gram per gram than most other tomatoes. Flavour-wise it isn't too shabby either, with a sweet, exotic-fruit flavour and thick meaty texture that pairs incredibly with ham or gammon in sandwiches or on pizzas in the place of pineapple.

'Ildi'

This quirky fella offers up great big bunches of more than 50 grape-sized fruit at a time, with a refreshing sweet/tart flavour – a bit like the sweet corn kernels I loved eating straight from the tin as a child. 'Ildi' is conveniently also one of the earliest ripening tomatoes around, with its bunches having the unusual property of being able to last for weeks, hung in a cool, dark place, without losing flavour or freshness.

☆ 'Orange Paruche' *The Best for Sweetness*

They say that 'knowledge' is knowing that a tomato is a fruit, but 'wisdom' is knowing not to put it in a fruit salad. Well, whoever came up with that saying has clearly never tried 'Orange Paruche'! Its lychee/passion-fruit fragrance, syrupy juice and lack of all but a hint of umaminess mean that it could easily work in dessert dishes. A perfect tomato for people who think they don't like tomatoes.

'Artisan Sunrise Bumble Bee'

An adorable mini orange plum tomato, quirky both in name and in appearance. Streaked with bright red, like a tiny Fabergé egg, this tomato is a tad mealy when raw, but a few minutes of heating transform its flesh into a deep, smooth richness. Wonderful grilled, roasted or fried.

GREEN

These tangy and citrusy tomato varieties are green even when fully ripe and have fresh, bright acidity and grassy, herbal flavour. They contain tomatidine, a compound that may help build muscle mass according to the University of Iowa.

☆ 'Green Zebra' *The Best for Salsa*

This semi-beefsteak type replaces watery pulp with a thick, meaty and intensely umami flesh that combines a silky texture and zesty richness. Equally delicious raw or cooked and truly spectacular in an emerald-green mozzarella salad scattered with shards of basil.

'Green Envy'

A real winner of a cherry variety, producing bunches of grape-sized fruits with a depth charge of tanginess and a curious lingering sweetness that stays with you for several minutes after eating it. Perhaps my favourite for its sheer intensity of flavour.

BLUE & PURPLE

True purple tomatoes are the result of a recent breakthrough in crop breeding at Oregon State University that successfully crossed wild South American species to produce tomatoes containing the purple pigments known as anthocyanins that may give fruit like blueberries and black grapes their purported health benefits. Although initial breeding was guided mainly toward enhanced nutrition, recent developments have created some very tasty lines that have a complex, smoky flavour with an intense umaminess.

Their skins have the curious habit of morphing into vivid purple where light hits the fruit, long before they are actually ripe. The more intense the sunshine, the deeper the colour. The best way to tell if they are ripe is when they feel soft yet firm, and the skin under the leafy bits that are around the stem (which usually shield the skin from light) are the same shade as the rest of the fruit. With their wild-tomato genes, these varieties need far less moisture. In fact, normal irrigation can result in watery fruit, so keep them as dry as possible to release their true flavour potential.

'Clackamas Blueberry'

Frequently topping taste tests as the most flavourful blue variety, 'Clackamas Blueberry' was bred from **'Indigo Rose'** – the first ever blue tomato to be created in the quest for fruit with added nutrition by the scientists at Oregon State University. Its fresh, sweet flavour comes with a hint of plum and blackberry, then a distinct smoky, pipe-tobacco flavour – in a (very) good way. Other flavour-enhanced alumni of the Oregon State programme include the small, sweet and smoky **'Indigo Cherry Drops'** and **'Indigo Pear Drops'**.

CHERRY OR BEEFSTEAK?

The chemicals responsible for the unique flavour of tomatoes are not distributed equally throughout the fruit, but are concentrated in different tissues. The varying arrangements of these structures can result in a diverse eating experience from one variety to the next.

CHERRY

Glutamates and acids are concentrated in the jelly-like pulp.

Bitter, soapy flavours are found in the seeds.

BEEFSTEAK

The flesh contains proportionally the most sugar.

Antioxidants like lycopene and other carotenes are concentrated in the skin.

The small size of cherry tomatoes means they have proportionately far more skin and seeds than the big beefsteaks, which are dominated by flesh. With many nutrients concentrated in the skins, however, some cherry types contain up to 20 times the antioxidants of beefsteaks.

The seed-filled pulp contains six times as much glutamate as the flesh, making cherry tomatoes far more savoury. As a result they are sometimes recommended by experimental chefs for making pasta sauce with an almighty umami kick.

Unfortunately, tomato seeds also contain saponins - soap-like chemicals, which can give the cherry types a nasty bitterness when cooked, not to mention chunks of seeds and skin in your teeth! Best eaten fresh.

The best beefsteak tomatoes contain almost no pulp or seeds, packing in wall-to-wall flesh, which on average contains 20 percent more sugar and 50 percent less acid than the pulp. Happy days!

Containing less glutamate can also mean they have a fruitier taste and less potential 'off' flavours that taste panels report in varieties that are particularly high in glutamate ('off' is the term used in trials to describe flavours that are bitter, fishy, rancid or otherwise unpleasant). However, having proportionately less skin means that they often contain much less antioxidant gram per gram.

Their lower water content also means they have a meatier texture when raw, creating smoother, silkier soups and sauces when cooked - far superior to the cherry types.

SALAD VARIETIES

Salad varieties are far higher in water, giving them a fresher, juicier texture. They are best eaten raw and tend to be tart and sweet, rather than rich and meaty.

Fresh & Tart: The sugar in these babies is balanced out by bright acidity, which gives them a more complex, tangy flavour. To me, they are by far the best choice for fresh, clean salsas and salads, cutting through rich or oily foods like ready-made tomato-shaped jars of chutney growing on your plants.

Supersweet: Most modern breeding for flavour has concentrated on upping sugar levels, producing new varieties so sweet they are more like dessert fruit than vegetables: some are even sweeter than strawberries. This all sounds grand, but try making pasta sauce out of them and it will taste like jam. Trust me, I have made that mistake more than once!

FRESH & TART

'Green Zebra'

'Ildi'

'Gardener's Delight'

'Flamingo'

SUPERSWEET

'Sungold'

'Rosella'

'Green Envy'

'Orange Paruche'

'Russian Rose'

'Corazon'

'Clackamas Blueberry'

'Artisan Sunrise Bumble Bee'

'San Marzano'

'Tomaccio'

JUST FOR COOKING

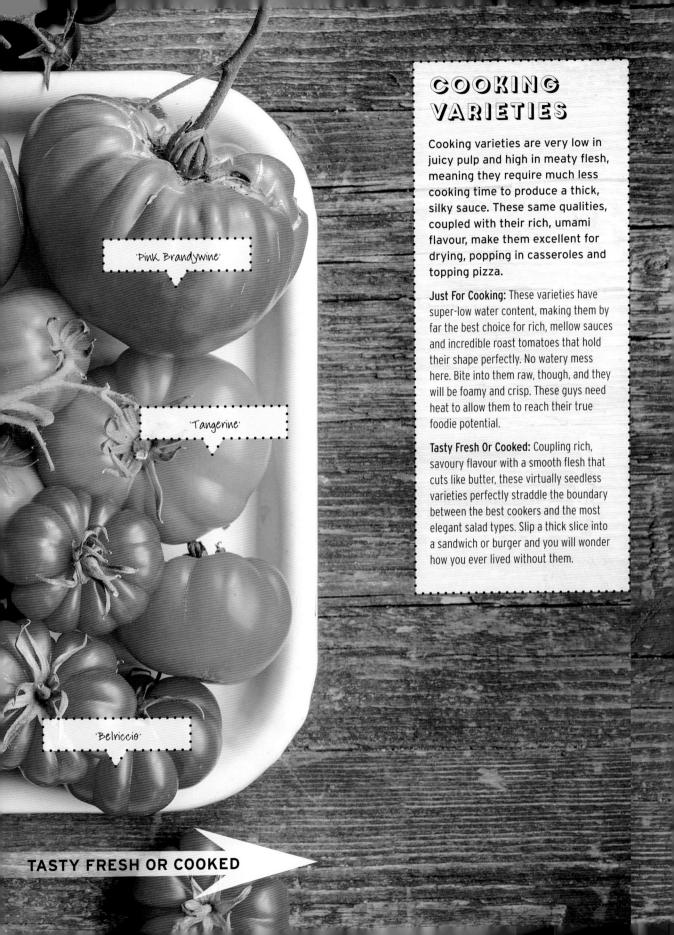

'Pink Brandywine'

'Tangerine'

'Belriccio'

COOKING VARIETIES

Cooking varieties are very low in juicy pulp and high in meaty flesh, meaning they require much less cooking time to produce a thick, silky sauce. These same qualities, coupled with their rich, umami flavour, make them excellent for drying, popping in casseroles and topping pizza.

Just For Cooking: These varieties have super-low water content, making them by far the best choice for rich, mellow sauces and incredible roast tomatoes that hold their shape perfectly. No watery mess here. Bite into them raw, though, and they will be foamy and crisp. These guys need heat to allow them to reach their true foodie potential.

Tasty Fresh Or Cooked: Coupling rich, savoury flavour with a smooth flesh that cuts like butter, these virtually seedless varieties perfectly straddle the boundary between the best cookers and the most elegant salad types. Slip a thick slice into a sandwich or burger and you will wonder how you ever lived without them.

TASTY FRESH OR COOKED

TIPS & TRICKS

Genetics aside, four main growing factors have been demonstrated significantly to affect the eating quality of tomato fruit: light levels, watering, fertiliser and pruning. Sadly, the great paradox for home growers is that much of standard gardening advice seeks to manipulate these factors to water down your crops' flavour, in the quest for maximum yield at any expense. Here's how to change all that.

Ditch The Glasshouse

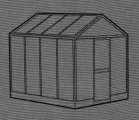

As with all fruit crops, the sugar content of tomatoes is pretty much directly proportional to the amount of light they receive. The apparently transparent glass panels of glasshouses can in fact block as much as 40 percent of the sun's rays, scuppering your flavour-growing goals. **If you have a sunny, sheltered spot, planting your crops outside in the sunniest site you have can result in a noticeable spike in sweetness.**

It is, surprisingly, light, not heat, that is the most important factor at play here; in fact, **overheating in glasshouses has been scientifically demonstrated to result in a poorer flavour and lower yields**. Add the fact that many of the resinous, herbal and fruity aroma compounds that create classic tomato flavour are produced by the plant using sugar as a building block and you could be in for a real double whammy.

Note that planting tomatoes outdoors in the UK significantly increases the potential risk of their becoming infected by blight, a disease that is rarely a problem in glasshouses.

Forget The Grow Bags

Grow Bags and pots of compost may be the most popular way to grow tomatoes, but in my experience they virtually guarantee inferior-tasting fruit, not to mention loads more work. This is because almost all potting mixes are based on materials (such as peat) which naturally have a low level of minerals and nutrients. This ties gardeners into relying on high-cost liquid feeds that are designed to boost yield not flavour. **Incidentally, if you follow the instructions on standard liquid tomato fertiliser, you will almost certainly spend as much money on liquid feed as you save on not buying tomatoes!**

Plants grown in well-managed ground, by contrast, have access to a far broader range of naturally occurring minerals, including micronutrients not found in most liquid feeds. This results in toms with a far richer, more well-rounded flavour without the time (and cost) of excessive feeding.

Give 'Em The Sweet Stuff

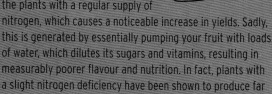

The massive levels of fertiliser often recommended for tomatoes provide the plants with a regular supply of nitrogen, which causes a noticeable increase in yields. Sadly, this is generated by essentially pumping your fruit with loads of water, which dilutes its sugars and vitamins, resulting in measurably poorer flavour and nutrition. In fact, plants with a slight nitrogen deficiency have been shown to produce far better-quality fruit – containing up to 17 percent more sugar.

As most well-tended garden soils contain adequate levels of the major nutrients, I prefer to ditch conventional fertiliser in favour of a simple molasses feed (see below). This by-product of sugar processing is very high in potassium, which has been shown not only to improve the flavour and yield of tomatoes, but also to boost their lycopene content. It has even been shown to cause them to ripen faster – a potential life-saver in short summers. **Molasses is also a great source of the minerals your plants need, with its sugars helping boost the growth of friendly bacteria and fungi in the soil.** These microbes have the knock-on effect of mopping up excess nitrogen, which has been demonstrated to improve not only the sweetness, but also acidity and vitamin C in tomatoes by keeping your plants slightly under stress. A real virtuous circle (see page 27).

If you'd like to experiment with this for yourself, dilute 450g (1lb) molasses in 9 litres (2 gallons) water in a watering can and sprinkle this mix over your soil every two weeks from the time the first flowers appear on your tomato plants. Unless you have a particularly poor or sandy soil, this should be all the additional fertiliser necessary on a well-maintained bed high in organic matter.

Spray On The Love

Unlikely as it may sound, the occasional spritz of dilute aspirin could increase the sugar concentrations in your tomatoes by over one-and-a-half times, as well as boosting their vitamin C content by 50 percent. By mimicking a naturally occurring plant hormone which triggers their immune system into action, such sprays have been shown by some research to give your plants an extra resistance to drought and cold too.

As a matter of academic interest, some trials have shown that this can also improve their ability to fight off two major diseases to which tomatoes are prone: early blight and fusarium wilt. According to one trial, it may even cut the risk of late blight – scourge of the outdoor tomato grower – by almost 50 percent. Impressive! I must stress, however, that while aspirin is recognized as safe for use as a flavour-boosting treatment, it is against EU legislation to recommend it for pest control (for more info on exact dilution rates for the spray and on how aspirin works, and details of current legislation, see pages 28-29).

GROWING MYTH NO. 7

Some 80 percent of sugars in tomatoes are manufactured in their leaves, so please ignore advice that tells you to defoliate these to help ripen their fruit. It is not based on sound science.

My recommended twice-yearly application is based on the findings of trials at Rutgers University in New Jersey; at a super-dilute concentration of just 2 percent, there should be no risk of it building up in the soil – it is soon washed away by rainfall and normal watering (instructions on exact dilution and application rates can be found on page 52). Although demonstrated to work on a variety of crops, this isn't a treatment I would advocate for all your plants: some fruit, including strawberries, are sensitive to even small amounts of salt.

Adding a splash of mineral-rich seaweed extract to this mix will ensure your plants have all the micronutrients they need. It also provides an extra hit of sweetness-boosting potassium.

Add Salt Water (No, Really!)

In the mid-20th century, researchers in Israel made an unexpected discovery while experimenting with whether they could save precious resources by irrigating their arid fields with diluted seawater: **tomatoes grown with salty water taste better**. Not just that but, by hampering the absorption of water into the fruit even at very small concentrations, the salt caused levels of vitamin C, lycopene and beta-carotene in fresh fruits to shoot up by as much as 35 percent. These findings have since been echoed by US, Italian, Japanese and Spanish research teams, with scientists further discovering that salt water also made the fruit mature faster, ripening days, sometimes weeks earlier.

Attributed by some scientists to the sodium content (a minor plant nutrient linked to the production of flavour chemicals), this flavour-boosting effect has also been noted in olives, pears, melons and wine grapes. Israeli tomatoes irrigated with salt water are now commercially sold across Europe under the name 'Desert Sweet'. The US Department of Agriculture further noted as far back at 1980 that fleshy fruit grown on saline soils were 'markedly softer and juicier at the normal harvest stage'. There is one slight downside to this practice, however. What you gain in flavour, you sadly lose in total yield. Your plants will be smaller, and frankly quite sad looking, but your tomatoes will taste great.

Tomatoes soaked in salt water contain over $1/3$ more antioxidants than those that are not.

Keep Them Down At Heel

In the 1960s Dr Allen Cooper, a British researcher trying to find a way to reduce the massive amounts of labour needed to prune and train tomatoes, hit upon a novel idea. Why not simply pinch out the tops of the plants after they had set their first truss (bunch) of fruit, turning them from rampant vines into squat 50cm (20in) high munchkins? Little staking or further pruning is needed, and, as these dwarf plants can be packed in far closer together, their total yield in a given area stays the same. Bingo!

The unexpected side effect of this one-truss training technique was that without the need to generate masses of new leaves and fruit, the plants' resources were focused 100 percent into swelling and ripening the fruit, creating much larger tomatoes with a far superior flavour. Sceptical? Check out this technique in action in my front garden in the photo below. These short plants also make more efficient use of light by not shading each other out, creating fruit with excellent compositions of sugars and acids even under low light conditions.

When combined with the salt-water treatment (see page 49), these larger fruit offset the usual reduction of yield associated with saline soils and made the crop ripen even faster. In addition to potentially sidestepping the risk of late blight, this earlier ripening can suddenly make some of the wonderful Mediterranean heritage varieties that fare poorly in short summers a viable option in those conditions. Full info on how to train them is provided on page 52.

WIMPY & WATERY
Normal four-truss tomatoes were nearly four weeks behind.

MASSIVE & MEATY
My one-truss tomatoes were almost three times larger.

HOW TO GROW TOMATOES

Sow & Grow

SPARK your seeds into growth in early to mid-spring in pots or seed trays on a warm, sunny windowsill indoors. Tiny seedlings should emerge within 1-2 weeks and be kept at 18°C (64°F). Transplant them into small pots when four leaves have formed and grow them on in the same environment.

20cm (8in)

GIVE your young plants a good spritz with my aspirin booster spray when they just begin to form their first flowers. Plant out into the border 20cm (8in) apart (ideally not in pots nor Grow Bags) at least one week later, after all risk of frost has passed in late spring.

PLANTS FOR FREE

Tomato seed can be very expensive. Up to 50p *each* for some varieties! **By rooting the first sideshoots your little plants produce** in small pots of compost on a sunny windowsill in spring and early summer, **you can more than double your number of plants** in just a couple of weeks. **These cuttings are far quicker growing than plants grown from seeds,** being ready to plant in early summer, providing you with a second wave of **harvests for free.**

GROWING ON

Watering
Be Mean With The Hose
Water the plants regularly for the first month after planting, gradually tapering this off to an absolute minimum. Once your plants are established, water them only very lightly when they show visible signs of wilting.

Pruning & Training
Embrace Single-truss Pruning
For Regular & Beefsteak Varieties: As soon as the first bunch of fruit sets, pinch out the growing tip of the plant three leaves above this truss and remove all sideshoots – you should barely need to stake or prune ever again.

For Cherry Varieties: Allow the super-vigorous 'king shoot' (the sideshoot immediately below the flower truss) to develop to create a short Y-shaped plant before pinching out the tip three leaves after its first fruit set. Japanese studies have determined that the yield of cherry varieties trained according to this system can be doubled without a detrimental impact on the quality of the fruit. The only downside is that plants pruned this way may need a little staking.

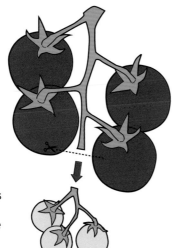

Snipping off the tip of each truss to leave a maximum of 4–5 fruit on regular tomatoes or 8–10 on cherry varieties ensures they ripen easily, at the same time improving their size and flavour.

Feed
Get Out The Big Guns
Apply liberal doses of aspirin booster spray and soakings of molasses tonic once a month throughout the summer, ideally in the mid-morning, as this is when tomato plants are growing at their fastest (see under Harvest & Storage, right).

Drench with Sea Water
When the small, green fruits have just begun to swell to the size of a pea, drench the soil around the plants in a sea salt solution. Use 60g (2oz) sea salt and 3 litres (5 pints) water to every square metre (10 sq ft) of ground, being extremely careful not to wet the leaves. Repeat the process two weeks later, then don't do it again for a year.

Harvest & Storage
Harvest In The Afternoon
Tomato plants grow most actively in the morning, drawing up loads of water from their roots, making this the ideal time to water. By late afternoon the sun will have dried the plants out a little, concentrating the sugars and flavour chemicals in the fruit, making this the best time to harvest. For maximum flavour punch, some growers even let their plants wilt for a day or two before picking, to guarantee honey-like sweetness.

Avoid The Fridge At All Costs
Tomatoes can be stored for a good few days without losing their rich flavour. This is because the fruit continue to develop their aromatic compounds to replace those that are being continually evaporated off into the air – that is, unless you put them in the fridge. As we saw earlier (see page 33), temperatures below 10°C (50°F) can have a disastrous effect on their taste. Far better to keep tomatoes in the fruit bowl or just on the kitchen counter.

FLAVOUR FROM FOLIAGE

Love the intoxicating herbal scent of fresh tomato leaves? Well, why not use them to cook with? Despite the popular misconception that they are toxic (they are part of the deadly nightshade family, after all) tomato leaves are fast becoming a popular ingredient with top US chefs, for their ability to impart the foresty, 'green' flavour aroma of the vine to soups and sauces.

Although tomato leaves do contain very small amounts of a toxic chemical called tomatine (also incidentally found in all green-fleshed tomato varieties and of course in green tomato chutney!), this is at such a low dosage you would have to eat literally kilograms of them on a regular basis to have any noticeable effect – making them arguably as safe to eat as crops like rhubarb or almonds that also contain small quantities of toxins.

ONE-POT TOMATO-LEAF PASTA

When added to even the most boring shop-bought jar of pasta sauce, just a few leaves are enough to cheat a fresh-from-the-garden flavour. But I like to go one better and add them to my own one-pot recipe, where the pasta is cooked in its own sauce. Yes, I know it sounds implausible, but it really does work. Perfect for lazy foodies who love home-grown flavour, but hate washing up!

What You Need:

350g (12oz) spaghetti

2 tomato leaves, whole

350g (12oz) tomatoes: I've used **'Russian Rose'**, **'Yellow Pear'** and **'Green Zebra'** varieties

1 red chilli, sliced

1 litre (1¾ pints) stock

1 onion, thinly sliced

2 tablespoons olive oil

5 cloves garlic, chopped

What To Do:

BUNG everything into a wide shallow pan, boil for 10 minutes, fish out the tomato leaves and get greedy!

SUPER SALAD GREENS

With their short shelf life and delicate constitution, salad leaves are some of the most expensive items on the fruit and veg aisles. Yet they are also rather conveniently some of the quickest and easiest to grow. As almost any plant with tender, edible leaves can be used as a salad green, there is much more to these crops than watery iceberg and flavourless-to-a-fault baby spinach. Check out my guide to growing the most tender, succulent leaves, including some unexpected options.

PICK YOUR FLAVOUR

The same salad crop can be made either mild and sweet or more full on and fiery simply by how you choose to grow it. Of course, you can always go down the third route of meeting these criteria halfway, picking and choosing a mix of the above approaches to create 'Goldilocks' leaves that are not too hot, not too mild, but just right for your own personal taste. Let me explain...

Mild & Sweet

Looking for the tenderest, most delicately flavoured greens? Follow the mainstream advice and you'll be fine.

Shady Site

As most flavour chemicals develop best in full sun, **opting to grow salads in a spot with light shade will suppress any potentially fiery or bitter notes in your leaves.** Out of direct sun the leaves will also expand wider as they stretch out to grab hold of as much light as possible, making them less fibrous, softer and even more delicately flavoured.

In Pots

Growing salad leaves, in trays or pots of soilless compost, rather than in the ground, can make them even more mild flavoured. This is due to the lack of trace minerals that plants use to manufacture pungent or fiery flavour chemicals.

High Water

Generous waterings and applications of dilute nitrogen-rich feed will enhance the effect of growing salad leaves in partial shade, pumping the expanded leaves full of water, reducing the concentration of any potentially strong flavours and giving them a juicy, fresh crunch. This regime will also prevent the plants from flowering, which is another factor that can trigger the development of strong flavours or tough fibres.

Baby Leaves

The immature leaves of most plants are not only the most succulent and tender, but have also yet to develop the chemicals that give the adult plants of some species their strong or bitter flavours (see page 159).

Full On & Fiery

If it's peppery pungency you want, be a horticultural rebel and do the exact opposite...

Sunny Site

Siting your salad patch in the sunniest spot you have **will allow flavours to develop to their maximum potential.** Growing this way will also significantly raise the levels of phytonutrients such as glucosinolates in the leaves as these are the same chemicals that create bitter, fiery flavours.

In The Ground

Your salad plants are likely to have access to a far more complete range of minerals, which can be vital to producing the fullest flavour, when grown in the garden soil. True lovers of fieriness have even been known to scatter a tablespoon or two of Epsom Salts (magnesium sulphate, available at any chemist) over the soil before planting, as they are a rich natural source of sulphur, which plants such as rocket and mustard use to manufacture pungent flavour chemicals.

Low Water

A good guide is to water only when the plants have begun to wilt. If you are gardening on heavy soil you could even dig plenty of grit or sand into the bed to improve drainage and prevent the plants' roots from soaking up masses of moisture from damp, waterlogged soil. This water stress will often also induce your plants to flower, which can trigger the formation of yet more pungent flavours in some species.

Mature Plants

Delaying harvesting until the plants are larger gives them a chance to ramp up the production of flavour chemicals, resulting in an altogether more punchy crop.

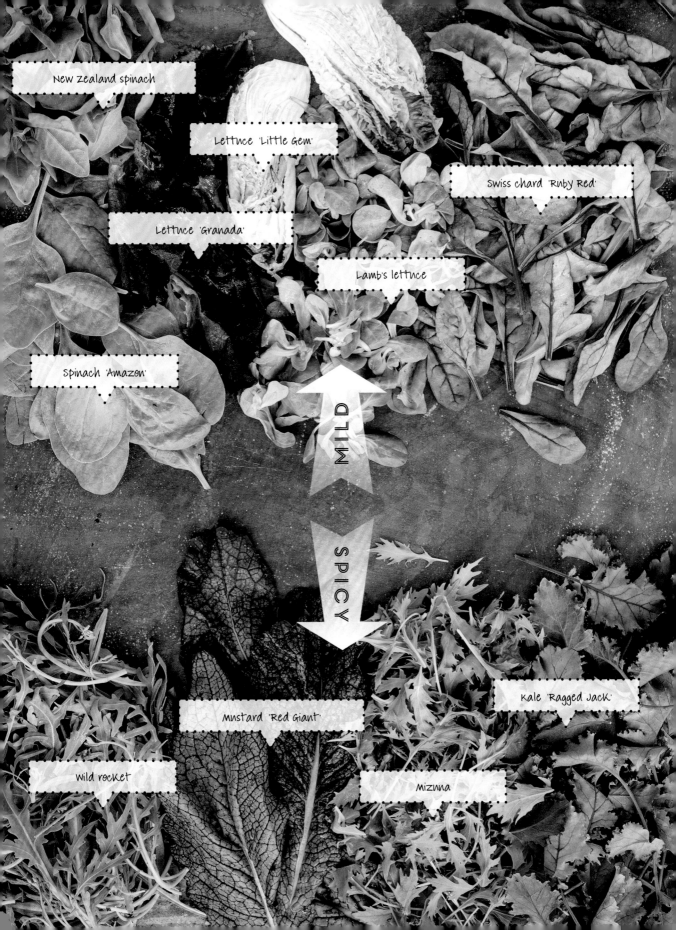

New Zealand spinach

Lettuce 'Little Gem'

Swiss chard 'Ruby Red'

Lettuce 'Granada'

Lamb's lettuce

Spinach 'Amazon'

MILD

SPICY

Kale 'Ragged Jack'

Mustard 'Red Giant'

Wild rocket

Mizuna

Rocket 'Dragon's Tongue'

Radicchio 'Castelfranco'

Nasturtium 'Empress of India'

Radicchio 'Rosso di Treviso'

Land seaweed

Marsh samphire

MAVERICK LEAVES

Keen to explore the world of salad leaves that lies beyond supermarket staples? Well, these gourmet greens are some of the best-tasting and easiest of all to grow.

NASTURTIUM

Tropaeolum majus

The Peppery One

Despite being possibly the most flavourful and versatile of all salad crops, and one that will grow almost anywhere you like, **this exotic Incan vegetable has been unfairly relegated to the flower border for over a hundred years.** Yet give it a chance in your veg patch and it will adorn your beds with an almost inexhaustible supply of peppery leaves, watercress-flavoured flowers and crisp seed pods for literally months on end. All nasturtiums are edible, but I particularly love **'Empress of India'** for its dwarf stature and purple-blushed leaves.

Nasturtiums are one of the easiest edible plants to grow from seed: sow them 1.5cm (½in) deep in a finely prepared bed of well-drained soil, where they are to flower. For quicker crops, start them off earlier in the season in little pots, 2-3 seeds in each, and put them on a sunny windowsill or in a glasshouse. Once the seedlings are up and growing, and all risk of frost has passed, they can be planted out in the garden.

WILD ROCKET

Diplotaxis tenuifolia

The Fiery One

For hard-core spice fiends like me, I cannot recommend any salad green more highly than wild rocket. It has been specifically selected for its nose-tingling, horseradishy/wasabi flavour - like regular rocket doused with a fancy wasabi vinaigrette. Being packed full of glucosinolates, the powerful antioxidant chemicals found in broccoli and watercress, wild rocket is as good for you as it is tasty.

Like most rocket varieties it will enthusiastically self-seed everywhere in your garden, giving you a perpetual supply from the five minutes it takes to sow it. I particularly love the variety **'Dragon's Tongue'** with its deep burgundy veins that not only look great on the plate but also make them easy to pick out when they spring up in the most unexpected of places.

LAND SEAWEED

Salsola soda

The Weird One

These shaggy tufts of wispy leaves are massive in Japan, where they are known as *okahijiki.* On the other side of the world, under the name *agretti* or *barba di frati* (literally 'monks' beard'), they are a regional delicacy in Italy. Yet the curious culinary charm of land seaweed has remained, until very recently, a well-kept secret from the rest of the world.

The thick-skinned leaves are crisp on the outside but curiously succulent and slippery within; they have a mild grassy flavour with subtle sour and bitter hints. **They are delicious eaten raw or very briefly steamed and dressed with oil in summer salads or tossed in pasta.**

These are easy-to-grow, vigorous plants that will better tolerate constant bouts of clipping throughout the summer, not to mention drier conditions, than almost any other salad leaf. There is one slight catch, however: the seeds have a notoriously short viability, meaning they are stocked only by specialist catalogues, usually online. Even then only about half the seeds you plant will actually germinate. On the plus side, to counteract this, packets are usually very generous (containing up to 2,000 seeds) and the plants that do come up are extremely productive.

Order seeds to be delivered in mid-spring and sow them immediately 1cm (½in) deep in moist garden soil in a sunny spot. Water in well. Germination should be rapid, taking 7-10 days, so you will soon know if you have not received a viable batch. My experience is that most retailers are extremely responsible and only advertise freshly gathered stock. When they reach 10cm (4in) tall, thin them to 10-15cm (4-6in) apart. Alternatively, some catalogues sell young plug plants via mail order, meaning you get to sidestep the germination problems.

> Both wild rocket and nasturtium are prolific self-seeders and will soon pop up all over your garden, making them crops that quite literally plant themselves.

MARSH SAMPHIRE

Salicornia europaea

The Salty One

This native salt-marsh plant seems to have come out of nowhere to become one of the trendiest new veg on restaurant menus and the fish counters of upmarket supermarkets all over the place. **Its strange, crisp fingers are packed full of a succulent, salty-flavoured gel, tasting like a breath of fresh ocean air.** Being rich in vitamin C and with a truly unusual flavour, marsh samphire works best served with seafood dishes, either raw, flash-fried in a little butter or even pickled in vinegar.

For a plant specifically adapted to grow only in an extreme coastal environment, marsh samphire can be surprisingly easy to get away with at home if you are willing to provide it with its two finicky requests: **frequent dousing with salty water and plenty of sunshine.** I water mine twice a week using 1 litre (1¾ pints) of tap water mixed with 6 teaspoons sea salt. Sea salt is by far preferable to regular salt as it contains a broader range of minerals that can help fuel the growth of your plant. Although I have found it will grow relatively well without this, marsh samphire does lose its characteristic salty flavour and can start to develop lanky, lax foliage. The plants can be grown from seed, but germination can be a little erratic. You can also buy young plants by mail order from a specialist nursery.

The easiest way to grow this plant is in a medium-sized tub or trough of gravel with no drainage hole. While it doesn't demand slavish devotion to a saline schedule, the one thing it will not compromise on is sunlight. Pick a bright spot that enjoys direct sunlight all day, remember to add briny water now and then, and your plants will be quite happy to take care of themselves.

RADICCHIO

Cichorium intybus

The Bitter One

The stunning burgundy-coloured leaves of this Italian chicory look incredible in an autumnal salad, and their exceedingly bitter taste makes a wonderful contrast to many of the sugary sweet flavours of the season, like apples and pears. Add a honey-mustard dressing, a handful of walnuts and a crumble of Wensleydale and you will be in greedy grower heaven. The bitter flavour and intense colour of radicchio are caused by a high concentration of phytonutrient chemicals, making them a fantastically healthy choice.

I sow mine in mid to late summer, directly into beds of soil in full sun (if you are going to grow a bitter crop, it might as well taste bitter). Once the seedlings are up I thin them out to 35cm (14in) apart and let them get on with it. **Keeping on top of the watering makes their leaves nice and crisp without diluting flavour**, with the occasional high-nitrogen feed helping boost this further. By early autumn you should be able to make your first harvests, and the plants are hardy and slow-growing enough for you to pick them continuously right through to the following spring.

For both flavour and taste I recommend **'Grumolo Rossa'**, a late-maturing variety from Verona, whose foliage looks like burgundy-coloured roses. Likewise there is **'Castelfranco'** with its beautiful smattering of red on green foliage. **'Orchidea Rossa'** (literally 'Red Orchid') has stunning blooms of claret foliage early in the season. The super-hardy spears of **'Rosso di Treviso'** turn red and white after the first hard frosts, resisting sub-zero freezes and coming packed with up to 10 times the antioxidants of most salad greens.

HEALTH GEEK FACT

The open-leaved, purple radicchio cultivar 'Rosso di Treviso' has **X10** the phytonutrients of green radicchio varieties.

USE SEAWEED TO BOOST NUTRITION & FLAVOUR

Several studies suggest that you can increase the content of key phytonutrients in leafy crops like spinach, cabbage and broccoli simply by spraying them with a dilute solution of seaweed extract. In fact, in spinach the result can up to double normal levels! Just a single soaking in a solution of 1g commercial seaweed extract per litre of water (⅙oz per gallon) two weeks before harvest can be enough to send the content of potent plant nutrients like phenolics and flavonoids soaring.

For flavour junkies this spike in flavonoids is particularly exciting, as research at Pennsylvania State University has demonstrated that these slightly bitter compounds can help to improve the flavour of a wide variety of cooked foods. Adding these health-giving compounds appears to block the production of 'off flavours' that result from scalding or overcooking foods, without any noticeable increase in bitterness.

BETTER THAN PARSNIPS

I might as well confess right now, I *cannot* grow parsnips. They are my horticultural nemesis. I've tried every trick in the book, from controlled chilling in the fridge to whacky lunar planting, but they seem determined either never to germinate or to fork out almost immediately into fibrous rooty masses. Fortunately for me they are cheap and widely available in all supermarkets, with a flavour that (I am reliably informed) varies little from home-grown.

The unexpected silver lining to my parsnip-growing trials and tribulations, however, was that my furious research unearthed some of their long-lost relatives which, to my great surprise, are not only easier to grow and harder to buy, but downright better tasting. Hallelujah!

CHERVIL ROOT

Chaerophyllum bulbosum

What Is It?

With their sky-high sugar content and fluffy starchiness, these short, stubby roots, also known as turnip-rooted chervil, are probably best described as tasting like a cross between syrup-sweetened parsnips and floury, buttered baked potatoes.

Once one of the most highly esteemed of all root veg, chervil root's delicious thumb-sized morsels have mysteriously disappeared from our diets over the last century or two. In my opinion this is nothing short of a culinary tragedy, as they are positively **the sweetest, creamiest root vegetable that can be grown in temperate climates** (and believe me I have grown my fair share of the weird and wonderful). They are still adored by the foodie-minded French, who traditionally consider parsnips a fodder crop fit only for livestock. Trust me, if you try chervil root, you'll soon think the same.

They are extremely low in terpenes (the group of chemicals with a turpentine-like flavour that are found in the roots of most of the carrot family), so any of that metallic harshness carrots and parsnips can have is entirely absent. In chervil roots the terpenes have been replaced with fragrant aroma compounds whose unique, almost floral hint of fragrance perfectly complements the sweetness of the vegetable.

How To Grow Them

Chervil root can be grown like parsnips or carrots (see pages 73-74) with two slight adjustments. First, the seeds need to be stratified in order to germinate, which basically means subjecting them to a few weeks of cool, damp temperatures. Sow them in autumn and the winter chill will naturally spark them into growth the next spring.

As with all members of the carrot family, chervil's seed is extremely short-lived and can germinate erratically, although in my experience nowhere near as erratically as that of parsnips. To get around this, it is important to buy new seed each year and resist the temptation to use the leftovers from last season. It is even advisable to store the seed in the fridge if you cannot plant it immediately.

The other key difference between chervil roots and parsnips or carrots is that they take far longer to grow, first reaching maturity late in the summer the year after sowing. They then become infinitely sweeter after the first autumn frosts start to break their starch down into sugars. In short, this means a full 12 months between sowing and harvest, but boy are they worth it!

How To Eat Them

Use chervil root in all the same ways you would parsnips or potatoes: mashed with cream and nutmeg, roasted in goose fat, blitzed into soups with sautéed leeks or simmered in a veggie curry with roast pumpkin and cauliflower. I think I may have gained a good half-kilo just typing this...

A LOT'S IN A NAME
Chervil root is actually a totally different species to the herb chervil (*Anthriscus cerefolium*). To be 100 percent sure, look for the name *Chaerophyllum bulbosum* on the pack.

HAMBURG PARSLEY

Petroselinum crispum var. *tuberosum*

What Is It?

This large-rooted form of parsley is the perfect horticultural multitasker, producing masses of flat-leaf parsley up top and skinny, sweet mini parsnips below. As a vegetable it is of major importance to Eastern European cuisine, where the roots are added to soups, stews and casseroles, as well as being sliced and eaten raw in salads, just as you would a carrot. **The flavour is similar to that of parsnips, but with the cleaner, grassy freshness of parsley.** Funny that.

How To Grow It

You grow it exactly as you would parsnips, only it's easier. The roots are nowhere near as prone to forking, the seeds are far easier to germinate and, being relatively quick growing, they can be ready to harvest in half the time. All that plus a harvest of fresh parsley leaves while you wait. What's not to like?

How To Eat It

For me, Hamburg parsley is essential for truly first-rate stocks and soups, providing a double hit of sweet carrotiness along with the herby fragrance of parsley. Try it sliced into a clear chicken soup with garlic, red chillies and plenty of ginger for a winter pick-me-up that works every time. Serve scattered with spring onions and a drizzle of sesame oil.

SKIRRET

Sium sisarum

What Is It?

Ladies and gentlemen, I present to you skirret, one of the best-tasting, yet least-grown veg crops out there.

Now here is a proposition for you: how about a heritage root veg with double the sweetness of parsnips and with frothy panicles of white flowers that will come back year after year from a single sowing? Skirret plants produce big bunches of long ivory roots that taste similar to parsnips, albeit more starchy and with a significantly higher sugar content. **The very name skirret comes from the Dutch for 'sugar root'.** Widely eaten until the early part of the 20th century, the roots are no more than 1cm (½in) thick and with thin, edible skins, I like to think of them as pre-peeled, pre-sliced parsnips that are sweet enough to eat raw.

How To Grow It

Skirret's biggest boon is that it is a perennial, meaning that once you are over the initial hurdle of getting the seeds to germinate (which can be a nightmare with all the carrot/parsnip family), they will flourish for years and even spread enthusiastically through your beds.

Some specialist suppliers (usually herb nurseries) sell small, ready-grown plants in the spring, meaning you can skip the germination stage altogether. Plant them up in a sunny spot in deep, rich, well-drained soil and let them get to work. Unlike most members of the carrot family they will cope with even quite heavy soil, though your yields may be lower and the resultant roots a tad more fibrous.

Harvest your underground bounty in autumn or early winter, after the first frosts have withered the plants' leaves. You will be faced with a big mass of long, white, pencil-thick roots. Snip off about 80 percent of these, leaving the ones surrounding the base intact, and put the plant back in the ground. When kept moist with the odd quick boost of liquid feed each summer, a single planting will keep you in stock with skirret for years to come.

EDIBLE ORNAMENTAL Skirret's frothy white flowers are so pretty, yet they are capable of hiding incognito in any flower border. A true horticultural multitasker.

How To Eat It

Given nothing more than a quick scrub, skirret roots make spectacularly sweet, crisp crudités – team them with posh hummus scattered with pomegranate seeds and a drizzle of unfiltered olive oil for a match made in heaven. For something altogether less virtuous, **try parboiling them and frying them in goose fat to make positively the most addictive 'chips' ever.** A perfect trifecta of fluffy carbs, fat and sugar.

For unbridled comfort-food cosiness I turn skirret roots into the gratin to end all gratins. Layer the parboiled roots in a baking dish with caramelized onions and crispy fried bacon. Then slather over a rich béchamel, top with grated cheese and pop in the oven at 200°C/400°F/gas mark 6 for 10 minutes or so until golden.

Hamburg parsley 'Eagle'

chervil root

skirret

CORN

Corn has to be one of the easiest gourmet veg around, offering up jaw-dropping flavour without the need for any special cultivation tips and tricks. Step out of the supermarket comfort zone of boring, canary-yellow cobs and you'll discover a world of flavour, texture and colour so varied you'd never believe it could come from the same plant.

VARIETY GUIDE

Field Corn

You may have noticed this page is entitled not 'sweet corn' but 'corn'. This isn't a typo. In fact, there are hundreds of corn varieties out there that are not sweet at all, possessing instead an altogether richer, more rounded flavour and starchy texture, ranging from chestnut-like flouriness to the waxy creaminess of a new potato. These are so wildly different in flavour from sweet corn (think the difference between popcorn and corn on the cob) that even the most ardent sweet corn haters could fall for their charms – especially when they find out they are significantly easier to grow in a cold, blustery climate!

I am a particularly big fan of **'Blue Jade'**, which produces uber-cute 7cm (2½in) pods of tender violet kernels on tiny 1m (3ft) high plants. **'Bloody Butcher'** may not have the most glamorous name, but this US heirloom variety does exactly what it says on the tin, producing bicoloured kernels of deep red and black that have a moreish, chestnutly crunch. **'Fiesta'** is a popcorn variety whose fresh, waxy kernels knock the socks off any Jersey Royal. **Ditch the spuds for a couple of these technicoloured wonders at your next barbecue and I promise you'll never, ever look back.**

Sweet Corn

'Old-fashioned' Sweet Corn, 5–10 Percent Sugar

The original sweet corn varieties were the result of a random genetic mutation discovered by Native Americans. This impairs the ability of maize plants to convert the sugars in their kernels into stores of starch efficiently, creating sweet-tasting cobs with between 5 and 10 percent sugar.

Bucking the trend of modern crop-breeding efforts, there has been a huge amount of work in the last 60 years driven almost entirely by flavour. In the quest for ever-increasing sweetness, geneticists have discovered two further sweet corn mutations, resulting in a massive near 10-fold leap in the sugar content, producing cobs that can be almost 50 percent pure sugar by weight.

'Sugar-enhanced' Hybrids, 14–25 Percent Sugar

This is my favourite of the two main types of modern, sugar-charged sweet corn varieties. First developed in the 1970s, it contains a naturally occurring gene which boosts its sugar content without impairing its characteristic 'corny' flavour. This same gene conveniently also causes the skin of the kernels to be far thinner, resulting in a much more tender, creamy texture. The flavour of old-fashioned corn, with the sweetness of modern hybrids. What's not to like?

I particularly love **'Ruby Queen'** for its brilliant scarlet ears with the silky tenderness of rice pudding. **'Sugar Baby'** is a bicoloured variety of golden and pearly white kernels that thrives even in cool weather, offering up ears laced with hints of malt loaf and barley sugar. Finally, there is the tried-and-tested UK favourite **'Swift'**, with home-grown kernels that are far sweeter than anything you can buy in the shops.

'Supersweet' Hybrids, 28–44 Percent Sugar

Sweetest of all are the modern 'supersweet' hybrids, which contain a third gene that can make their cobs 10 times more sugary than conventional sweet corn, though in so doing they lose much of their characteristic flavour and texture. However, if you are after an unbridled sugar rush you simply cannot beat **'Illini Xtra Sweet'**, which can be up to twice

'Mirai White'

'Indian Summer'

'Illini Xtra Sweet'

'Ruby Queen'

'Sugar Baby'

'Fiesta'

'Bloody Butcher'

'Blue Jade'

SUGAR CONTENT

UP TO
44%

LESS
THAN
5%

as sweet as other supersweets, with up to *four times* the sugar of conventional sweet corn. It produces good yields from sturdy plants. **'Indian Summer' AGM** is a stunning variety with kernels in white, yellow, blue and pink all on the same cob, as sweet as they are colourful. **'Earlibird'** has been granted a prestigious RHS AGM medal after proving a top performer in its UK trials, while **'Mirai White'** AGM

is a pure white form, with an almost pavlova-like creaminess and it has the superior ability to soldier on through cold, wet soils.

Traditional sweet corn is given its silky, creamy texture by a slippery starch called phytoglycogen. In the headlong pursuit of unparalleled sweetness, in 'supersweet' corn even the phytoglycogen has been transformed into sugar, making the kernels tough and crunchy.

TIPS & TRICKS

Unlike so many other crops, home-grown sweet corn's flavour doesn't appear to be much affected by growing techniques. Watering levels don't seem to have any significant impact on sugar content, and trials into fertiliser rates have turned up mixed results. This means that aside from picking a great-tasting variety, all you have to do for maximum flavour is to harvest and cook it right. It doesn't get easier than that!

Harvesting
Choose Your Moment

Sweet corn is ready to harvest when its silks (the long female threads at the end of their cobs) have dried and turned brown, yet their leafy sheaths are still fresh and green. **The gold-standard test is to peel back the sheaths gently and pierce a kernel with your fingernail.** If the kernels are plump and exude a milky white fluid, they are perfectly ripe and ready to eat. Commercial growers refer to this stage of maximum sugar content as the 'milk stage': any earlier and your crops will taste watery; any later and they can take on a doughy consistency and flavour. This window can be quite short, particularly in some of the old-fashioned varieties, so it is worth checking back every day or so once the silks have dried.

Eating
Freeze-frame The Flavour

After variety choice, to me the single most important factor in ensuring maximum flavour lies not in growing, but in cooking. **From the moment a cob is picked off the plant, chemical triggers within each kernel are set in motion to turn any remaining sugars into starches.** Even in the modern supersweet varieties, a delay in getting it from plot to plate can seriously dent the flavour you have worked so hard to get your teeth into. **In fact, some corn varieties can lose more than half their sugar content within just 12 hours of storage.** That's a 4 percent drop in flavour for every hour you delay the scoffing process!

The old-school tip to get around this is to get your pan of water boiling before dashing straight out to harvest your cobs. I have always found this advice rather strange, as the sugars (and other flavour chemicals) in corn are water soluble, making boiling it one of the most efficient ways to leach out flavour, not to mention nutrients. Steaming has a milder version of the same effect. Instead, **I like to dunk the newly harvested cobs, still in their leafy sheaths, into a bucket of ice cold water before chucking them straight over the hot coals of a barbecue, under a grill or even a microwave.** This helps seal in the flavour, with the water preventing the sheaths from charring. Alternatively, you can bung your cobs in the freezer to stop this chemical reaction in its tracks, which is fantastically handy if you are growing loads of the stuff.

NUCLEAR-STRENGTH SWEETNESS?

All 'supersweet' varieties can trace their origins back to a single mutant gene discovered in a random batch of seeds from the Maize Genetics Center at University of Illinois. This unique stockpile of thousands of mutant corn strains sourced the bulk of its chromosomal aberrations from a series of bizarre US military experiments. No, really.

Documents first declassified in 1997 reveal that in the late 1940s US naval scientists subjected healthy corn seeds to the radiation of atomic bomb blasts to test the effect of nuclear warfare on plant growth, and in so doing created an almost infinite diversity of mutations unknown in nature. A treasure trove for breeders. The rest is history.

Field corn powering through a chilly summer.

The 'supersweet' variety next to it is lagging weeks behind.

THE GREAT SUGAR TRADE-OFF

Just by looking at the seeds, you can see why 'supersweet' corn is the trickiest type to grow. Its shrunken appearance is due to the fact that its supersweet status hampers its ability to generate the stores of starch that power the growth of young seedlings.

'Supersweets' also demand to be planted at least 80m (250ft) away from all other forms of corn lest they lose their thoroughbred sweetness by cross-breeding through wind-borne pollen. Not easy if you are an allotmenteer!

IN SEED FORM

Field Corn

'Supersweet'

HOW TO GROW CORN

Sow & Grow

• **Start off in late spring by soaking your corn seeds for 12 hours in my camomile and aspirin seed-sprouting solution.** Dilute solutions of aspirin-like compounds have been demonstrated in some trials greatly to improve the cold tolerance of sweet corn seedlings, potentially doubling their growth rate in chilly springs. Camomile contains natural anti-fungals. Applying this as a tonic can work to help ensure your resultant seedlings are healthy and disease resistant. To make it, drop ⅛th of a 300mg soluble aspirin tablet into 1 litre (1¾ pints) of cold camomile tea and give it a good shake.

• **Sow seed indoors on a warm, sunny windowsill.** Corn seedlings hate root disturbance, so plant in deep root trainer or coir 'Jiffy' pots to minimize transplant stress.

• Standard advice is to plant two seeds per pot, later thinning out the weaker seedling. However, **my trials in Devon have shown that, by leaving both seedlings to mature side by side, you can up yields by as much as 60 percent without affecting flavour.** Get in!

• Once your new seedlings are kicking out their fourth leaf and after all risk of frost has passed, they should be ready to plant out into the ground in the sunniest, warmest location you have.

• **Corn is wind-pollinated**, so planting your seedlings not in rows but in blocks at least four plants across (45cm/18in apart) will result in much larger, better-filled cobs.

Growing On

• **When plants start to develop 8–10 leaves, give them a boost with a high-nitrogen fertiliser like chicken manure.** According to some (but not all) studies this could help raise the aroma compounds that give corn its characteristic flavour, plus nudge up the sugar content of your cobs by more than 25 percent.

• Chucking a 1cm (½in) layer of grass clippings around the base of your corn plants each time you mow is a great way further to boost the soil nitrogen, while sealing in water and cutting down on weeds. No lawn? Compost will work, too.

• Plants generally don't require slavish devotion to the hose; however, **generous watering is key while seedlings are establishing**, and then again when the plants are flowering. This will help increase yield, without watering down flavour.

• **Tapping the tops of the plants when the antennae-like male flowers (tassels) open will rain pollen down to the female (silks) below, helping ensure nice, full cobs.**

SKIP THE SYNTHETICS?

A study from the University of California showed that organically grown corn had more than 50 percent more vitamin C and significantly more polyphenols than conventionally grown corn. While the jury may be still out on this issue and results may vary, I'd prefer to skip the synthetics.

NEVER SHUCK CORN AGAIN!

Following this simple trick means no fiddly peeling or fuzzy silks.

COOK your corn with the sheaths on as described on page 54, then slice the bottom 2cm (¾in) off the cooked cob. Careful, it's hot!

TWIST the bottom of the cob and gently pull it away. Watch as it pops out perfectly clean.

DOUSE in butter and get greedy.

FROZEN
CORN POPS

In Japan whole frozen corn cobs are eaten like ice lollies as a popular late-summer treat for kids. They are so sweet and creamy that little sugar monsters will barely notice how healthy they are. This is veg serving via deception.

FOLD back the leaves around each sheath and tie them back in a bundle with a piece of string. This will form your lolly 'stick'.

POP the cobs into a plastic bag and freeze until solid (about 6 hours).

DRIZZLE over some cream and a sprinkle of (all natural) hundreds and thousands as soon as the cobs leave the freezer – they will stick solid and persuade even the most five-a-day-phobic young 'un to get stuck in.

PEAS, ONLY BETTER

If you were to set up a blindfold taste test ranking crops according to the flavour difference of home-grown versus store-bought, peas would come close to the top spot almost every time. But unless you want to turn over your entire plot to growing them, the sad truth is you'd struggle to get more than a single meal's worth, not to mention the hours of fiddly picking and shelling involved.

Luckily for pea junkies like myself, in the course of my experiments I have stumbled upon a range of close pea relatives that offer up the same sugary, green creaminess for a fraction of the time and space. They're peas, only better.

MINI BROAD BEAN PODS

Sadly, old-school gardening advice will tell you to harvest broad beans when they are actually way past their best. This delicate spring veg, picked in Spain and France when still no bigger than your little fingernail, will have swelled into sacks of leathery-skinned starchiness by the time they reach familiar supermarket size. Sacrilege!

Yet I think we can go one better by harvesting young pods when they are tender and green and eating them like mangetout. There are even two gourmet varieties that are grown for this purpose: **'Statissa'**, with its creamy seeds and thin, succulent skins, and **'Stereo'**, which is famously the finest tasting of all varieties, with an intensely sweet, nutty flavour.

Pick the pods off when they have reached finger length and slice them raw into a salad of goats' cheese and roasted red onions, or grill them whole and scatter with shards of *jamón ibérico*, lemon rind and walnuts.

PEA SHOOTS & FLOWERS

It's not just pea pods themselves that are edible, but the whole plant, with the tender shoots and flowers also packed with the same fresh vegetal sweetness. In fact, in the Far East, pea shoots are considered a high-end ingredient, costing much more than the peas themselves. While in the US and Europe, pea flowers are sold for a fortune to swanky restaurants.

'Twinkle' produces masses of succulent leaves on its tiny shoots. **'Bingo'** is its opposite, with leaves replaced by masses of curly tendrils. I love the pretty pink flowers of **'Shiraz'** or **'Blauwschokker'**, which rival anything in the flower border.

SUGAR SNAPS & MANGETOUT

These two culinary gems are easier to grow and harvest than regular peas, yet far more expensive to buy, which makes me wonder why anyone grows regular peas. Eating them whole also means no fiddly shelling and twice the potential yield, not to mention the fact that the crisp, sweet pods contain loads more fibre and antioxidants than the peas themselves.

I love the deep burgundy-podded forms like **'Shiraz'** or **'Blauwschokker'**, with their savoury, almost chestnutty taste. These are definitely best eaten raw, though, as cooking degrades the colour and delicate flavour. **'Golden Sweet'** is a mangetout form which, as its name suggests, is particularly sugary, with a fresh grassy green bite. **'Sugar Ann'** is a snap variety famous for its unsurpassed flavour and stringless pods, produced on stout bushy plants that never need staking.

CHICKPEA "EDAMAME"

Chickpeas that are harvested tender and green and eaten cooked in their pods, just like edamame, are probably the most underrated veg in the whole pea and bean family. They have an outstanding pistachio flavour and are as easy to grow as they are tasty. Sow the seeds straight into the ground in spring just as you would dwarf peas. The variety **'Principe'** will perform well in temperate conditions. The drought-tolerant, hardy, undemanding plants will soon produce hummocks of knee-high, feathery foliage, followed by masses of small pods in mid- to late summer. To prepare, boil the pods whole for a minute or two in salted water or pan-roast them in a large frying pan until they begin to char. **Serve drizzled with olive oil, sea salt and smoked paprika or sea salt and sesame oil.**

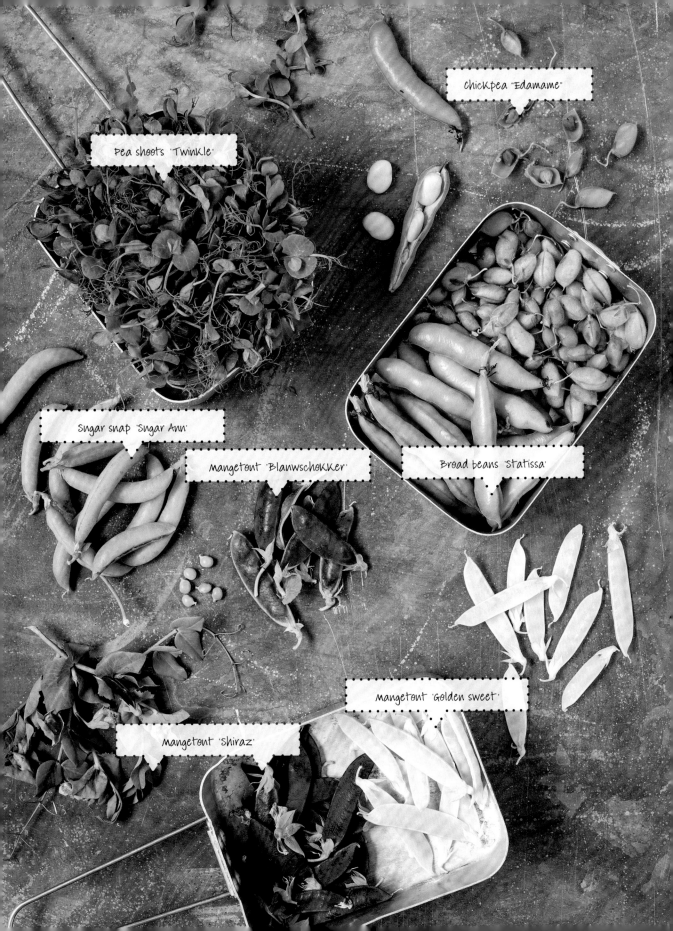

chickpea "Edamame"

Pea shoots 'Twinkle'

Sugar snap 'Sugar Ann'

Mangetout 'Blauwschokker'

Broad beans 'Statissa'

Mangetout 'Golden sweet'

Mangetout 'Shiraz'

CARROTS

Growing your own carrots not only opens up a dazzling array of colours and flavours far beyond anything the chilled bags of jumpsuit orange ones can offer, but with a few tips and tricks you can make them measurably sweeter and better for you. But don't take my word for it.

Researchers at the Norwegian Food Research Institute discovered that the tumbling and shaking that commercially grown carrots go through during machine washing and freighting causes a spike in the production of a group of chemicals known as terpenes that have a bitter, metallic flavour and ethanol-like odour. Oxygen-deprived in sealed plastic bags, their sugar levels start to dip, causing these acrid flavours to come to the fore. Sound familiar? Grow your own and discover how a carrot really should taste.

VARIETY GUIDE

Just like the chocolates in those big tins you buy at Christmas, the flavour of carrots is conveniently linked to their colour. Here's my guide to what's inside the wrapper.

Purple

Sceptical about new-fangled coloured varieties? Then you will love purple carrots, which actually predate the 'proper' orange varieties by centuries. They are also sweeter, contain fewer bitter chemicals and come packed with up to twice the nutritious carotene and a hefty dose of anthocyanins. Not a bad trade-off, in my opinion. They are incredible roasted, grated in salads or stir-fried. Do not boil them, though, as these purple pigments are water-soluble, meaning much of the colour and nutritional value will leach out if cooked this way.

I prefer to sidestep the commonly available 'Purple Haze' (which is actually just plain orange at its core) and go for the almost black 'Purple Sun', which is inked with maroon through and through, getting increasingly dark as the carrot matures. Hunt out seeds online and thank me come harvest time.

White

White carrots came out the top of blindfold taste trials in *Journal of Agricultural and Food Chemistry* and were demonstrated to contain the highest amounts of aromatic flavour chemicals of all varieties. I love 'Crème de Lite' for its almost artificial, flavour-intense carrotiness, with a slightly spicy aftertaste and skins so thin you don't have to peel them. Sadly, what they have in flavour they lack in nutrition, containing virtually no carotene or anthocyanins. But with flavour this good, who cares?

Red

Red carrots have traditionally been the dominant form of this root vegetable found in East Asia. They combine watermelon-red skin and rosy pink flesh and have a similar flavour to that of the classic orange carrots, but their larger cores (the sweetest part of most carrots) gives them a more sugary flavour. I'd go for the Japanese-bred variety 'Red Samurai', whose red hue comes from lycopene, the antioxidant found in tomatoes.

Orange

These are paradoxically the most recent of all carrot colours. After appearing only in the 17th century as a random mutation in the Netherlands, carrots were enthusiastically promoted for their colour, which is symbolic of the Dutch Royal House of Orange. They are pleasantly sweet, but can have a stronger, more earthy flavour than other varieties.

Within this familiar group there is a surprising diversity of flavour. Arguably the best is 'Nantes 2', an early variety from France with a rich, almost caramel-like flavour to match its coreless, tender texture. Research suggests that cultivars specifically bred for their high carotene levels are generally ranked more highly in taste tests, almost on a par with white carrots. 'Ingot', for example, to me tastes almost radioactively sugary, while 'Juwarot' is said to have double the carotene of any other orange type.

Yellow

These forms generally have the lowest concentrations of aroma chemicals which, combined with a high sugar content, gives them a mild, sweet flavour. They are a great option for people who don't like the intense, diesel-like taste that stronger carrots can have. If I had to pick one it would be 'Yellowstone'.

'Purple Sun'

'Purple Haze'

'Red Samurai'

'Nantes 2'

'Yellowstone'

'Crème de Lite'

TIPS & TRICKS

The flavour of carrots is the result of a fine balance of sugars and terpenes, bitter chemicals that have a strong turpentine-like aroma. Too high a dose of terpenes and carrots take on an acrid taste, like the smell of fresh varnish. Too much sugar and they will be sweet but bland, lacking that characteristic carrotiness. Here's my guide to getting this spot on.

. . . .

Forget Baby Carrots

Contrary to standard gardening advice, carrots are not sweeter when picked as baby veg – just more tender. In fact they accumulate sugars steadily throughout their growth cycle, becoming increasingly sweet (although admittedly more fibrous) as they age. Harvesting them when the tops showing above ground have reached the diameter of a bottle cap will give you a good balance between maximum sweetness and minimum fibre.

Keep Them Cool

Carrots grown in cooler conditions have been demonstrated to taste significantly sweeter than those allowed to bake in hot sun, and are consistently ranked as having a superior flavour in most taste tests. Ironically, this is not because they produce more sugar, but because they produce fewer terpenes to mask the sweetness we crave. Simply avoiding sowing carrots that will be harvested over the hottest months can measurably up the perceived sugariness of your crops.

Sugar Frosting

Several root veg taste noticeably sweeter after a touch of frost. This is because tumbling temperatures cause the plants to convert the starches in their roots to sugars, which they stockpile as a natural antifreeze. With all that dissolved sugar floating around their cells, the water cannot freeze, thus protecting the plant from damage. The lower the mercury falls, the tastier your harvests are likely to be.

Cook Them Whole

The most common way for many people to cook carrots is by plunging them peeled and sliced into boiling water. This is an excellent way to extract as much flavour and nutrition as possible out of the crop into the water. Too bad we then pour this down the sink! The UN's Food and Agriculture Organization reports that carrots can lose as much as 25 percent of their sugars cooked that way, along with much of the vitamin C and carotene. Steaming, roasting or baking them whole and slicing them up at the table will not only make them taste sweeter, but also conserve more of their water-soluble vitamins and minerals.

Flavour Anatomy Of A Carrot

Although the sugars are distributed fairly evenly through the roots, varying levels of terpenes result in different flavours in each part of a carrot.

The green bits that can sometimes form when the tops are exposed to the sun contain such high levels of terpenes that eating them is pure punishment. Earthing them up (i.e. covering the tops of the roots with soil) will help prevent this from happening.

Terpenes are generally concentrated in the tops and skin, making these bits taste much more bitter. If you like your salad sweet, peel and top your carrots for an instantly less acrid flavour.

Lower terpene levels at the core and tip make these parts taste milder and sweeter – perfect for salads and crudités. Use the strongly flavoured tops for intensely carroty soups and stews.

HOW TO GROW CARROTS

Although garden writers seem to insist on labelling them as easy to care for, carrots can be rather tricky to grow (well). Perilously susceptible to a pest called carrot fly, whose larvae riddle the roots with tunnels, carrots also have a habit of forking out into contorted masses if the soil is too rich, too stony, too wet or too heavy (which covers pretty much every patch I know). However, through much trial and error, I think I have finally hit on a winning formula to sidestep most of these challenges and give newbies a fighting chance.

Site & Soil

Growing plants in large pots can solve most problems in one fell swoop. A tailored growing mix gives plants a lightweight, stone-free soil that their roots can expand into uninterrupted. A low-fertility mix, such as the one recommended below, prevents the carrots from forking and improves their flavour at the same time. Trials show that carrots growing in a low-nitrogen mix contain more sugar and are described as tasting 'fruitier', 'less bitter', 'more intense' and 'less earthy'. Leave the soil to stabilize for a week before sowing.

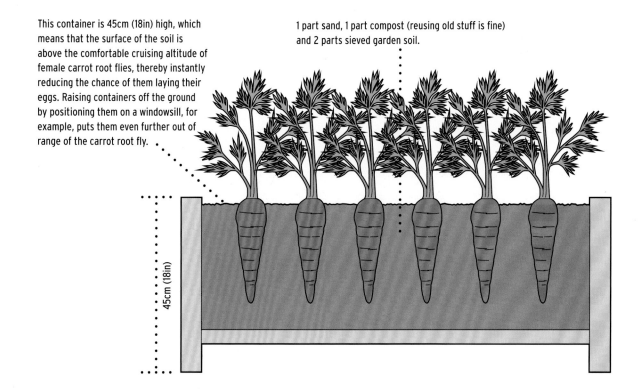

This container is 45cm (18in) high, which means that the surface of the soil is above the comfortable cruising altitude of female carrot root flies, thereby instantly reducing the chance of them laying their eggs. Raising containers off the ground by positioning them on a windowsill, for example, puts them even further out of range of the carrot root fly.

1 part sand, 1 part compost (reusing old stuff is fine) and 2 parts sieved garden soil.

45cm (18in)

Sowing

Sowing seeds sparsely reduces the amount you will have to thin out later on. This not only reduces labour but also the chances of your patch being detected by the dreaded carrot root fly.

15cm (6in) apart

2cm (¾in) deep

Planting seeds in very early summer misses out one of the main egg-laying windows of the carrot root fly, and ensures harvesting will occur during the cooler months of the year – leading to better flavour.

Thinning

Once seedlings raise their heads, it's time to select the best of the best. Ideally, do this in early evening, when carrot root flies are at their least active.

Thin the seedlings to 5cm (2in) apart by pulling them up gently with your thumb and forefinger. Water them first to avoid their roots breaking off and emitting their scent.

The pungent smell of garlic may mask the scent of thinned carrot seedlings from the carrot fly, which locate their prey (your crops) by smell. To capture it in all its pongy glory, blitz four garlic cloves in 500ml (17fl oz) of water, tip into a spray bottle and spritz over your seedlings as soon as you have thinned them out.

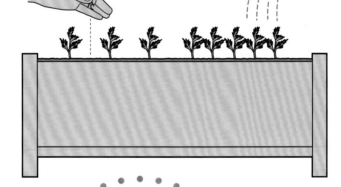

Mulching

As your crops mature, their heads may peek out over the surface of the soil. A thin layer of compost mulch excludes the light that can turn the tops green and bitter.

Scattering a little wood ash (if you have it) at this time boosts the soil's levels of potassium, which research suggests may also help promote sweetness.

Storing

According to trials at the University of Massachusetts, Amherst, **the sweetness of carrots actually improves with winter storage, peaking after about three months.**

CHEAT YOUR WAY TO SPEEDY SOWING SUCCESS

Using pre-spaced seed tape is a nifty way to turn hours of fiddly spacing into the work of mere minutes. These can be picked up at garden centres or online.

After this point, however, there is a marked decline, with the roots becoming increasingly bitter, so don't forget them!

The best way to store carrots, as well as many other root veg, is simply not to harvest them. The chilled yet aerated environment of the soil will (surprisingly) keep them fresher for longer than your fridge. That is, after all, what carrots' swollen roots have evolved to do. Laying a blanket of cardboard and straw over the surface of the soil and covering this in a sheet of polythene adds an extra layer of insulation to protect your buried stash from hard frosts.

What You Need:

FOR THE BASE

250g (10oz) digestive biscuits

125g (5oz) butter, melted

FOR THE FILLING

1 x 125g (5oz) packet lemon jelly crystals

2 'Purple Sun' carrots, about 20cm (8in) long

1 thumb-sized piece of ginger

250g (10oz) cream cheese

225g (8oz) caster sugar

1 teaspoon vanilla extract

½ teaspoon mixed spice

1 x 410g (14oz) can evaporated milk, chilled in the fridge for at least 6 hours

What To Do:

SEAL the biscuits in a plastic bag and whack them with a rolling pin until they are crushed, then mix with the melted butter.

PRESS the biscuit/butter rubble onto the base of a 25cm (10in) spring-form cake tin.

BAKE for 10 minutes in a preheated 150°C/300°F/gas mark 2 oven and leave to cool.

DISSOLVE the jelly crystals in 200ml (⅓ pint) hot water.

GRATE the carrots and ginger using a microplane (extremely fine grater). The goal is a fluffy confetti, not chunky shards.

BEAT the cream cheese, sugar, vanilla extract, mixed spice, carrots and ginger in a mixing bowl until well combined.

WHISK the chilled evaporated milk in a large mixing bowl until it thickens like whipped cream. This only works if it is well chilled, so make sure it is icy cold before you start.

FOLD in the cheese/carrot mixture and, last of all, stir through the lemon jelly liquid.

POUR the mixture over the cooled base and refrigerate overnight or for at least 8 hours.

SERVE decorated with carrot leaves (which are edible, by the way) and slices of carrot.

'PURPLE SUN' CARROT CHEESECAKE

Serves 6

This fluorescent purple cheesecake takes the best bits of carrot cake (the creamy frosting and spices) and ditches the worst (the baking and fuss). It's coloured entirely by the natural hue of the carrots, but if you don't like purple there are plenty of other shades to pick from. Miss the walnuts? Just shove a handful of chopped ones in the base mix.

BEETS

Once considered fit only to be embalmed in over-sweetened vinegar and dished out over iceberg and salad cream, the humble beetroot is now experiencing a truly dramatic reversal of fortune. Beets in every colour of the rainbow popping up on trendy restaurant menus are one thing, but beetroot juice in the chiller of every fancy supermarket? Now that I didn't see coming.

Beets are among the richest sources of phytonutrients of all vegetables and can yield surprisingly large crops of sweet, candy-coloured roots in even the smallest spaces. They are true horticultural multitaskers, too, producing masses of tasty, Swiss chard-like greens atop their familiar roots. Some varieties are even pretty enough to hide incognito in the flower bed, giving flashes of colour to rival the most disco-hued bedding plants. Asking more from a plant is really just being greedy.

VARIETY GUIDE

Whether it's all-consuming sweetness, old-fashioned earthiness or a nutrient powerhouse you are after, there is a beet variety out there for you. Here are my top picks for true taste heavyweights that came up trumps in my trials of dozens of varieties both in my garden and at RHS Garden Wisley.

'Detroit Dark Red'

In my opinion these are the tastiest of all beets: intensely red, intensely sweet and with no soil-like hints. They also happen to contain one of the highest concentrations of the red pigment betalain, a phytonutrient with demonstrated antioxidant properties in test-tube studies. I also love the similar variety **'Red Ace'**, which has been bred to be just as tasty but even easier to grow. Its in-built vigour means it's more disease-resistant and quicker growing, kicking out whopping great leaves as big as chard. Probably the best variety for offering up massive yields of tasty crops both above and below the soil line.

If you are after something a little bit different, try **'Bull's Blood'**, a beet variety originally bred as an ornamental for its deep crimson leaves during the Victorian craze for carpet bedding. It's proper tasty, too, with sweet, nutrient-packed leaves and flavourful roots. Best harvested young, though, as it can become a little tough and increasingly earthy with age.

'Burpee's Golden'

Introduced by American seed company Burpee way back in the early 19th century, this has swapped its red betalain pigments for the yellow hue given by lutein, another celebrated phytonutrient. With a flavour very similar to traditional red varieties like **'Detroit Dark Red'**, albeit with honey-like hints, this is a real dual-purpose beet, with very little earthiness in its tender roots and tasty leaves. It has an inherently lower germination rate, though, so sow it more thickly than other varieties.

'Chioggia'

An old Italian heirloom from the town of Chioggia (pronounced kee-oh-ja) near Venice, much loved by the celebrity chefs. This beet is one of the sweetest varieties around, but its high sugar levels are matched with an almighty earthiness. **Perfect for lovers of gutsy, classic beetroot flavour, but one to skip for soily-flavour phobics like me.** Sadly, its sorcerer's pinwheel of colour can fade once cooked. Boil whole, then peel and slice just before serving to retain maximum colour.

'Albina Vereduna'

Sugar fiends, this one's for you – an old Dutch variety that was originally bred not for eating but as a sugar beet. As you might expect, it has an exceptionally sweet flavour and little earthiness, complemented by a slightly denser, potato-like texture that holds its shape well when cooked. Its tender, wavy-edged leaves make excellent eating too. **A great all-rounder.**

Its lack of betalain pigments also means it won't leave your kitchen (not to mention hands!) indelibly stained serial-killer red. An excellent candidate for when you want the flavour of beetroot, without the inevitable tainting of the colour of the other ingredients in the dish that happens with the red varieties. There is a downside to this, however: as it is the pigment itself that provides much of the phytonutrient content of regular beetroot, the lack of staining power puts a serious dent in any claim this beet may have to 'superfood' status.

WHAT'S IN A NAME?

Despite often being thought of as totally different crops, beetroot, sugar beet and chard are merely different varieties of the same plant. The boundaries between them are blurry at best, with so-called 'beetroots' like supersweet 'Albina Vereduna' being more like sugar beet and leafy cultivars like 'Red Ace' very similar to chard. Hence the reason I have named this section 'beets', not 'beetroots'.

'Detroit Dark Red'

'Chioggia'

'Burpee's Golden'

'Albina vereduna'

REALLY HATE AN EARTHY TASTE?

Put off beetroot by its earthy, soil-like flavour? Well, take it from an ex-beetaphobe like me, beets and muddy flavour need not go hand in hand. The roots derive their dusty flavour from a substance called geosmin, which is the self-same chemical released into the air by soil after a rainstorm. To me, it's an instant flashback to being forced to play rugby at school in Singapore, trudging through mud in 35°C (95°F) heat. There are drawbacks to being the biggest kid in school. Fortunately, the amount of geosmin that beetroot create is genetically determined, and scientists at Washington State University have been able to rank varieties along a sort of Richter scale of earthiness. With some containing three times more geosmin than others, you can pick a variety to suit your personal taste.

	Variety	Geosmin Level (mg/Kg)	
SWEET — Sweet, rich deliciousness, with almost no hint of soil.	'Detroit Dark Red'	2.02	Intense sweetness and a silky texture. Tender even when large, with no hint of woodsiness. One of the highest phytonutrient levels of all varieties, too.
	'Lutz Green Leaf'	3.88	An old-school heirloom selected for its particularly tender, green leaves. The roots can swell to a massive 2kg (4½lb) and store for ages. Nicknamed 'Winterkeeper'.
	'Mr Crosby's Egyptian'	4.15	A rare US variety from the 1870s, bred from seeds collected in Egypt. Renowned for excellent flavour, tender texture and resistance to bolting.
	'Cylindra'	4.28	A fine, smooth texture with next to no fibre that has earned it the nickname 'Butter Slicer'. Proper sweet, too. Described as having an earthy-caramel taste.
EARTHY — A powerhouse of soil flavour. Ideal for lovers of intense earthiness (you weirdos).	'Chioggia'	6.09	Popular for its Willy Wonka coloration, this high-sugar/low-pigment beetroot is great if you want to avoid stained fingers. It also contains three times the geosmin of some varieties, making it (to me) inedibly earthy, like swallowing a puddle.

TIPS & TRICKS

How you should grow your beets depends entirely on what you want to use them for, with subtly different growing methods capable of creating radically different eating experiences. Whether its 'superfood' juice or tender roast beetroot you are after, these tips will allow you to grow tailor-made crops to match your foodie requirements.

. . . .

For Beetroots To Roast
Sweeter & More Tender

There are few things tastier than sticky-sweet roast beetroot. The fact that this, according to research at Berlin University of Technology, conveniently doubles its antioxidant activity compared to eating it raw is just a delicious bonus.

For the most syrupy, caramelized and melting soft beetroot ever, your objective is to up its sugar content while reducing its fibre, both of which are easily done.

Sow Early

US studies have shown that sowing beetroot in cooler conditions leads to increased sweetness, along with more intense colour. To reap these benefits, sow bolt-resistant varieties such as 'Detroit Dark Red', 'Mr Crosby's Egyptian' or 'Bolthardy' under cloches or fleece from late winter to mid-spring. After 4-6 weeks the coverings can be removed and the beets grown on unprotected.

Harvest Young

Unlike carrots, beetroot start stockpiling their sugars from an early age. Harvesting them early means your crops will be far more tender, without sacrificing sweetness.

As the geosmin that gives beetroot its earthy flavour increases with age, the smaller you pick them, the less earthy they will taste. For real earthiness-haters like me, a nifty trick is to splash a little balsamic vinegar over them as it goes into the oven, as geosmin is degraded by acid.

For Beetroots To Juice
More Concentrated & Vitamin-packed

Beetroot juice has recently attracted scientific interest because of its potentially significant health benefits, including lowering blood pressure, improving cardio-vascular health and even enhancing athletic performance. More research is underway.

Fortunately, while we wait for these results to come in, us hort geeks have already cracked how to send soaring the contents of the two key substances said to be behind these reported benefits - nitrate and betalains.

Sow Late

Waiting till mid-summer to sow your seeds and applying a high-nitrogen fertiliser have been shown to raise the nitrate said to produce beetroot's cardio-vascular benefits by a whopping 300 percent. However, I would opt for a balanced fertiliser like blood, fish and bone, whose potassium content prevents the beets from being all leaves and no roots, as can happen if nitrogen alone is used to excess.

Skimp On The Water

Lack of water has been shown to concentrate both the nitrate and the betalain content of beetroot, with drought stress causing the content of phytonutrients to spike by up to 86 percent. According to Italian research, it also makes beets richer in zinc and iron. An easy way to achieve this is to plant in sandy soil and be miserly with the the hose.

The downside of this treatment is that the lower water content of the beetroot can cause it to become fibrous, woody and lower in sugar. As you are running it through a juicer, however, who cares? All you get is richer, more nutritious juice.

Don't Forget The Leaves!

Closely related to both spinach and Swiss chard, **beets boast leaves that are not merely edible, but to me positively tastier than those of their more common cousins**. Richer and more flavourful than spinach, they won't cook down into a khaki mush in seconds, but will keep their vibrant colour like a delicate chard. The fact that they grow attached to a tasty root veg, giving you double the crop for the same amount of space and effort, just clinches the deal.

If you harvest when the roots are between golf- and tennis-ball-sized, the leaves also happen to be at their peak of deliciousness. I love varieties like 'Lutz Green Leaf', which was specifically bred as a multipurpose crop with loads of tender leafy greens above giant roots – both of which have a low geosmin content. If you want something bolder, there are always the dark burgundy leaves of the appropriately named 'Bull's Blood' that turn even darker as cold weather sets in. Many people find it has a pleasantly earthy flavour.

HOW TO GROW BEETROOT

Beets like a rich, well-drained soil. Unlike most vegetables, they will let you get away with growing them in part shade, but **in my experience they will produce better flavour and higher betalain content when grown in full sun.**

Sowing & Growing

For the best beets for eating, sow the beet seed from late winter to mid-spring. Plant three seeds at 10cm (4in) intervals along the row.

Once your seedlings have reached 5cm (2in) high, thin them out to leave just one plant per interval. These thinnings make tasty spring salad greens.

Growing On

The great thing about beetroot is that it is fairly drought-tolerant, actually becoming higher in many nutrients if kept slightly on the dry side. That said, do not be too mean with the hose, as severe drought can make the roots fibrous and woody and dent their sweetness. The key, as always, lies in moderation.

The tops of some varieties will protrude out of the soil surface as they grow. Keep them cool by covering the tops in a mulch of compost as they appear. This will also provide them with added nutrients to fuel their growth.

Harvest

For very best flavour and texture, harvest beets when they reach between golf- and tennis-ball size.

ROASTED BEETROOT & LENTIL SALAD

Serves 4 as a starter or a light lunch

OK, I'll admit it, this recipe is pretty much directly lifted from a delicious lunch I had sitting in the sun at my favourite London plant-lovers' haunt, The Chelsea Physic Garden. So sticky-sweet and satisfying, you won't even notice how virtuously healthy it is.

What You Need:

1kg (2¼lb) small **'Detroit Dark Red'** and **'Burpee's Golden'** beetroots, peeled

1 red onion, peeled

1 tablespoon honey

2 tablespoons unfiltered olive oil

2 tablespoons balsamic vinegar

salt and pepper

250g (10oz) precooked beluga lentils

1 handful of beet leaves, finely shredded

juice and rind of 1 orange

a few sprigs of mint and dill

100ml (⅙ pint) crème fraîche

What To Do:

CUT the beetroot and onions into quarters. Arrange in a roasting tin and drizzle over the honey, olive oil and balsamic vinegar. Do not toss them together as the red beets will stain the yellow ones. Season with salt and pepper.

ROAST the beetroot in a preheated 200°C /400°F/gas mark 6 oven for 45 minutes or until tender.

SPOON the lentils onto a plate and arrange the beet leaves around them. Top with the roasted beetroot, drizzle with the orange juice and scatter over the herbs and orange rind.

SERVE with a dollop of crème fraîche and extra oil and vinegar. This salad is a match made in heaven with goats' cheese or grilled mackerel.

6X

MORE GEOSMIN IS CONCENTRATED IN THE SKINS. SIMPLY PEELING BEETROOT WILL MAKE THEM TASTE LESS EARTHY.

SUMMER SQUASH

If you know anyone with an allotment, there is a time of year around late summer that you will have learned to avoid them, for fear of falling victim to the unloading of their biblical glut of watery courgettes.

Although quick-growing, low-maintenance and massively productive, the crop itself is not to blame. In my opinion, the problem lies with the choice of varieties. Swap the bland modern cultivars, bred in the relentless pursuit of massive yields, for some of the tasty heirloom or speciality types and all that changes. Get ready to discover what a real courgette should taste like.

VARIETY GUIDE

'Costata Romanesco'

This Italian heirloom from Rome is widely described as being the best-flavoured of all summer squashes. Nutty and creamy with an exceptionally dense, non-watery texture, it is at its most delicious picked at 15cm (6in) long with its flowers still attached and fried whole in garlicky olive oil. Speaking of flowers, **this variety also throws up dozens of large male blossoms, which can be harvested freely without denting your fruit crop.** Plants produce half the yield of modern 'improvements' on this variety that carry similar names, but that smaller quantity has infinitely better flavour. Always go for the real deal.

'Tromboncino'

This wacky Italian cultivar from Liguria **is actually a variety of butternut squash**, picked while still tender and green. As well as looking incredibly ornamental in the garden, its big benefit in the kitchen is that it tastes sweeter than most regular courgettes. Lovely, mild artichoke flavour and a long neck that's 100 percent free of seeds.

'Early Golden Crookneck'

These early and prolific yellow squash have a clean lemony flavour and wonderfully tender flesh. Hugely popular in the US, they are only just becoming available in UK catalogues. **Best harvested at their most tender and succulent while still 15cm (6in) long.** Plants are vigorous and disease-resistant, but will fare best in a warm, sheltered spot.

'Parador' AGM

Tender and creamy with a delicate flavour like a cross between chestnut mushrooms and egg custard. These guys grow on super-productive plants, meaning **just two plants are more than enough for the average family.** Excellent flavour, excellent disease-resistance.

'Sunburst' AGM and 'Peter Pan' AGM

Known affectionately in the States as 'UFO squash' because of their quirky flying-saucer shape, **these are probably my favourite of the lot, picked when no more than 5cm (2in) across, then steamed whole and doused in olive oil and garlic.** They have a nutty flavour and melt-in-the-mouth texture. Buttery and mellow, their greater ratio of skin to flesh means they have a firmer bite than most courgettes with no hint of wateriness.

SIDE-STEPPING BITTERNESS

The ancestors of most squash, in the wilds of South America, were absolutely packed full of bitter chemicals called cucurbitacins, whose acrid flavour and toxic effects helped protect the fruit from being eaten.

Millennia of human intervention have bred most of this out, creating the tasty fruit we know today. However, in times of stress – when the plants are subjected to searing summer heat, drought or wide swings in temperatures, for example – these chemicals can raise their heads again. Apart from creating crops with a nasty bitter flavour, their noxious effects can result in severe stomach cramps and nausea in a condition known as 'toxic squash syndrome'. Not good!

Fortunately, this is easily avoided by planting crops outdoors in the open air, instead of in a glasshouse, and keeping them evenly watered in hot weather. If squash is allowed to cross with its non-edible relatives, such as decorative gourds, which are high in cucurbitacins, this trait may be passed on to their offspring, so always purchase new seed instead of saving your own.

'Costata Romanesco'

'Sunburst'

'Early Golden Crookneck'

'Tromboncino'

'Parador'

'Peter Pan'

BAKED COURGETTE CRISPS

Serves 2 as a snack

This glut-busting recipe will magically transform even the most colossal mountain of courgettes into super-healthy, moreish crisps. This baking process concentrates the natural umami chemicals found in the fruit and creates a low-fat, low-carb snack with a flavour to satisfy even the most resolute junk-food fiend.

PREHEAT the oven to 110°C/225°F/ gas mark ¼.

SLICE 2 courgettes thinly – about 1mm (½₅in) thick. Using a mandolin will make this a breeze. Pat dry with kitchen paper.

TOSS the slices in a mixing bowl with 1 tablespoon olive oil and a pinch of salt, then scatter the slices over 2 large baking sheets. Scatter over 2 tablespoons each of panko breadcrumbs and Parmesan cheese.

BAKE in the oven for roughly 1½–2 hours or until crisp but not browned.

TURN off the oven and leave inside the oven to cool to room temperature. Serve with salsa and home-made guacamole.

HOW TO GROW SQUASH

Squash grow at their very best in full sun in warm, sheltered locations. They are greedy feeders and will respond to a good few shovelfuls of well-rotted manure dug into the soil by kicking out loads more fruit. The best thing is that, unlike so many other crops, the higher yield generated by lashings of fertiliser has been shown in trials not to affect their flavour or nutritional content significantly, so don't be mean with the manure.

Sowing & Growing

In mid- to late spring, soak your seeds overnight in my camomile and aspirin solution (see page 66). This could improve the cold-tolerance of your plants and may even help keep them strong and healthy.

Sow these soaked seeds in 10cm (4in) pots on a sunny windowsill, two to a pot. After germination, remove the weaker seedling and grow on at 18-21°C (64-70°F) until the plants have five leaves.

In early summer, transfer your little plants outside and water in well. Be careful not to damage their roots. Plant compact, bushy varieties 80cm (2½ft) apart, spacing trailing types 1.2m (4ft) apart.

Growing On

Scatter a mulch of biochar around your plants. This will act as a weed control, reduce soil moisture loss and in my experience even help deter slugs from attacking the seedlings.

Keeping your plants evenly moist will help maximize yields and reduce the chance of them succumbing to mildew without diluting their flavour. Apply my Supersquash Tonic Spray (see below) liberally throughout the summer to keep them in tip-top condition.

With summer squash, regular harvesting when the fruit are small and tender makes for not only better flavour, but also higher yields. **The more you pick, the more they'll grow!**

For winter squash, slipping a tile or piece of slate under the fruit prevents contact with the ground, reducing rotting.

SUPERSQUASH TONIC SPRAY

Trials at the US Department of Agriculture have shown that a foliar spray rich in potassium improved the fruit quality in the squash's close relative the melon by improving both firmness and sugar content, while astonishingly also increasing vitamin C and beta-carotene. Working on this hypothesis, **I have concocted my very own tonic spray, specifically developed for squash plants, to help maximize their health and improve their cold tolerance.** It may even improve the flavour of their fruit. If you fancy experimenting with this for yourself, here's how I do it.

Add a splash of seaweed extract, which is high in potassium, to a 1 litre (1¾ pint) spray can of water along with a quarter of a 300mg soluble aspirin tablet. **Trials have demonstrated that chemicals closely related to aspirin can act as a tonic to help boost squash plant defences against some of their greatest foes – drought and cold.** Experimental evidence suggests that aspirin spray can also improve their resistance to diseases such as mildew and mosaic virus.

Finally, I like to add a quick splash of full-fat milk (not skimmed or soy!) for added nutrient content. By handy coincidence, the fatty acids in milk have also been shown in some trials to inhibit the growth of mildew. I spritz this tonic spray over my plants once a month throughout the summer to saturate their leaves as much as possible. See the results for yourself and, trust me, you will never look back.

For EU residents it is worth pointing out that neither aspirin nor milk are formally approved as a registered pesticide or for the treatment or prevention of plant diseases. It is entirely legal, however, to apply them to boost plant growth and crop flavour. All references to pests here are therefore strictly for academic interest. (For more information on exact dilution rates, how aspirin works and details of current legislation, see pages 28–29.)

WINTER SQUASH

Winter squash are one of the easiest of all foodie crops to grow and can kick out kilos of sugary, caramel-flavoured squash in exchange for next to no work. Add to this a few deceptively simple harvest and storage tricks and you will get jaw-dropping flavour that even the most fancy farmers' market will never be able to compete with. Understanding which varieties to use for what, and which ones you should avoid altogether, can mean the difference between culinary triumph and your dinner guests voting you off the island. Whether it's the world's best pumpkin pie, comfort soup or an awesome carved jack-o'-lantern you are after, trust me, Halloween will never be the same again!

VARIETY GUIDE

Meet the Family: *Cucurbita*

OK I'll admit it, winter squash is a bit of a 'catch all' category. You see, despite most gardening (and food) writers lumping them all together, they are actually made up of three distinct species, which, while behaving similarly in the garden, perform radically differently in the kitchen.

MAXIMA
The Tasty Ones

This single species is what the vast majority of highly esteemed culinary squash varieties, with their richer, denser flesh, descend from. **If it's classic caramel-nut, 'pumpkin' flavour you are looking for, you will find it here in spades**.

The big paradox is that the classic, jack-o'-lantern type pumpkin does not belong to this species, but instead to *C. pepo* and has a far more watery, fibrous flesh. It's good for carving, and very little else.

There is a surprisingly wide variation between the different cultivars, from the silky smooth and sweet **'Crown Prince'** to the floury and chestnutty **'Kabocha'**.

These plants may be a little less cold-tolerant than *C. pepo*, but to me their flavour is far and away the best.

This includes all the best-rated squashes and 'pumpkins'.

PEPO
The Pretty Ones

This group is dominated by varieties usually picked and eaten as tender, immature fruit - think courgettes, marrows, patty pans and so on.

Their flesh is juicy and cucumber-like when young, but stays pretty much the same when fully ripe - just encased in a rock-hard, enamel-like shell. **When mature they can develop grassy, bitter or tea-like notes on top of the standard marrow flavour**.

Although some acorn *Cucurbita* varieties have quite an intense sweetness, they generally make inferior eating to *C. maxima*. Adding sugar to courgettes doesn't exactly make them tastier.

Sadly, some of the most beautiful-looking varieties belong to this family.

This group includes courgettes, marrows, acorn squash and jack-o'-lantern pumpkins.

MOSCHATA
The Ready-meal Ones

This third, entirely distinct species hails from the tropical zones of Central America. As it's specifically adapted to its exceptionally hot, humid, home climate, you can imagine just how much it loves being planted out in the soggy North Atlantic.

The flesh is low-sugar/high-moisture, making it bland and watery compared to other varieties. But don't take my word for it. In a University of New Hampshire trial of a wide range of varieties, butternuts were demonstrated to be considerably lower in starch, sugars and super-nutritious carotene than almost all other squashes. The reason these are so beloved by supermarkets is mainly that they store well and are easy to slice and peel for the ready-meal market.

Trickier to grow and inferior tasting. Why would you do it to yourself?

This includes butternut squash.

'Marina di Chioggia'

'Galeux d'Eysines'

'Sweet Dumplin'

'Sunspot'

'Crown Prince'

'Tonda Padanaw'

'Zucca da Marmellata'

'Honey Bear'

'Bonbon'

'Queensland Blue'

'Munchkin'

'Celebration'

CUCURBITA MAXIMA TYPES

Without a doubt the best flavoured of the three main winter squash species. I have personally taste-tested dozens of cultivars of *Cucurbita maxima* to shortlist the best of the best.

. . . .

☆ 'Crown Prince' *The Best for Roasting*

Sweet, sticky, golden goodness beneath a steely blue skin: ask any allotment veteran their idea of the best-flavoured winter squash and you can pretty much guarantee 'Crown Prince' will come out top of their list. **Its nutty, honey-like depth and smooth, pudding-like flesh make it to my mind by far the best for roasting.** Even its skin crisps up to a toffee-apple like sweetness. It also happens to be one of the most long-storing of all squash, produced by plants ideally suited to temperate climates.

☆ 'Galeux d'Eysines' *The Best for Soup*

The pale pink skin of this old French heirloom is so packed with sugar that it erupts through its surface as the fruit ripens, creating curious peanut-shaped warts. A staple in the kitchens of French chefs, 'Galeux d'Eysines' has a velvet-smooth texture and creamy caramel-butter flavour when it is simmered down slowly into sauces and soups.

☆ 'Tonda Padana' *The Best for Breads and Baking*

A beautiful squash from northern Italy's Po Valley that is as delicious as it looks. **Rich and intense, it has a chestnut-like texture and deep, savoury, almost smoky flavour.** Its dense, dry, floury flesh makes it perfect for home-made breads, gnocchi and cakes. Roast until golden in oil, mash and knead into your mix. Pretty damn spectacular in soup, too.

☆ 'Bonbon' *The Best for Pie*

Bred specifically with flavour in mind, the smooth, fibre-free texture and rich sweetness of this modern hybrid make it the perfect candidate for turning into pumpkin pie: roast it with plenty of butter and brown sugar before puréeing it and folding it into the batter. The plants themselves are compact and upright, making this a great choice if space is limited. It even displays tolerance to the dreaded powdery mildew.

'Sunspot'

This variety of the Japanese onion squash has an exceptional sweet potato-like flavour and rich fluffy starchiness, with just a hint of spice. 'Sunspot' is perfect for soups and sauces or used in any way you would a sweet potato, albeit with a slight hint of popcorn and chestnuts. A favourite in Japan stirred into a smooth egg custard. **Fruit ripen early on neat, well-behaved plants, making it perfect for gardeners lacking space and patience.**

☆ 'Zucca da Marmellata' *The Best for Jams*

A variety bred specifically to simmer down into a spiced amber jam much loved in Italy. It is rather lacking in sugars, so I find it tastes watery and insipid on its own, but it is magically transformed by a few generous cupfuls of the sweet stuff, a sprinkling of lemon rind and a dash of cinnamon. When spread over hot buttered toast, the jam provides one of the most civilized breakfasts around.

'Marina di Chioggia'

Another Italian heirloom from near Venice, this striking-looking squash's rich orange flesh is much used as a ravioli filling as well as in pies and custard tarts. Like many squashes, **the flavour improves significantly on storage, which is just as well as the vigorous plants are heavy producers.**

☆ 'Munchkin' *The Best for Stuffing*

Adorable micro-pumpkins much used by upmarket florists in autumnal displays. Who would have thought they would also make such good eating? Slice them in half, stuff with anything that takes your fancy, from a savoury quinoa mix to a spiced pumpkin-pie custard, and bake in a hot oven for 30 minutes until soft and caramelized. Wonderful, sticky texture.

'Queensland Blue'

The deep orange flesh of this old-school variety from Australia is almost artificially sweet and fibre-free. **Its small seed cavity means its smooth-textured, creamy flesh stretches wall-to-wall, making kitchen prep a breeze.** The rich sugar and antioxidant content also make it as long-keeping as it is tasty: it'll last well into the spring if kept in a cool, dark place.

DON'T FORGET THE SEEDS!

To turn your pumpkin seeds from kitchen scrap to irresistible snack, clean and rinse them and scatter them in a thin layer over a baking sheet.

SPRINKLE with salt and pepper and drizzle with olive oil.

BAKE at 180°C/350°F/gas mark 4 for 15 minutes or until the seeds are crisp and have turned golden brown.

ALLOW them cool completely and scoop them into a preserving jar, where they will keep for a week.

CUCURBITA PEPO TYPES

I have chosen these varieties for fuller flavour and added sweetness - qualities which buck the trend for members of the *pepo* group. These squash can be almost as wonderful as the *C. maxima* types when baked with enough brown sugar and butter.

. . . .

'Honey Bear'

One of the sweetest of all acorn-type squashes, 'Honey Bear' has a fruity flavour like baked apples or pears. **These fruit grow naturally to an individual portion size and work well** stuffed and baked, looking great on the plate. Miniature plants don't take up any more space than a regular courgette, sprawling only to 1m (3ft).

'Celebration'

Said to be the very sweetest of all acorn squash, containing 50 percent more sugar than standard types and with stunning skin flecked with a confetti of coloured speckles. Easy-to-grow, high-yielding plants.

'Sweet Dumpling'

Not quite as sweet, but with one of the richest, most complex flavours of the group. The pale flesh combines a classic taste of courgettes with nutty, eggy overtones. Really versatile in soups, purées and dips.

TIPS & TRICKS

Apart from variety choice, there are three key factors that determine the eating quality of winter squash: thinning, harvest stage and proper curing. Fortunately, all these are very straightforward and have been scientifically demonstrated measurably to enhance their flavour. Think of them as the horticultural equivalent of MSG.

. . . .

Spare The Secateurs, Spoil Your Harvest

Some squash varieties can be incredibly vigorous, yielding up to 10 fruit. However, as with most crops, **thinning these out to a maximum of three fruit when they have swollen to the size of a golf ball will result in larger squash come harvest time**, each of which will be of vastly improved eating quality. Instead of being all skin and seeds, they will have thicker, sweeter, denser flesh.

Pick Them Ripe

In order to develop their fullest flavour, all squash should be harvested at their ripest point, when the starches within the fruit have peaked. Research at Cornell University has demonstrated, however, that many varieties tend to reach their full adult size and colour a good few weeks before this occurs, making knowing exactly the right time to harvest a potentially tricky business. If sliced off the vine before they are ripe, the harvested fruit will start to steal sugars from their flesh to ripen their seeds within - resulting in poor flavour, watery texture and impaired shelf life.

But there is a deceptively easy way to tell when winter squash are ripe. Simply lift up the fruit and inspect the patch of skin that touches the ground: if this has matured to the same colour as the rest of the fruit, you are good to go. If it is still pale green or light yellow on otherwise fully coloured fruit, leave for a week or two before re-inspecting.

In order for the fruit to ripen fully, it is crucial that the plants remain as healthy as possible for as long as possible, and do not succumb to mildew attacks late in the summer. My SuperSquash tonic spray just might help minimize the risk of this happening (see page 85). Place each fruit on a piece of slate to stop it going mouldy through contact with the ground.

TASTE WITH YOUR EYES

Surprisingly, you can often get a good idea of how tasty a squash is likely to be by looking at the cut flesh. This is because several of the key flavour compounds in many crops (not just squash) are derived from carotenes, the chemicals that give everything from carrots to tomatoes and peppers their orange colour. The darker orange the flesh (not just skin), the more flavour it is likely to produce. I find this particularly noticeable in squash, with the brightest, richest coloured ones always by far the best flavoured.

Curing Is Key

Contrary to popular belief, **not all crops taste better freshly harvested** and winter squash are a perfect example of this. While those from the watery *Cucurbita pepo* group are generally fine to eat cut straight from the vine, those from the *C. maxima* and especially the *C. moschata* groups are often just a big block of floury starch at this stage, with very little sweetness and pale, stodgy flesh.

It is only with curing (that is, sitting around) for a few weeks that these starches are broken down to create the sugars that give these veg their characteristic sweet, buttery flavour. This may sound like an unnecessary step for impatient foodies like me, but trust me when I tell you that it makes a major difference. In fact, **the sugars in butternut squash have been shown to more than quadruple after three months' storage!** During this process the carotenes also start to increase steadily, giving your crops added aroma, colour and potential health benefits in exchange for zero hard work from you. **It is important, however, not to leave them for too long as this peak is soon followed by a crash in flavour.**

Fortunately, the team of supergeeks at Cornell University have calculated how much curing each species generally requires to hit the sweet spot that taste tests suggest creates the 'perfect' squash (approximately 10 percent sugar).

HITTING THE SWEET SPOT

Squash Species	Months After Harvesting (stored at 10–15°C/50–59°F)					
	1	2	3	4	5	6
Curcubita pepo	☆	☆				
Curcubita maxima		☆	☆	☆		
Curcubita moschata			☆	☆	☆	☆

☆ = best time to eat them

SPICED PUMPKIN, TARRAGON & MARSHMALLOW SOUP

Serves 4

Yes, this savoury roast pumpkin soup is indeed garnished with caramelized marshmallows. An idea I picked up from my American uni friends who served marshmallow-topped sweet potatoes at a Thanksgiving dinner, the combination of pumpkin and marshmallows may sound terrible, but it tastes wonderful.

What You Need:

1 **'Crown Prince'** squash (about 1.5kg/3lb), seeded and sliced

1 large onion, peeled and sliced into chunks

2 tablespoons honey

2 tablespoons unfiltered olive oil, plus a little more for drizzling

750ml (1¼ pints) chicken stock

250ml (⅖ pint) full-fat milk

50g (2oz) butter

2 sprigs tarragon, chopped

a little fresh nutmeg, grated

4 marshmallows

smoked paprika, for sprinkling

What To Do:

SCATTER the pumpkin and onion over a baking sheet, drizzle with the honey and 2 tablespoons olive oil and season.

ROAST in a preheated 240°C/475°F/gas mark 9 oven for 25–30 minutes until soft and golden brown.

BLITZ the roast squash and onions with the stock, milk and butter until smooth.

TRANSFER the liquid to a saucepan, add the tarragon and nutmeg, then bring to a gentle simmer for 15 minutes.

POUR the soup into 4 bowls and lay a marshmallow on each one. Pop them under a hot grill for 5 minutes, just until the marshmallows have begun to melt and brown.

SERVE the soup with a sprinkle of paprika, a drizzle more olive oil and a hunk of crusty white bread.

STRAWBERRIES

Every single article that has ever been written on strawberry growing opens by proclaiming how much better home-grown fruit taste. But where is the evidence? Ladies and gentlemen, I give you exhibit A.

According to *Journal of the American Society for Horticultural Science*, strawberries traditionally harvested at the pink, half-ripened fruit stage for maximum supermarket shelf life can contain as little as 1 percent of the aroma compounds of ripe, red fruit. That's 99 percent of the flavour you could be missing out on, before we even get started on sugar content. Incidentally, ripe fruit contain up to a whopping one and a half times the sugars of semi-ripe fruit. Trust me with stats like this: growing your own strawberries is well worth the 30 minutes it takes to plant them.

VARIETY GUIDE

As with most crops, the single overriding factor that determines the flavour of strawberries is cultivar. With some varieties producing up to an astonishing 35 times the aroma compounds of others, this is worth taking the trouble to get right. Fortunately, I have done the work for you, munching through more than 30 varieties to bring you my round-up of the best for flavour. There are three main types of strawberries, each with its unique pros and cons, spanning dozens of varieties – June bearers, everbearers and wild or alpine strawberries.

JUNE BEARERS

Far and away the most popular group, June bearers have the biggest, sweetest fruit borne in one generous summer flush. Huge crops in a short window make these the perfect choice for jams and jellies.

The big downside is that their season is very short, lasting only about 2-3 weeks per variety. Collecting a mix of early, mid- and late-fruiting varieties, however, is a nifty way to stretch the season to its limit, giving you a conveyor belt of fruit over several months.

'Honeoye' *Early*

In early summer this throws up a brief but massive harvest of fruit with a bright acid twang - perfect for jam making. Uniquely among strawberries, 'Honeoye' contains the flavour compound hexyl acetate, which is also found in passion fruit and Fuji apples, giving them a tropical fruit-like flavour.

'Korona' *Early*

The huge, almost kiwi-sized fruit of this heavyweight Dutch variety don't just offer mere size, but also outstanding flavour and even super-fast ripening - making it one of the first of the season, extremely juicy, though with a shelf life of mere minutes. Plants are also resistant to a wide range of pests and diseases. It's almost too good to be true!

'Gariguette' *Early*

This French variety from the 1930s offers pointy, orange-red fruit with a rich perfume. It is a favourite of top chefs, grown for direct sale to fancy restaurants, but for some reason all but absent from shops outside of swanky food halls. The plants lack vigour and yields are low, but the flavour is really exceptional.

'Manille' *Mid*

With both 'Gariguette' and the celebrated 'Mara des Bois' in its ancestry, there was no doubt 'Manille' was going to be a culinary starlet. The fruits are high in sugar, low in acid and have a distinctive aromatic flavour, while the plants are even conveniently rather pest-resistant.

'Marshmello' *Mid*

With a excellent balance of sugars and acids, the incredibly soft flesh of 'Marshmello' virtually melts in your mouth (and in the punnet), meaning you will never spot it at even the fanciest farmers' market. **Described by chef Raymond Blanc as the sweetest of all.**

'Frau Mieze Schindler' *Mid*

Measly crops of small berries that require another variety growing alongside it if you ever want to see any fruit meant this German variety from 1925 almost never made it to market. Yet its irrepressible, winner-takes-all flavour has seen it become

'Snow White'

'Garignette'

'Mara des Bois'

'Honeyoye'

'White Surprise'

'Frau Mieze Schindler'

'Candy Floss'

'Manille'

the most commonly grown variety in its country of origin. Like 'Mara des Bois', it produces methyl anthranilate, the same compound that gives woodland strawberries their unmistakable floral/candyfloss aroma. As the plant's flowers are male sterile, it is essential to grow a surrogate pollinator such as **'Cambridge Favourite'**, that flowers at the same time, nearby.

'Senga Gigana' *Late*
Truly gigantic, egg-sized fruit that astonishingly have not traded in their flavour in the process. Sweet and aromatic, the fruit unusually contain Heptan-2-one, a flavour chemical with a banana-like aroma, and linalool, the compound responsible for the scent of basil and bay leaves. A bizarre cocktail that somehow just works!

'Malwina' *Late*
The favourite of my childhood hero, garden writer and broadcaster Bob Flowerdew, **these large, exceptionally flavourful berries round the regular strawberry season off with a bang.** Considered 'too dark' for supermarket shelves, their deep red colour is provided by anthocyanins, giving the berries enhanced potential health benefits.

EVERBEARERS
Some of the best for flavour in my opinion, their light cropping does mean, though, that you need quite a few plants to fill a punnet at any given time. Being smaller and tarter, the berries of this group often make up for their initial shortcomings with a rich aroma, which after all is the hardest fruit quality to fake. **As their name implies, they will give you a drip feed of fruit over an incredibly long season, from as early as late spring right up until the first frosts.** Like June bearers, they also won't throw up runners all year, making pruning (by far the most labour-intensive task) a breeze. With a sneaky dusting of sugar, I feel these beat the blowsy June bearers hands down in the flavour stakes.

'Mara des Bois' *Mid-summer to Mid-autumn*
Probably the most highly rated gourmet variety, this captures all the aroma of the best wild strawberries but has the size and succulence of modern cultivars. It contains large quantities of methyl anthranilate, resulting in a fruit with a candyfloss, almost bubble-gum-like flavour. Frequently described as 'heritage', this French cultivar actually only dates back to the early 1990s, making it no more of an heirloom than a Nirvana album.

'Aromel' *Mid-summer to Late Autumn*
As the name suggests, the intense fragrance of these little flavour bombs really sets them apart. The fruits' notoriously soft, delicate texture also gives them an incredible juiciness,

causing the flavour to linger on your tongue and leaving you wanting more. Unfortunately, it also makes them impossible to store for supermarkets. Eat before you get to the kitchen door.

'Albion' *Early Summer to Mid-autumn*
Said to have twice the flavour compounds of other strawberries, according to a study at the University of Nottingham. This Californian variety's sky-high sugar content can edge upwards of 10 percent, making it one of the sweetest around.

'Buddy' *Early Summer to Mid-autumn*
Developed specifically for flavour at the East Malling Research Centre in Kent, **'Buddy' consistently ranks as possibly one of the best-tasting varieties it is possible to grow in Britain with a sweetness that can match any June bearer.**

'Snow White' *Early Summer to Mid-autumn*
All today's modern strawberries descend from an accidental cross between a species from Chile and another from Virginia that spontaneously popped up in a French botanic garden centuries ago. When attempting to create a variety with truly superior flavour, plant breeders went back to the drawing board to recreate the original cross, with some delicious consequences. The result was 'Snow White' whose knock-out aroma and unparalleled sweetness belies its ivory colour.

WILD OR ALPINE STRAWBERRIES
Adored by European foodies since the Stone Age, wild strawberries have an incredible aroma that has recently become all but lost. Since the large hybrids were introduced a couple of centuries ago, they have been slowly but steadily crowding the wild strawbs out of our gardens. Actually a totally different species from the regular strawberry (*Fragaria vesca* as opposed to *F. x ananassa*), **these alpine types are tiny by comparison but crammed with truly explosive strawberry flavour.** Like everbearers, these plants provide a steady trickle of fruit throughout the summer. What they have in flavour, though, they lack in monster yields, so plant up as many as you have space for. Fortunately, their compact plants and ease of cultivation mean they are enjoying a bit of a renaissance, ideal for getting maximum flavour out of minimal space.

I love the lipstick-red **'Candy Floss'**, whose flavour really does live up to its name, and **'White Surprise'** with a creamy-coloured flesh that complements its pineapple/banana fragrance. My favourite, however, has to be **'White Soul'** for its knock-out tropical-fruit aroma. Old favourites from the final throes of the golden age of wild strawberry breeding in the early 20th century include **'Baron Solemacher'** and **'Mignonette'**.

TIPS & TRICKS

Growing the best-flavoured strawberries is really very simple. Give them loads of light, don't overwater or fertilise them, and keep on top of pruning. Of course, for true taste geeks I have one or two further tricks up my sleeve to help you create flavoursome strawbs the mere memory of which will delight you in your old age. That's quite a promise(!), so I'd better get going.

Let There Be Light

The aromatic compounds that give strawberries their characteristic flavour are directly related to the amount of light they receive. In fact, **trials have shown that, if you halve the light, you quite literally halve the flavour.** That's before we even mention sweetness, which can plummet sevenfold for plants in deep shade. I know it's prime garden real estate, but **treating your strawberry plants to the sunniest spot available really will pay dividends.**

Make 'Em See Red

According to studies at Clemson University, South Carolina, strawberries grown through a red plastic mulch produced fruit that were not only significantly sweeter and more aromatic, but also a whopping 20 percent bigger. The fruit were even shown to contain more Vitamin C and anthocyanins to offset their jump in sugar content.

The researchers concluded that the invisible spectrum of far-red light reflected off this mulch mimicked the light reflected by neighbouring plants, 'tricking' the strawberries into perceiving the threat of nearby competition. They responded by ramping up their defences, directing energies into producing bigger, tastier fruit.

Get Them On Acid

Plant geeks in Ireland have demonstrated that **strawberry plants grown on acidic soils with high potassium content yield fruit with measurably better flavour.** If you do not live in an area with acid soil, plant your strawberries in raised beds with plenty of organic matter such as a peat-free ericaceous compost.

Apply a potassium-rich fertiliser like comfrey solution or molasses tonic (see page 27) once every two weeks throughout the summer. Commercial strawberry food often contains large amounts of nitrogen, an excess of which has been shown in trial after trial to result in a crunchy (not juicy) texture, poor flavour and lacklustre yields, not to mention stimulating the growth of loads of pesky runners.

Planting Is Key

Simply plant them right and you could raise the average sugar content of your strawberries by 14 percent - at least that is what US Department of Agriculture research suggests. According to their results, planting strawberries in raised beds through a sheet of plastic mulch and removing the runners as they appear, rather than letting them run freely over the bare soil, not only causes the jump in sweetness, but also boosted the fruit's vitamin C by 10 percent.

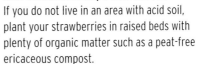

Dose Up On Comfrey & Aspirin

Believe it or not, some research suggests that the characteristic flavour of strawberries is partially provided by a symbiotic bacteria called *Methylobacterium extorquens* that lives on the plant leaves. In one study at Austria's Graz University of Technology, strawberry plants sprayed with the friendly bacteria produced almost three times the normal quantity of strawberry-scented furanoid compounds, sending the flavour of the crop soaring. In the future this could prove a natural, low-cost way dramatically to improve the tastiness of commercial strawberries.

If you want to set up your own experiment at home, spraying your strawberries with a dilute comfrey liquid could in theory boost the populations of these flavour-enhancing bacteria by providing them with a supplemental food source to kick-start their growth. It's always worth a try!

To get brewing comfrey liquid, cram a bucket half-full with comfrey leaves. Drop a brick on top to keep them weighted down and fill the bucket up with water. Place a lid over the top (this stuff is great for plants, but smells truly awful) and leave it to stand for four weeks. Funnily enough, it is the methane that creates this awful smell that the bacteria feed off, hence methylobacterium. The smellier, the better! Dilute one part comfrey liquid with 15 parts water and spray it over your plants once every two weeks, except when fruit are ripening.

Pick 'Em Ripe

The intensity of a strawberry's flavour is directly related to its ripeness and, while fruit picked pink may turn red in storage, it will never be as sweet or aromatic as when it is picked fully ripe. In fact, studies suggest that pink fruit can contain as little as 1 percent of the fragrance of deep red berries.

For real flavour obsessives, **strawberries harvested on sunny, dry afternoons are likely to be the most tasty,** as this is generally when sugar levels in the plant are at their highest and water levels at their lowest, leading to richer, more concentrated fruit. Be patient and you will reap the rewards.

IS ORGANIC BEST?

Several studies suggest that organically grown strawberries have significantly more antioxidants, including vitamin C, and potentially more flavour than conventionally raised fruit. More research is needed. Why not test it out for yourself?

Wait Four Days

The flavour compounds in strawberries continue to develop significantly after the fruit is picked. In fact, according to one Canadian study they can shoot up to seven times their normal levels after four days stored in a cool room at 15°C (59°F). Sadly, bunging them in the fridge does not count, as the chemical reactions that generate these flavour chemicals will not take place if it is too cold.

Waiting a few days should also result in a peak in anthocyanin content, making these berries not just tastier, but potentially healthier too. In the trial, however, four days of steady increase was followed by a dramatic crash, so don't forget them!

Cheating The Flavour

Fruit late in the season, particularly those set during periods of heavy rain and grey skies, can be on the bland side, with low light and high water levels conspiring to dilute flavour. But all is not lost. **With these four simple tricks you can rescue the flavour of end-of-season strawbs.**

1) Slice the fruit finely, as this increases their surface area, causing you to perceive them as tasting stronger (this is also the reason grated cheese often tastes better than sliced).

2) Sprinkle them with a little sugar, or even better use fructose (sold in most chemists or health-food shops) to cheat the sweetness. Fructose is one of the chief sugars found in strawberries, resulting in a more convincing 'fruity' flavour.

3) A spritz of lemon juice, containing the same citric acid found in strawbs, will add depth and brightness.

4) Finally, leaving this concoction to macerate for one hour at room temperature will draw out the juices from the fruit, bumping up their flavour by converting the contents of their cells into a solution more easily perceived by your taste buds. And lastly, always, always serve them at room temperature. Not only will they contain more aroma compounds but they will also be more easily detected by your taste buds.

TIP

Adding half a 300mg soluble aspirin tablet per litre (1¾ pint) of this spray could, according to some trials, not only improve your yield but also their earliness, sugar content, vitamin C and anthocyanins.

WOW!

HOW TO GROW STRAWBERRIES

Sow & Grow

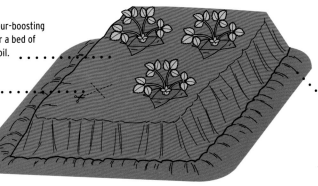

Lay the sheet of flavour-boosting red plastic mulch over a bed of moist, recently dug soil.

Create a small hole with a mound in the middle. Trim the tips of the roots and spread them out. Make sure the crown is level with the soil. Backfill with soil and water in well.

Anchor down the edges of the sheet with soil. Cut 10cm (4in) crosses along the row about 35cm (14in) apart.

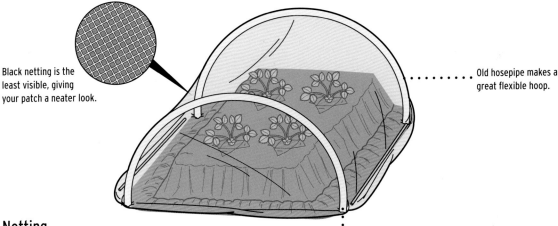

Black netting is the least visible, giving your patch a neater look.

Old hosepipe makes a great flexible hoop.

Anchor lengths of hosepipe firmly into place with bamboo canes inserted into the soil.

Netting

Eco ideas of sharing your harvest with wildlife are lovely. If only they were willing to do the same. Birds and squirrels love strawberries as much as people do, meaning if you don't net your crops you may not ever see a single fruit.

Growing On

To give your crops the best chance of success, apply a low-nitrogen/high-potassium fertiliser like molasses tonic once every two weeks throughout the summer.

If you fancy experimenting with some hardcore flavour tips and tricks, give your plants a good spritz of comfrey and aspirin spray once every two weeks throughout the spring and summer, except when the fruit are nearly ripe.

Reducing watering to a minimum, just when leaves begin to wilt slightly, has been demonstrated to improve the flavour of several strawberry cultivars. And lastly, don't forget to remove all runners as they appear.

Post-harvest Care

Once June-bearing varieties have finished fruiting, trim off their leaves and give them a good watering with a high-potassium feed. This reduces the risk of disease and encourages the growth of next year's flower buds.

Replace plants every three years, as the number and fruit quality of strawberry plants declines with age.

FIGS

Figs really are one of those crops whose shop-bought relations are just a pale shadow of their true flavour potential. Planting your own will take you little more than 30 minutes and could reward you with decades of syrupy sweet fruit. Not to mention fragrant leaves that fill your garden with the scent of a Mediterranean holiday right through the summer. So what on earth is stopping you?

VARIETY GUIDE

Sadly, the fig variety that is far and away the most frequently recommended by books and seen in garden centres also happens to be the most insipid and watery, chosen purely for its cool-weather tolerance rather than its taste. If you see the label 'Brown Turkey' on a little potted plant, put it down quietly and step away slowly before you condemn yourself to a lifetime of flavourless figs. I have always been puzzled about why this variety remains so widely recommended (and therefore sold) when there are several equally hardy varieties out there with far superior flavour. Introducing my top contenders for Spanish holiday flavour growable in blustery climes.

'Rouge de Bordeaux'
(syn. 'Petite Negri' and 'Violette de Bordeaux')
Perhaps the best flavoured of all outdoor figs I have tasted, and believe me I have scoffed my way through my fair share. **Its dusty purple skin hides a bright red flesh that tastes just like home-made strawberry jam**, albeit with a deeper, more exotic, characteristic 'fig' fragrance.

Despite being widely labelled as a glasshouse variety, this has sailed through several pretty Arctic winters with me, taking temperatures far lower than even the average winters in northern Scotland. It is also one of the most widely grown varieties in the Pacific Northwest region of the United States, which has a broadly similar climate to the UK, meaning that this should thrive on a sunny wall across most of Britain. If you don't fancy risking it, the plant's conveniently compact stature makes it a perfect choice for a pot, which can always be bunged in a porch or glasshouse should a truly apocalyptic winter strike.

'Brunswick'
These massive brown and green fruit with dusky pink centres have one of the best flavours of all, with a rose-scented fragrance and a sugar content so high it literally drips from the eye (the hole at the base of the fruit) when the fig is perfectly ripe. **Exceptionally large, exceptionally tasty and exceptionally tolerant of damp, cool weather – if you can only grow one fig make this it.**

'Osborn's Prolific'
Good news, cool-climate growers! This is one of the best-flavoured figs for areas with chillier summers, with its pink-streaked pulp needing far less heat to ripen than most other cultivars. A rich, sweet flavour fused with a jam-like texture makes this one a real winner.

'Excel'
This is an exciting introduction from the States whose greenish yellow skin belies both the intensity of its sweetness and the fragrance of its amber flesh – like a light, floral honey. The tree has excellent cold tolerance too, fruiting easily as well as 'Brown Turkey' in my experience. **This variety is a particularly vigorous grower so it is even more essential to limit its plans for world domination by restricting its roots to a pot or lined 'fig pit'** (see page 100) and (as with all figs) planting it against a wall in a sunny position.

'White Marseilles'
Don't let the name fool you, these figs are actually light green to pale yellow and not white at all. But one bite of these super high-sugar fruit with their silky smooth texture and outstanding aromatic flavour and you will instantly forgive their rather confusing name. Grown in the UK since the 1500s, they don't come much more tried-and-tested than this.

'Excel'

'Brunswick'

'Rouge de Bordeaux'

'White Marseilles'

'Osborn's Prolific'

Figs help to hold moisture in baked goods, meaning that they can reduce the amount of fat added to recipes by up to 50 percent. Try replacing half the amount of butter or oil in a recipe with half its weight again in fig purée.

HOW TO GROW FIGS

Despite their Mediterranean origins, with a little groundwork figs can be one of the easiest of all fruit to grow even in cool temperate regions. Supplied with full sun, a sheltered site and a restricted root run, they are capable of producing huge harvests for decades to come.

Planting
Create A 'Fig Pit'

Planted into moist, fertile ground, figs will soon grow into huge, spreading trees, quickly swamping your plot in masses of leafy growth that produces very little fruit. Constraining their roots in a fig pit (essentially a large, buried pot) will force them to divert their energies from foliage to fruit - maximizing both the size and the flavour of your harvest.

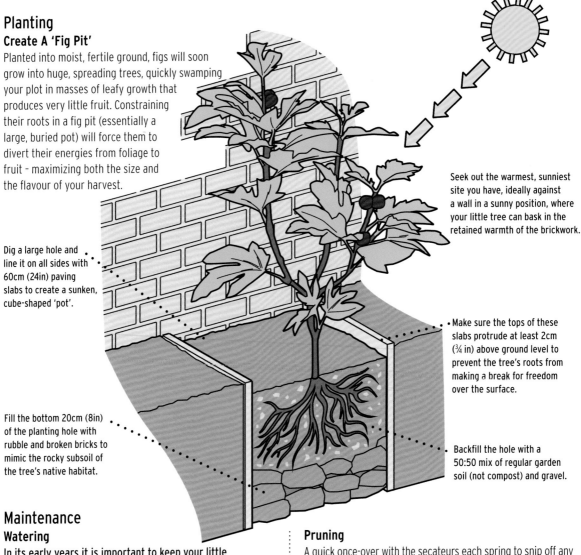

Seek out the warmest, sunniest site you have, ideally against a wall in a sunny position, where your little tree can bask in the retained warmth of the brickwork.

Dig a large hole and line it on all sides with 60cm (24in) paving slabs to create a sunken, cube-shaped 'pot'.

Make sure the tops of these slabs protrude at least 2cm (¾ in) above ground level to prevent the tree's roots from making a break for freedom over the surface.

Fill the bottom 20cm (8in) of the planting hole with rubble and broken bricks to mimic the rocky subsoil of the tree's native habitat.

Backfill the hole with a 50:50 mix of regular garden soil (not compost) and gravel.

Maintenance
Watering

In its early years it is important to keep your little sapling well watered and fertilised to ensure its rapid establishment. At this stage it doesn't matter if it explodes into vegetative growth, as it's not likely to fruit for a good year or two. Once it has really got its roots down, however (usually after the first two years), a tree planted in a fig pit should need little to no supplemental feeding and watering.

Pruning

A quick once-over with the secateurs each spring to snip off any frost-damaged or crossed branches, as well as any suckers that are shooting up from the base, will keep your plants in tiptop condition. **Pinching out the tips of the new branches to five or six leaves long in mid-summer will encourage the formation of embryo fruit for next year.** Watch out for the sticky white latex that exudes from the cut branches, though, as this is corrosive on the skin, particularly when exposed to strong sunlight. Take it from someone who has been on the (very) sore receiving end of stupidly deciding to prune in a vest on a hot mid-summer's day.

AN OVERLOOKED DELICACY

After your harvest of ripe figs comes to a close in mid-autumn, most books will recommend that you snip off any large, unripe green figs and toss them in the compost bin. The first part of this advice is very sound, as these fruits will almost certainly never have the chance to ripen fully before being trashed by winter frosts, and so they'll become an unnecessary drain on the tree's resources. However, consigning what could be kilos of fruit to the garbage is nothing short of sacrilege. Green, unripe figs are a much sought-after ingredient in the cuisines of Latin America, the Middle East and the Med – places that know a thing or two about figs – and making use of yours will give you two harvests for the effort of one.

COOKING GREEN FIGS

To transform the hard, green fruit into a delicious sweet treat it is first necessary to precook them. This removes their bitterness and renders them safe to eat.

To get started, just snip off their tough stems and pop them into a pan of rapidly boiling water for 10 minutes. Drain off the water, replace it with fresh and subject the figs to a second 10-minute boiling session. This helps leach out the last of their latexy, 'green' flavour. Your figs are now ready to sweeten and serve as you like. Here are a few ideas.

• In the eastern Mediterranean precooked green figs are sliced and simmered in jam sugar and lemon juice to make a translucent conserve that is amazing over hot toast.

• In Latin America green figs are boiled in brown sugar syrup and served with cream.

• In the Middle East, they are candied by being boiled whole in a heavy syrup, then stuffed into all manner of pies and pastries.

GREEN FIGS IN SPICED SYRUP

My unashamedly lazy option is to simmer the figs briefly in the leftover syrup of a jar of stem ginger with a red chilli and a cinnamon stick thrown in. Serve cold with grilled Halloumi cheese.

PEARS

Apples may remain the undisputed king of tree fruit in the popularity stakes, but, as any self-respecting food snob (like me) knows, it is really their close relative the pear that offers the very best culinary quality of the family. With an altogether more complex, aromatic flavour and chin-drippingly buttery texture, to me home-grown pears are easily the most luxurious of the orchard fruits.

VARIETY GUIDE

If you want true gourmet harvests from your backyard orchard sidestep supermarket staples and track down these flavour heavyweights. Personally tried and tasted by me after hours of scouring RHS Garden Wisley's massive pear tree collection, these rare gourmet treats will have you lusting after autumn even in the height of summer.

Dessert Pears

For proper pear-drop flavour, the classic continental variety 'Glou Morceau', dating back to the 1750s, is about as old school as it gets. Its extremely sweet, almost spicy fruit start to come into season in late autumn and will keep well into winter. **For the best conceivable flavour, plant in a warm, sheltered location and leave the fruit to hang on the tree for as long as possible before harvesting.**

For sheer aroma, however, there is probably no contender that comes near the pear 'gold standard' that is 'Doyenné du Comice'. Widely regarded by fancy French chefs as the finest flavoured of all pears since its introduction way back in 1849, it fuses intense sweetness and unparalleled fragrance with an irresistible 'melting' consistency.

If it's a pure sugar hit you're after, you cannot fail with the exceptionally syrupy, uber-cute fruit of 'Seckel Early'. With a spicy, brandy-like aroma in pears that can be as tiny as cherries, they are proof positive that good things come in small packages. Absolutely stunning jarred whole, sliced in half to garnish a cheeseboard or popped into the kids' lunchboxes as a E-number free treat. Its larger-fruited offspring 'Worden Seckel' is a super-size version, with an identical flavour, just in much more generous portions.

Looking like home-grown Fabergé eggs decorating your trees, the old Ukrainian variety 'Humbug' could easily be dismissed as a novelty, but a single bite instantly dispels that idea. Keeping their sugary sweetness well into spring the following year without refrigeration, these candy-striped fruit are known as 'Easter pears' in their native land. Hardy and holding their shape well when cooked, this crossover dessert/cooking variety does not develop its full flavour until at least two months after being picked.

Love the fragrance of pears, but not a fan of their smooth, slippery consistency? I have a solution! Asian pears such as 'Hosui' descend from an entirely distinct species, *Pyrus pyrifolia*. They have a crisp, apple-like texture and a refreshing sweet-sour flavour, all rounded off with a burnt-sugar aroma.

Cooking Pears

Tracing its origins as far back as the 13th century, the classic English cooking variety 'Black Worcester' must be one of the most ancient (and delicious) cultivars still in cultivation. Pre-dating the sugary, buttery-fleshed European pears that shot to popularity in Victorian England, **cooking pears are tooth-shatteringly hard when eaten fresh and flecked throughout with gritty sand-like particles. An hour or two of slow simmering, however, magically transforms them into fragrant orbs of creamy-fleshed goodness.** With an altogether more intense flavour and dense texture than the normal dessert types, they are by far the best choice for pies, jams and jellies. I also love 'Catillac', an ancient French variety straight from the court of King Louis XIV and the continental cousin of 'Black Worcester'. Sadly, both of these are triploid varieties, which means that they require two different pollination partners nearby if you want to see fruit. One taste of them slowly poached and smothered in dark chocolate sauce, however, and you will forgive them this single fussy point.

HORTI HOOK-UP
Most pears need to be teamed up with a tree from another variety in order to produce fruit. As playing matchmaker can be tricky, I've done the legwork for you. All varieties on this page are compatible with each other, so pick any two you like.

'Glou Morceau'

'Worden Seckel'

'Seckel Early'

'Humbug'

Asian pear 'Hosui'

'Doyenné du comice'

'Black worcester'

'Catillac'

Quince 'Portugal'

HEAVY SOIL, HEAVYWEIGHT FLAVOUR

Pears are widely believed by old-timer gardeners to taste far better when grown on heavy clay soil rather than free-draining sands. Although I have yet to find any conclusive scientific evidence to prove this, it is true that the plants themselves will tolerate heavy clay better than most tree fruit, so it is definitely worth a try.

Can't Make Up Your Mind?

Good news! You don't have to. If you're an indecisive foodie like me, the kind of person crippled by the fear of food envy at the mere thought of being handed a menu, I have the solution for you: family trees.

As if by magic, **these special trees are capable of bearing multiple varieties of fruit on the same plant**. Achieved through an ingenious horticultural technique known as grafting, the branches of different cultivars are effectively 'cut and pasted' onto the same tree to create these surgically enhanced beauties. They are great if you are short on space or, let's face it, don't want to go to the trouble of assessing pollination groups and ensuring the compatibility of several trees. The horticultural matchmaking has been done for you. Ready-grafted family trees are sold in all the catalogues.

THE ROOT TO FLAVOUR

Always choose varieties that have been grafted onto a dwarfing rootstock. This has been demonstrated in trials to create larger and often more flavourful fruit, not to mention giving you a compact 2.5–3m (8–10 ft) tree instead of a 6m (20 ft) giant. In my experience, one of the best for this purpose is called Quince C – think '70s TV detective. Look out for it on the plant label/catalogue entry.

Want Even More Fragrance?

Quince are an old-school relative of pears, which have swapped sweetness for an almighty hit-you-over-the-head fragrance. Once a staple all over Europe, they have (at least in Britain) mysteriously dropped from favour in recent years. Yet, with a small bowl of the fruit enough to fill a room with a rich, honeyed spice scent that simply no other fruit can offer, I believe this is a culinary travesty!

OK, so they may be severely lacking in the sugar department, but this is easily rectified. **Grow exactly as you would a pear and use exactly like a cooking apple.** Guaranteed to make the world's best crumble, liqueur, pie and a jam (see page 213) that will transform even the most ordinary grilled cheese sandwich into an altogether more exotic treat.

My Idea Of The Perfect Tree-some

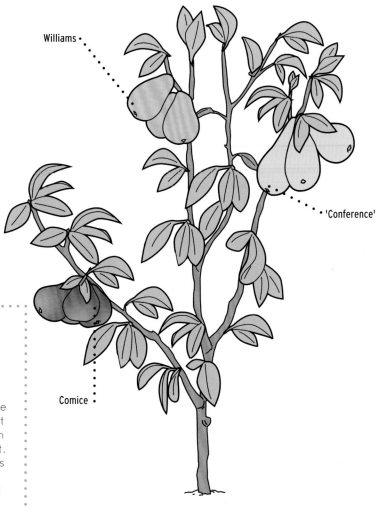

Williams

'Conference'

Comice

TIPS & TRICKS

The wonderful thing about pears is that they don't need a lot of coaxing to produce outstanding flavour. Pick the right variety, give your little tree a warm, sheltered site, and you will soon be kicking out gourmet pears with the best of them. There is a simple trick, however, that will dramatically improve their taste and texture, and that is never to harvest them fully ripe from the tree. Let me explain…

Unripe For The Picking

Pears allowed to ripen on the tree can develop a mealy, 'woolly' texture, with their cores breaking down to a soft, bitter mush. This is what the old boys referred to as 'sleepy'. However, it doesn't end there. You know those horrible grainy bits that pears sometimes get? Those are caused by structures called stone cells. These are made up of the same rock-hard substance as cherry stones, and are produced by the plant as the fruit ripens on the tree.

Picking the fruit when they have reached full size but are only just on the verge of changing colour instantly eliminates both these problems. **It may sound totally counterintuitive, but pears really do develop a better flavour and texture when picked early and ripened indoors.**

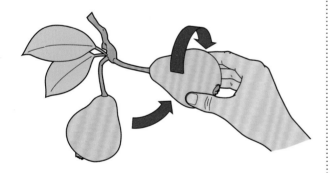

To tell if a fruit on a branch is ready, lift it up to a horizontal position and give it a gentle twist. If it detaches itself easily from the tree, it is ready to pick. Fruit do not mature to picking size all at once, but in waves over the season, so check back every few days.

Once you've picked it, ripen your bounty by placing the fruit in slatted crates or cardboard boxes in a cool, dry place such as a garage or shed. **When the flesh gives under the slight pressure of your thumb near the stalk, it will be at its very tastiest.** Depending on the variety, pears can ripen in just a few days like 'Williams' Bon Chrétien' and 'Red Williams' or take many months like 'Glou Morceau' (mid-winter) and 'Humbug' (early spring).

Forget Watering

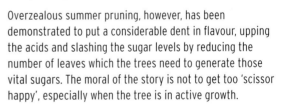

Once established, **pear trees will need very little extra watering and feeding.** In fact, trials at New Zealand's Massey University, among others, have demonstrated that generous irrigation, apart from having little or no effect on yield, results in fruit with a bland, watered-down flavour.

Similarly, large quantities of fertiliser, particularly if it is high in nitrogen, have been demonstrated to generate flavourless fruit with a tendency to rot, not ripen, in storage. **A couple of soakings in a high-potash fertiliser like seaweed extract or molasses tonic (see page 27) in the spring should be more than enough to keep your trees in top condition.**

Let In The Light

Improving the penetration of sunlight into the canopy will result in measurably intensified colour and possibly flavour of fruit, even causing them to swell to up to 20 percent larger. The occasional winter prune to clear out any crossed, dead or congested branches is all that is needed to create the open shape that allows this to happen.

Overzealous summer pruning, however, has been demonstrated to put a considerable dent in flavour, upping the acids and slashing the sugar levels by reducing the number of leaves which the trees need to generate those vital sugars. The moral of the story is not to get too 'scissor happy', especially when the tree is in active growth.

Like most tree-fruit trees, pears will naturally shed some of their developing fruit in early summer in a phenomenon known in the northern hemisphere as the 'June drop'. Helping this process along by thinning them out to one fruit per cluster after the initial drop will result in larger but more importantly tastier fruit with a higher concentration of sugars and aroma chemicals. You are looking to leave just one fruit along every 15-20cm (6-8in) of branch.

HOW TO GROW A PEAR IN A BOTTLE

Easily the quirkiest home-grown gift of all, these bottles of fancy pear liqueur come complete with a whole golden pear encased within, in a mysterious 'ship in a bottle' kind of way. Yet committing this act of horticultural alchemy is far easier than your mates might think.

1

PRUNE in late spring, when the fruitlets are about marble-sized. Trim off all but one from the tip of a skinny horizontal branch. Snip off the leaves around this, too, so all you have is a mini pear on a stick.

2

INSERT the tiny fruit into a bottle until it is near the bottom end. Use a length of wire to hang the bottle on the tree, attaching it to adjacent branches. Leave the neck of the bottle open and hang it so that it is pointing downwards, to allow any condensation to dribble out. The fruit should be hanging free from the sides of glass.

3

LEAVE over the next few months while the fruit swells and eventually ripens within the bottle, at which point it can be snipped off.

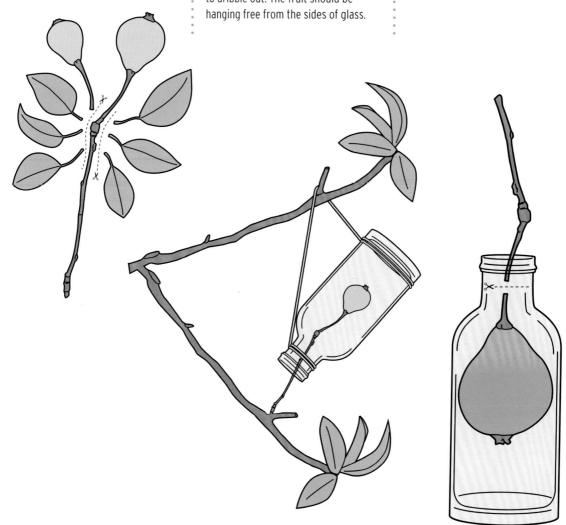

4

SWEETEN some grappa to taste, stirring until the sugar is completely dissolved and pour it into the bottle using a funnel. Seal and leave in a cool, dry place for at least a month to absorb all the fragrant peariness, then offer it up for all to behold!

SOUR CHERRIES

Cherries start to lose both their flavour and their rich phytonutrient content as soon as they are picked, making home-grown fruit potentially not only measurably tastier, but also better for you. Yet while low-acid 'sweet' cherries are infinitely more popular in the catalogues, to true food geeks nothing comes close to the grown-up, bitter-sweet tang of a ripe, red **'Morello'**. Think the difference between the dayglo glacé fruit of '80s kids' parties and the fancy French ones that come in jars of aged brandy.

Add to that the fact that sour cherries are far easier to grow, not to mention the exciting emerging research behind their potential health benefits, and you will wonder why you ever entertained the idea of growing the sweet ones in the first place.

Sour Cherries Are:
Higher in Phytonutrients
Tart cherries are thought to be a far richer source of antioxidants than the regular kind. **Emerging studies suggest that drinking tart cherry juice might potentially have a wide range of health benefits,** including significantly improved sleep duration in insomnia sufferers, reduced muscle damage from intensive exercise, and even reduced pain and inflammation. More research is clearly needed, and the sample size of most trials has been small, but I for one can't wait to learn what further investigation might uncover.

The Best For Bakers, By Far
When the fuller flavour and bracing acidity of sour cherries meets the sweetness of sugar, something magical happens. Far superior to the gloopy, bland sweetness of regular cherries, they make truly exquisite pies, jams and liqueurs.

Easier To Grow
Sour cherry trees are far tougher than their sweet cousins. For starters, they are one of the only fruit to crop well on shady sites, making them a great choice for cold, sun-starved locations. They are self-fertile, smaller and more manageable in size and even far less prone to bird attack. Happy days!

WHY DO YOU NEVER SEE THEM IN SHOPS?

Before the Second World War there were more than 50 varieties of sour cherries in Britain; now you would be lucky to find more than one in the catalogues – a trend that has sadly been echoed around the world.

This is partly due to the fact that the little flavour bombs have an exceptionally short season and are so delicate they are unlikely to last a day or two on the shelf.

According to *Journal of Food Science*, even when chilled to –20°C (–4°F), sour cherries lose up to 75 percent of their phytonutrients after just six months in the freezer, so if you want to sample the world's best ever cherry pie, jam or uber retro black forest gateaux, I am afraid the only way is to plant a little tree for yourself.

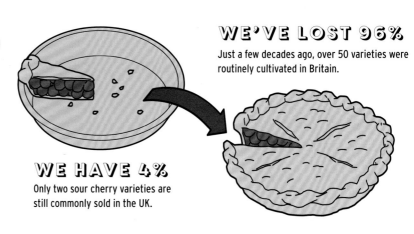

WE'VE LOST 96%
Just a few decades ago, over 50 varieties were routinely cultivated in Britain.

WE HAVE 4%
Only two sour cherry varieties are still commonly sold in the UK.

VARIETY GUIDE

Sour cherries such as **'Morello'** actually have a similar, if not higher sugar content than many of the so-called 'sweet' varieties like **'Stella'** that dominate supermarket shelves. It's just that this sweetness is balanced out with a bracing acidity, resulting in a more intense, less watery flavour. After munching my way through countless varieties on a trip to the UK's National Fruit Collection at Brogdale in Kent (they have 300 cherries cultivars alone!), I finally managed to whittle them down to these three 'best of the best'.

'May Duke'
Best for Eating Fresh
My personal favourite, though, is **'May Duke'**. The result of mixed parentage between sweet and sour varieties, it really does capture the best of both worlds with a deliciously tangy flavour. Scrumptious ripe from the tree with a glass of very cold, very sweet vermouth. Growing them on a sunny site and harvesting them fully ripe will further spike their sugary potential.

'Morello'
Best for Pies and Jams
By far the most commonly sold sour cherry in the UK is the dark red old Kentish heirloom **'Morello'**, with its rich wild-fruit flavour and grown-up hint of bitterness. Halfway between **'May Duke'** and **'Montmorency'** in the sweetness stakes, its deep red juice is evidence of quite how packed of anthocyanins it is. For me, it's the best variety for pies and jams by far.

'Montmorency'
Best for Syrups and Liqueurs
It is well worth making the extra effort to track down **'Montmorency'**, a traditional French variety that makes up over 95 percent of the North American market, with its glistening scarlet colour and biting acidity. Much sourer than **'Morello'**, this is the variety that has attracted the most interest from medical researchers.

SWEETNESS

To me it's simple:

more sugar + more acid

= MORE TOTAL FLAVOUR.

Pick Your Flavour

The same variety of sour cherry can have a very different flavour – and therefore culinary use – depending on its stage of ripeness.

DEEP RED 'MORELLO' CHERRY

Sour cherries are ripe for cooking when they are deep red. Great for pies, jams, syrups, cordials and home-made liqueurs. Incredible as a glaze for roast pork or duck and the perfect base for an adults-only ice-lolly with a splash of kirsch.

BLACK 'MORELLO' CHERRY

Leave them till almost black and you can eat them fresh. Great in salads, sandwiches and summer drinks. Their bright acidity is a perfect sparring partner for rich ingredients such as cheese or roast game, as well as bitter flavours like rocket salad or iced black tea. Oh, baby!

An Unexpected Fan Base

Scientists as far back as Darwin have noted that **children between the ages of approximately five and nine prefer foods with an acidity level far beyond the threshold of what most adults and babies perceive as unpalatable.** Hence the plethora of super-sour candies and gummy sweets that sweet manufacturers have churned out to satisfy this craving. So sour cherries may counterintuitively be a monumental hit with your little ones.

Pits Add Flavour

Deep inside the hard shell of cherry pits, minute levels of toxic cyanide compounds give the kernel an intensely bitter flavour. Developed by cherry trees to protect their seeds from being eaten, these chemicals give their close relative the bitter almond their characteristic nutty flavour.

Popping these whole pits, along with the fruit themselves, into recipes for syrups, cordials, jams and jellies is an age-old tradition to impart an altogether deeper, darker mellowness, while dispensing with the need for hours of fiddly pitting. Straining before serving will instantly remove every stone and with them any potential risk of toxicity.

HOME-MADE CHERRY SYRUP

Makes 500ml (17fl oz)

I like to use a mix of **'Montmorency'** and **'Morello'** for this 'no-pitter required' recipe. Dilute with three parts soda water for simply the best cherryade known to man – if I do say so myself.

SQUISH 500g (generous 1lb) sour cherries between your fingers in a large mixing bowl to create a rough pulpy mush. Do not bother to remove the stones. It's gloriously messy, but I promise you the results are worth it.

SPRINKLE over 250g (10oz) sugar and toss roughly to combine. Cover with a plate and leave to rest on a sunny windowsill for 24 hours.

ADD the juice of 1 lemon and simmer the mix very gently on a low heat for 15 minutes, just until the crushed fruit softens and goes slightly transparent.

PRESS the piping hot fruit through a sieve using the back of a spoon to remove the stones.

POUR into sterilized jars: it should keep in the fridge for at least a month. Or freeze it in ice-cube trays and defrost as needed.

P.S. This is equally incredible drizzled over Greek yogurt and granola or – for the less virtuous – used to lace a glass of Prosecco.

CHERRYADE

Fill a sundae glass one-third full with Home-made Cherry Syrup and top up with ice-cold soda water. Crown with a slick of whipped cream and dot with fresh cherries.

A sly shot of amaretto or brandy will transform this children's party favourite into an infinitely more grown-up libation, allowing even big kids to see the world through cherry-tinted spectacles.

HOW TO GROW SOUR CHERRIES

Sour cherries are famously more tolerant of less than prime horticultural real estate than their sweet cousins. This rugged disposition has made them *the* classic choice for a fruit tree that will still devotedly offer up good crops even when relegated to the confines of a cold wall. Spoil your little tree with a sunny site in deep, rich soil, however, and you will be justly rewarded with bigger, sweeter, more flavourful harvests.

Plant
Root Out The Flavour
Trials in Eastern Europe, where sour cherries are still immensely popular, have shown that **grafting the trees onto dwarfing rootstocks like 'Gisela 5' produces measurably better-tasting fruit**, with significantly more sugars and less of a watery texture.

This is great news for home growers, as it conveniently also results in trees that don't grow any taller than 2.5-3m (8-10ft), making picking, covering with netting and, let's be honest, fitting them into your overstuffed plot way easier.

Pruning & Thinning
Fan-train & Gain
If you want to add instant living structure to your garden, do away with any complicated pruning and supercharge the flavour of your crops in one fell swoop, go for a fan-trained specimen. Planted against a boring bare wall, a fan-trained tree will guarantee year-round interest and take up next to no space. Its flat, 2D fan shape also maximizes the amount of light reaching the leaves and developing fruit, which has been shown to increase the sugar, colour and aroma compounds in your fruit. Talk about win-win!

Maintaining the fan shape is easily done by thinning the new shoots that appear on the branches each spring to 10cm (4in) apart and snipping back any branches that grow out from the wall to stubs of just a couple of leaves. Tie in any new branches to the support framework and you are done.

It is important, however, that pruning be carried out only in summer; winter pruning can allow the dreaded silver leaf (a potentially deadly fungal disease) to take hold.

Implement a One-cherry Policy
Thinning the young bunches of fruit to leave just one cherry per cluster might seem harsh, but trial after trial has shown that this results in much larger fruits that are up to a third sweeter. Not just that, but according to Australian research the earlier in the season you get your gumption up and do it, the better the flavour will be.

Mulching
Don't Let Them Crack Up
Chucking a layer of mulch around the base of the tree once the fruit begins to swell is a nifty trick to prevent your cherries from splitting as they grow. This works by regulating the moisture levels at the roots, mopping up the excess water from heavy downpours that can cause the fruit to swell too rapidly and crack.

Netting
Defend Your Harvest
If you can manage to keep marauding birds away, sour cherries are otherwise pretty much 100 percent trouble-free. However, that is a pretty big 'if'. The good news is that **black netting is a cheap and easy way to protect your bounty: you can drape it over pint-sized trees in a flash**. Want more good news? Sour cherries are far less susceptible to bird attack, so you might even be able to risk skipping this step.

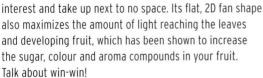

THREE-IN-ONE TREE PLANTING

Still can't make up your mind which variety to go for? Well, I have news for you – you don't have to! Being grafted onto dwarf rootstocks means that three or even four trees of the same species can astonishingly be planted in one large hole, giving you maximum variety from the same space as just one regular-sized tree. No, really!

To get this to work, take several young trees of the same age, all grafted onto the same dwarfing rootstock and plant them in a single large hole, spacing the rootballs 1m (3ft) apart. Prune out the branches toward the middle of the clump to create an open, airy centre, only allowing growth around the outer edge of your new mini grove.

This tip is based on the modern commercial orchard technique known as 'high density planting', and has been shown to work well on dwarf plums, cherries, pears and apples all over the world, as long as you keep on top of pruning.

No Cherry Pitter?
No Problem!

All you need is a chopstick and an empty bottle to pit cherries perfectly every time. Sit the cherry on the rim of the bottle and stab it with the chopstick. The stone will drop into the bottle, leaving you with a pit-free fruit.

CHERRY BLOSSOM & LYCHEE JELLY

Makes 500g (17oz)

A deceptively simple dessert idea picked up on a filming trip in Japan, which will guarantee you serious snob food points at your next dinner party for next to no work. It's concocted from the dregs at the bottom of a jar of 'Morello' cherry jam and the leftover syrup from a tin of lychees - just don't tell your guests!

SOAK 5 sheets of leaf gelatine in a little water for 5 minutes.

SIMMER the liquid reserved from a tin of lychees in a saucepan with 3 tablespoons sour cherry jam for a minute or two until fully combined.

STRAIN the liquid through a muslin cloth into a measuring jug.

DISSOLVE the soaked gelatine into the still-warm liquid and top with enough hot water to make up 500ml (17 fl oz) and sweeten to taste (I usually add 3 tablespoons caster sugar).

POP cherry blossom flowers into individual glass jars and pour over the gelatine mix while it is still piping hot. Allow to cool and leave in the fridge to set for 6 hours.

PLUMS & THEIR KIN

Think plums are boring? Well, consider this. Almost all the 'plums' sold commercially are not true plums at all, but a distinct species from Asia called the Japanese plum *Prunus salicina*. Their larger fruit and longer shelf life make them beloved by the big chains. Shame they come with a crunchy, mealy texture and intensely sour skins. In fact, if you have only ever tasted supermarket offerings, it is likely that you have never tasted real plums at all!

The true plum *Prunus domestica*, a species which includes damsons, gages and mirabelles, is altogether more aromatic and juicy, with a gel-like flesh that virtually melts on the tongue. Throw in a cocktail of hybrids that fuse these with apricots and a whole new world of flavour unravels before you.

The best news? Requiring no fussy pruning or training, plums are probably the easiest of fruit trees to grow in temperate climates. The perfect choice for gardening newbies, they almost come with stabilizers.

VARIETY GUIDE

Damsons

The dense, spicy flesh of damsons makes them the perfect choice for cooking, ensuring your pies and crumbles will be wall-to-wall flavour, without the watery runniness that dessert plums like **'Victoria'** can have. Super-hardy and self-fertile, they also are some of the most foolproof of all the family to grow.

My top picks for flavour include the dark and dusky **'Hauszwetche'**, which is a true culinary rarity, delicious cooked and yet sugary enough to be scoffed straight off the tree when fully ripe. The old Kentish variety **'Farleigh Prolific'** is one of the most heavy cropping of the damsons, its intense blue-black fruit an essential ingredient of jams and jellies. Perfect for small gardens, the compact trees are also one of the hardiest of all, capable of powering on through cold, wet climates where few others would cope. **'Blue Violet'** is one of the sweetest and most early ripening of the damsons. This old Cumbrian variety has the generous habit of the fruit falling from the branches when ripe. Yes, they effectively pick themselves. Lay out an old sheet, give the tree a good shake and watch as sugar plums come raining down. A tree straight out of a Roald Dahl book.

Plums

For lovers of classic dessert plum flavour I recommend sidestepping the ubiquitous **'Victoria'** in favour of **'Avalon'**. Developed in 1970, this modern variety takes all the best bits of the old-school English plums and sends their yields into overdrive without losing any of their flavour. I also love

'Excalibur', winner of independent taste tests for its sweet, juicy flesh. This early-season variety more than makes up for its slightly chewy skins with a rich, berry-like flavour offset by a hint of tannin.

For the best ever jams, pies and puddings, though, leave the dessert varieties behind and take the plunge with tarter cooking varieties like the refreshingly sharp and gently tannic **'Burton'** or the deep blue **'Stanley'**. The latter's wine-like flavour is complemented by seeds that obligingly fall away from the flesh, making de-stoning a breeze.

Mirabelles

Introduced to Europe from Asia at the time of the Crusades, the marble-sized golden orbs of **'Mirabelle de Nancy'** are a much-loved regional delicacy in France, prized for their honey-like sweetness and smooth, gelatinous consistency. Delicious straight off the tree or simmered down into jams, jellies and of course the famous tarte aux mirabelles, their fruit are even blessed with stones that come cleanly away from the flesh. It is worth thinning out the fruit, as the trees are so vigorous they can exhaust themselves, causing them to fruit only every other year.

Reine-Claude Gages

Thought to be the original ancestors of all greengages and still widely touted as probably the best tasting of all. Don't let the acid-green skin of many varieties in this group fool you; their succulent fragrance and almost syrup-like consistency leave no room for the slightest hint of

Plum 'Stanley'

Plum 'Burton'

Plumcot 'Flavor Supreme'

Damson 'Hanszwetche'

Aprium 'Cot 'n' Candy'

Pluot 'Purple Candy'

Mirabelle 'Mirabelle de Nancy'

Gage 'Reine-Claude de vars'

Damson 'Blue violet'

astringency. For truly outstanding flavour I particularly love the golden-fleshed **'Reine-Claude de Vars'** and the heritage French variety **'Red Reine-Claude d'Oullins'** with its rosy-blushed skin.

Pluots, Plumcots & Apriums

These complex, multi-generational hybrids muddle the fragrance of apricots with the sticky silkiness of plums. Like many interspecies crosses, the trees prove more vigorous than either of their parents, producing fruit that can grow to the size of a peach on self-fertile trees. I can't get enough of the US variety **'Purple Candy'**, whose deep, dark, plum-like flesh is a perfect storm of intense sweetness, bracing acidity and a candied apple-like aroma that sets every reward centre in your brain alight like the Fourth of July.

The mottled skin of **'Flavor Supreme'** might not win any beauty contests, but boy does it make up for it in taste. This 50:50 cross between the Japanese plum and the apricot combines the nutrient-rich red flesh of the former and the exotic aroma of the latter. By a streak of amazing good fortune, it has somehow also managed to escape the tart skin and crunchy flesh of the Japanese plum, while still inheriting its large fruit size and vigour. The one big catch is that the flowers are not particularly attractive to bees, meaning harvests can be light unless you hand-pollinate them with a paintbrush (for more on this see Pretend to Be a Bee on page 204).

When it comes to apriums, **'Cot 'n' Candy'** is one of the very best. Being three-quarters apricot, one-quarter plum, this apricot lookalike has a unique, almost tropical fruit flavour of its own, which then surprises you with a lingering plummy aftertaste. Partially self-fertile, the trees will fruit better if planted with an apricot nearby. **'Moorpark'** and **'Flavourcot'** are good choices for pollinators that are well adapted to temperate climates.

FERTILITY

Many plums, gages and mirabelles are not self-fertile, meaning they need to be planted within flirting distance of another variety if they are to bear fruit. Pick any other variety from pages 115–117 and your problem's solved.

FRUIT COCKTAIL

Exciting new breeding work coming out of California is creating a generation of complex hybrids that are blurring the boundaries between plums and apricots, with some truly delicious consequences. Here is my rough guide to navigating the newfangled names.

100% APRICOT

APRIUMS apricots that have inherited the gel-like texture and sweetness of plums

PLUMCOTS a perfect 50:50 fusion of plums and apricots

PLUOTS super-fragrant plums whose apricot genes create trees with added vigour

100% PLUM

| Apricot 'Late Cot' | Aprium 'Cot 'n' Candy' | Plumcot 'Flavor Supreme' | Pluot 'Purple Candy' | Plum 'Blue Diamond' |

'Pinot Noir'

'Concord Seedless'

'Gewürztraminer'

'Fragola'

'Cabernet Cortis'

'Kyoho'

'Müller-Thurgau'

your cup of tea, leave the grapes to ripen for as long as possible and clear the foliage from around the bunches, as exposure to sunlight will gradually degrade their pyrazine content.

THE 'CONCORD' ONES

The result of a bit of horticultural matchmaking between the European grape *Vitis vinifera* and an entirely different species from the wilds of North America known as the fox grape *Vitis labrusca*. These are the ones used to create US-style grape jelly and Welch's grape juice – they are famed for their staggeringly intense fruity fragrance.

'Concord Seedless'

America's favourite grape variety, just made seedless for easier eating. Almost jet black and exceptionally sweet, the fruits grow on vines with excellent hardiness, vigour and disease resistance. But that's not all. A British study published in 2007 in *Journal of Agriculture and Food Chemistry* reported that, of all fruit juices, theirs was the richest in anthocyanins and other polyphenols, plant compounds with potentially far-reaching health benefits.

'Kyoho'

This monster Japanese variety was bred back in 1937 by crossing European and American grapes, to produce what I can only describe as super-size **'Concords'**. Like its US relation it is what is known as a 'slip skin' variety, as the gel-like flesh is easily separated from the skins, literally slipping out as you bite into them. This curious habit, combined with the difference in flavour between the pleasantly tart skins and the nectar-like flesh, creates an unusual (and delicious) two-tone taste.

Traditionally eaten when they turn fully black for maximum sugar hit, I prefer them just as they start to turn pink, when their bracing tartness balances out what can otherwise be jaw-aching sweetness.

If you like the idea of making your own wine, but, like me, are daunted by the whole prospect of demijohns and testing kits, I have a solution for you. Run the fruit through a juicer and mix it with equal parts Shochu (a Japanese rice spirit) to make the popular Japanese cocktail Chuhai. Delicious poured over loads of ice, with a splash of soda water to dilute the sweetness.

'Fragola' (syn. 'Isabella')

With its incredible aroma of fresh, ripe strawberries, **'Fragola'** (Italian for strawberry) was once used to make a plethora of high-end wines across southern Europe, including the Veneto's famous Fragolino. However, in the last century, this once wildly popular wine has become impossible to buy as countries across Europe banned its production, starting with France in 1935. Thought to be a host to phylloxera, an insect that has a devastating effect on European grape varieties but to which 'Fragola' is immune, its musky aroma was also perceived as undermining the character of French wines. Today, however, many wine experts regard this ban as essentially an issue of nationalistic pride.

The good news is that it is still perfectly legal to grow and eat this variety – in fact, there are massive plantations in Italy for the fresh fruit market. You can even make wine out of it, as long as you don't then sell it. Gotta love a bit of bureaucracy, don't you?

WHAT ARE WINE GRAPES?

Richer and more aromatic in flavour, think of them as grapes for grown-ups.

The thicker skins and larger seeds are high in phytonutrients and, importantly, give the bitter, tannic flavours so sought after by winemakers.

Flesh contains far more sugar and has a softer, juicier texture.

WHAT ARE TABLE GRAPES?

Plants are bred to produce fruits that are not only much larger, but also have a harder, crispier texture to ensure they survive transport. They are also much lower in all-important sugars.

The thin skin and lack of seeds might make eating them more pleasant from a texture point of view, but it also results (as far as I am concerned) in grapes with a bland, 'two-dimensional' flavour.

TIPS & TRICKS

Grapevines are one of nature's true survivors, being resistant to drought, pests, poor soils and often complete neglect. Getting the best-tasting fruit, however, is another matter. Yet with just a few snips of the secateurs and a quick spray of fertiliser capable of supercharging their eating quality, your vines will repay your swotting up on these simple tips.

. . . .

Snip Your Way To Better Flavour

Probably the simplest way to improve the flavour of home-grown grapes is to get your pruning right. This really is crucial to reining back the vigour of these scrambling vines, turning their attention away from throwing up masses of leaves and focusing their efforts on top-quality fruit production. **Studies have consistently shown that hard pruning to restrict leafy growth measurably improves not only the yield, but also the sugar and polyphenol content of grapes.** For a beginner's guide that cuts through the mystery, check out page 123.

Spraying On The Love

Several studies have demonstrated that **applying dilute nutrient sprays over the canopies of vines creates not only higher yields, but also fruit with a greater content of sugars, acidity and tannins** (basically all the good stuff). This is surprising, as over-generous application of fertilisers to the roots of grapes has been shown to do the exact opposite, denting grape flavour by both promoting excessive leaf growth and making the plants more susceptible to disease. Foliar application of these nutrients, it seems, gives you all the benefits, without any of the drawbacks. Not a bad deal, really. **I would recommend using a seaweed-based fertiliser**, as these tend to have a more complete range of nutrients, including boron, iron and magnesium, which have been linked to enhanced flavour in grapes.

Let In The Light

Several studies suggest that removing the leaves from around ripening bunches of grapes can significantly boost the sugar and aroma content of the fruit. **Improving light access to the bunches can also dramatically reduce the time it takes for them to ripen, and even** boost the antioxidant content of some varieties four fold **according to one Australian study.** As light levels rise so does the temperature of the berries themselves, causing them to lose moisture, thereby further concentrating their flavour.

Although these improvements have not been consistently shown for every variety in all trials, the potential rewards could be significant given that it only takes a few minutes to make a few snips. **To give this a go, trim off the leaves around each tiny bunch of grapes as soon as the fruit have set in the early summer.** The extra light and air circulation that result may even help reduce the incidence of pests and diseases to boot.

Get Your Timing Right

Grapes do not reach their true flavour potential until they are 100 percent ripe. The trouble is that many varieties have the quirky habit of changing colour up to 40 days before they are actually ready to harvest, at which point they may contain only half the sugar and a fraction of the aroma compounds. **Simply tasting them can be a poor indicator of ripeness too, as some unripe grapes will taste pleasantly sweet, long before developing their full sugar and aroma potential.** Combine this with the fact that grapes generally do not continue to ripen once picked, and you will see why knowing when to harvest grapes can be a notoriously tricky business. Fortunately for the home grower there are a few tips and tricks that can make hitting that sweet spot a breeze.

As grapes ripen the plants start to cut off their supply of nutrients to the fruit causing the stem of the bunch slowly to wither, going from fresh green to an increasingly straw-like in colour. **Fully ripe berries will also feel slightly softer, come away easily from the bunch and have seeds that are light brown not green.** Remember that grapes ripen from the top of the bunch downwards, with the berries at the 'shoulders' of the bunch hitting maturity long before those at the tip, so always test the lowest hanging fruit.

The haunting strawberry-like flavour of 'Concord'-type grapes is provided by the chemical methyl anthranilate. This is found naturally in the blooms of gardenia, jasmine, wisteria and (unsurprisingly) some of the best strawberry cultivars, giving them their characteristic floral aroma.

GROWING WINE GRAPES

Although most grapes are perfectly hardy, they will produce the best possible flavour in the brightest, sunniest locations. Despite being popularly grown as a glasshouse crop, the varieties recommended on pages 119–121 will be perfectly happy outdoors as far north as Scotland, where (surprisingly) the longer daylight hours can result in a noticeable spike in flavour. Always ensure you buy plants from a reputable supplier and check that they are certified as being free from a pest called phylloxera.

Watering & Fertiliser

Grapes grown outdoors in the ground will generally only need watering in their first year and even then only during spells of particularly dry weather. Further irrigation is not only unnecessary, but in many Old World vineyards – those in Europe and parts of the Middle East – actually prohibited, as it is believed to ruin the quality of the grapes (in exchange for higher yields).

Forced to delve deep for water, the roots of non-irrigated vines are likely to have greater access to the key nutrients necessary to create truly first-rate flavour.

Pruning
Winter Pruning

The very idea of pruning grapes can fill even seasoned gardeners with dread. And given the hundreds of different traditional techniques there are, often with exotic-sounding names in regional French and Italian dialects, this is not without good reason. Let me cut through the confusion.

First, remember that **grapevines are pretty hard things to kill and will withstand even the most phenomenal amounts of clueless hacking** (yes, I have been there). At its very simplest, all you need to do is train a single vertical stem to form the central spine. Then, after the leaves fall each winter, trim back any lateral growths coming off this spine to two buds (roughly 3cm/1in long).

Once you have mastered this you can swot up on more advanced techniques, but even if this is all you do you will get far tastier fruit on more manageable plants.

Fruit Thinning

Preventing vines from fruiting might be hard for greedy growers like me, but I promise you that without this extra drain on their resources young vines will establish far better, allowing for greater, tastier harvests in the future. As a general guide you want to remove all flowers for at least the first two years after planting, allowing only three bunches to form on each vine for two years after that. After the fifth year, however, you can allow your vines to fruit normally.

Summer Pruning

It is a good idea to cut out bunches to allow for just one per 45cm (18in) length of vine. This results in fewer bunches of bigger, tastier grapes, rather than loads of tiny, misshapen ones that are all skin and seeds. Finally, trim the growing tip off each of the fruiting branches two leaves after each bunch as the bunch begins to form every summer.

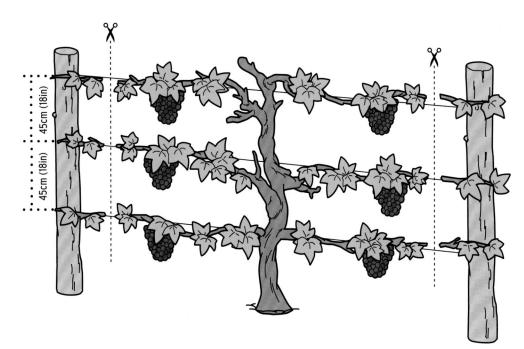

45cm (18in)

45cm (18in)

PERSIMMONS

With their rich sunset hue and tropical-fruit flavour, persimmons may seem just too impossibly exotic to grow outside the balmy climate of the Med. However, with the trees first introduced to Britain way back in 1796 and hardy down to a bitter –20°C (–4°F), I believe it is high time temperate-climate gardeners finally succumbed to the charms of this Far Eastern delicacy – the closest thing to a mango you can grow outside of the Tropics.

To me, however, the real point of growing them is not just the geek factor of telling your mates you can, but the simple truth that fully ripened, home-grown persimmons are almost unrecognizable from shop-bought offerings. Add to that the glorious shades of red and gold that these trees burst into each autumn, holding onto their dayglo orange orbs well into winter, and it is difficult to see why the persimmon doesn't rival the apple in our national affections. Well, that is until I tell you their one (rather large) catch.

In their early years the trees can be painfully slow-growing, which means that depending on the size of the specimen you start with, you could be waiting anything from 5–10 years for it to get into full production. I like to think about this philosophically, though: imagine, if only you had had the sense to plant one 10 years ago, what feasts would now await you!

VARIETY GUIDE

Generally speaking there are two broad categories of persimmon.

ASTRINGENT

The traditional types are normally eaten only once the flesh has ripened to a slippery, sweet gel. The ripe but still firm fruit contain astringent chemicals called tannins, which give crisp flesh a mouth-puckering dryness until fully softened.

'Rojo Brillante'

My favourite variety, this dominates the production in Spain for its rich, full flavour. Indeed if you see plants labelled persimmon in the UK with no variety name attached, nine times out of 10 this is it.

NON-ASTRINGENT

These **modern types have been bred to contain far fewer tannins, giving them a sweet, mild flavour even when they are still as crunchy as an apple.** They are, however, generally thought to be less cold-tolerant than the astringent types and in my opinion have a comparatively bland flavour.

'Fuyu'

A Japanese variety that is by far the most commonly sold form in the catalogues. Bucking the reputation for this group, 'Fuyu' luckily has a demonstrated iron-clad hardiness down to –20°C (–4°F) and even excellent resistance to late frosts.

Sadly in cool-summer climates, the distinction between these two categories becomes somewhat irrelevant, as even the so-called non-astringent types retain their tannins until they are fully ripe. But fear not! There is a crafty kitchen trick that will miraculously turn even the most astringent persimmons sweet when crisp (see opposite).

'Rojo Brillante' and 'Fuyu' are both self-fertile and seedless, although this is not true for all persimmons.

SO EASY, THEY ARE BOMB-PROOF. LITERALLY

Hardy, drought-resistant, pest-tolerant and needing no fussy pruning or training, these trees are notoriously tough contenders. One even survived the 1945 Nagasaki atomic bomb! If it can handle nuclear warfare, I think it stands a good chance in the average back garden.

TIPS & TRICKS: HARVESTING & RIPENING

Cool-climate garden writers can be quite dismissive of growing persimmons, claiming that summers like those of the UK are just not long enough for fruit to ripen on the tree. Just as well, then, that they will do this perfectly well in a fruit bowl! In fact, virtually all commercial growers, even in sweltering southern Spain, harvest them before they are ripe, as just as with pears this has been proven to result in far superior flavour.

Like 'Em Crunchy?

Follow this crafty, scientifically proven trick magically to turn the tongue-twisting dryness of even the most astringent persimmons into sweet, fragrant crispness in just a few short days.

SPRITZ the fruits in a fine mist of a high-proof spirit like vodka or brandy.

SEAL them in a large, loose-fitting plastic bag with an apple or a banana.

STORE at room temperature. Within 5-6 days, they will have lost all their 'furriness' and grown riper and sweeter.

Commercial growers use similar techniques to sell the easier-to-grow astringent varieties as if they were non-astringent. A clever bit of culinary trickery.

How does it work? The alcohol in the spirit combined with a natural gas called ethylene emitted by the apple or banana will render the tannins that cause the astringent texture completely unnoticeable. Still sceptical? Try it for yourself, and I'll be happy to accept your apology on Twitter.

Like 'Em Slippery & Gel-like?

When fully ripe, the flesh of all persimmons is transformed into a translucent, maple-flavoured jelly which will burst through their thin skins like a quivering water balloon.

SLICE in half and scoop away from the skins with a spoon to enjoy their mango/cantaloupe fragrance.

KAKIS CON JAMÓN

My favourite way to eat persimmons has to be at the halfway stage between crisp freshness and jelly-like mellowness, like they do in Spain, where they are known as *kakis*.

Serve thin wedges of the fruit with shavings of *jamón ibérico*, chopped pistachios and a drizzle of olive oil to create a simple Spanish-inspired autumn dish so good you won't care about the imminent onset of winter.

Combining high-fat ingredients with persimmons counteracts any remaining traces of astringency by providing smooth, emollient textures that make any dryness far less noticeable.

HOW TO GROW PERSIMMONS

Persimmons are among the least fussy of all fruit trees, but give them a warm, sheltered spot and a deep, well-drained soil and they will pay you back with faster growth and sweeter fruit.

Jump-start Their Growth

Young persimmon trees can take their time to establish. Fortunately, we crafty horticulturists have devised the means to kick 'em into action.

Go for plants grafted onto a *Diospyros virginiana* rootstock. This has been proven to supercharge their vigour, bringing their fruiting date forward by years and making the plants even more cold- and disease-tolerant. If in doubt, ask your supplier to confirm that a tree has been grafted before purchase.

A surface mulch of heat-retaining biochar will help warm the roots and power up growth.

A liberal splash of high-nitrogen feed each spring will fuel rapid development of young saplings. Never fertilise after mid-summer, though, as this has been demonstrated severely to dent cold-hardiness come winter.

Planting in large (preferably dark coloured) terracotta pots in a sunny spot means their roots warm up more quickly in summer, extending their growing season.

Once trees have reached fruiting size, they can be planted straight out into the garden and left pretty much to fend for themselves.

Pruning & Training

The most popular way to prune persimmons is using the vase technique, exactly as you would a plum (see page 118).

Trimming back new flushes of summer growth to four or five leaves will easily keep the trees a manageable size. Persimmons flower and fruit on the current season's growth.

If any vigorous young shoots - known as suckering growth - rear their heads from the grafting union or below ground level (as can happen on *Diospyros virginiana* rootstocks), snip these off flush with the trunk.

Fruit Thinning

Once the trees start coming into fruit, it is a good idea to thin them out as soon as they have set to leave a maximum of two fruits per shoot. Apart from improving the sweetness and size of your persimmons, it also reduces the load on the

branches - these trees are so ridiculously productive their fragile boughs can snap under the weight of their own fruit.

Harvesting

Gather up your golden bounty just before the first frosts are forecast, even if they aren't 100 percent ripe. **Contrary to standard gardening advice, it has been demonstrated that frost does not improve the flavour of the fruit, but actually results in it rotting before it ripens.**

Gently snip off your persimmons with a secateurs instead of picking them as you would an apple - the notoriously brittle branches can snap if you try to yank the fruit off with your hands.

Persimmons will ripen in a week or two in a fruit bowl in a warm room, turning first yellow and finally a bright, translucent orange.

BLACKBERRIES, RASPBERRIES & THEIR KIN

Despite being gram for gram easily the most expensive products in the fresh produce aisle, the wild vigour of these bramble relatives also makes them the easiest of all fruit crops to grow. If you fancy growing them for their potential health benefits, I have more good news for you. Several trials have demonstrated that growing berries outdoors (as opposed to under the plastic canopies some commercial growers use) leads to a spike in both their phytonutrients and their aroma chemicals. In one 2012 trial, raspberries grown in polytunnels experienced up to a 50 percent drop in some of their flavour compounds, particularly those responsible for their sweet, rose-like notes and buttery finish. Years of crops that could be twice as flavourful as shop-bought isn't a bad pay off, is it? Happy days!

VARIETY GUIDE

The wonderful thing about growing your own berries is the chance it gives you to access an enormous range of flavours that you would otherwise never get the chance to taste.

Black Raspberry 'Jewel'

If you could take those glinting pick 'n' mix sweets of childhood and magically turn them into a real-life berry, this would be it. With a flavour like bramble jelly laced with red raspberry cordial, the big surprise is that black raspberries *Rubus occidentalis* are neither a raspberry nor blackberry, but a totally distinct species from the forests of North America.

Containing nearly five times the antioxidant anthocyanins of popular blackberry varieties like **'Navaho'**, black raspberries have attracted the attention of medical researchers, with a growing body of studies unearthing some intriguing results. A phase 1 clinical trial at the University of Ohio suggested that consuming the fruit reduced the markers of DNA damage in oral cancer survivors. Additional test-tube and animal studies also suggest their consumption *may* be linked to the inhibited growth of oesophageal and other cancers. The researchers are careful not to make claims that go beyond their limited data and more clinical trials are underway to establish whether these results are replicated in humans. However, since these berries are delicious, massively productive and a cinch to grow, to me, any health benefits are just a great silver lining.

Raspberry 'Glen Coe'

The result of a cross between a Stateside black raspberry and the old UK favourite **'Glen Prosen'**, this transatlantic fusion combines the best of both worlds. Lurid purple, exceptionally aromatic berries are kicked out in great abundance on stems coated in a powdery silver bloom. **Spine-free and well behaved, this is also one of the few raspberries that won't try to make a break for freedom as soon as your back is turned.**

Raspberry 'Joan J'

Consistently voted one of the best for taste, if you are after a vintage, country-fair raspberry flavour then this is your best bet, offering up impressive yields from mid-summer right through to mid-autumn. Fruit have a high sugar content and delicate, juicy texture, which I did not expect given their above-average size.

Raspberry 'All Gold'

Discovered as a rogue seedling that popped up in a nursery among hundreds of young **'Autumn Bliss'** plants, this yellow-fruited raspberry has more to offer than mere visual novelty, with a flavour that easily knocks the spots of most of its conventionally coloured cousins. With production starting up in late summer, I have been eating these right into the dark days of late autumn. The plants are nice and compact, meaning they don't need staking, which more than makes up for its one tiny flaw: the fruit is so tender it tends to disintegrate as you pick it.

Blackberry 'Reuben'

Developed by the University of Arkansas, this has widely been described as a breakthrough in blackberry breeding for its extremely compact size. With berries containing up to 10 percent pure sugar, **this cultivar's neat, upright growth habit and enthusiasm, offering a light but continuous harvest of fruit over an extended season**, have made it a firm favourite of mine. I also love its thornless cousin **'Apache'**, another alumnus of the Arkansas programme.

Blackberry 'Reuben'

Raspberry 'All Gold'

Raspberry 'Glen Coe'

Japanese Wineberry

Raspberry 'Joan J'

Mulberry 'Chelsea'

Boysenberry

Loganberry

Blackberry 'Karaka Black'

Raspberry 'Glen Prosen'

Blackberry 'Black Butte'

Black Raspberry 'Jewel'

Blackberry 'Karaka Black'

No, I have not pulled any kind of photoshop trickery here. This modern New Zealand hybrid genuinely is that big. I was once deeply sceptical of its flavour potential on account of its sheer 'Honey I Shrunk the Kids' size, but, boy, was I proved wrong. This is one of the most floral and complex-flavoured of all the brambles, with its monster size giving the berries a gelatinous bite to complement its lychee-like fragrance. It's a rapid, vigorous grower, too, producing surprisingly sweet berries on the shady site I relegated it to. Plants are viciously thorny, but have the considerate habit of holding their extra-long berries up at an angle to the stem, making prickle-free picking a breeze.

An almost perfect doppelganger is **'Black Butte'**, bred by the US Department of Agriculture (USDA) in a trial looking to create a super-size berry. It has excellent flavour, like regular blackberries, but sweeter with leafy black currant-type notes and a hint of fragrant elderflower. An absolute must-try.

Boysenberry

A complex cross from the genetic melting pot of Napa, California, that fuses loganberries, European raspberries and North American blackberries – with delicious results. **With its great balance of sweet and tart, this 1920s heirloom makes probably the best pie known to man.** Its susceptibility to fungal diseases, however, means you should always plant it in well-drained plots. A thornless form does exist, but sadly in my experience when you lose the thorns you lose the flavour.

Loganberry

Tasting like a 50:50 mix of strawberries and raspberries with a spritz of lemon juice, **this old Californian hybrid makes the best ever jams and jellies**. Its delicate texture and drip feed of fruit over a long season (no brief gluts) means you'll never see it in the shops. What makes them a nightmare for farmers, strangely makes them great for gardeners.

Mulberry 'Chelsea'

OK, I'll admit it, this fruit is only remotely related to the other crops on this page, but boy is it tasty! **Perhaps the sweetest of all berries, its sky-high balance of sugars and acids combined with a gummy-sweet like texture has made them one of the world's most popular fruit for centuries.** Sadly, their perilously soft texture means they are unsuited to the production systems of modern supermarkets, leading to their dramatic decline in the last century. Trees can take a few years to come into fruit, but there are tricks to speed them up (see page 127). Grow them exactly as you would a persimmon.

Japanese Wineberries

The token Asian in this group which, despite having won an RHS first-class certificate in 1894, is often pitched as a new introduction. The plants are highly ornamental, with masses of furry red spines and glistening orangey-red fruit. Their small size and mediocre yield mean they have never caught on commercially, but their flavour is great: sweet and grape-like with hints of tropical fruit over a background of rich raspberry.

TIPS & TRICKS

The Sweet Smell Of Success?

Several trials have demonstrated that spraying a diverse range of fruit crops with a plant hormone called methyl jasmonate can produce a rapid escalation of both flavour chemicals and phytonutrients. Don't like the idea of spraying your plants with hormones? Well, methyl jasmonate is the exact same, naturally occurring chemical that gives jasmine flowers their gloriously sweet, seductive fragrance – hence 'jasmonate'.

A 2005 trial by the USDA found that spraying an incredibly dilute solution of the chemical over raspberry plants boosted the sugar content of the fruit by 18 percent, while almost doubling their anthocyanin content. A similar effect has been demonstrated for blackberries and strawberries, with the peak in anthocyanins also causing richer, darker-coloured fruit.

For experimental allotmenteers without lab access, methyl jasmonate is also found in natural jasmine floral water (an ingredient used to flavour posh cocktails and in aromatherapy). This is easy to track down online, but make sure it is edible grade, as some cosmetics companies add non-food grade preservatives to their jasmine water to extend its shelf life.

To mimic the trial at home, **pour the jasmine floral water into a small aerosol bottle and spray it over your plants to thoroughly wet their leaves and fruit just as the berries begin to ripen.** (Conveniently this is likely to have a broadly similar concentration of methyl jasmonate to that used in the USDA trial.) **Repeat the process twice more, leaving four-day gaps between sprays.** OK, so this homespun take on the formula used in a trial may be far from an exact science, but why not give it a go and see if you think it works for you?

BLACKBERRY, GOATS' CHEESE & PEA PIZZA

Serves 2

Sweet and fragrant meets salty and tangy, this quirky flavour contrast will hit your taste buds from all angles. Make it using frozen pizza dough, hide the box and your guests will never know.

What You Need:

2 tablespoons polenta

220g (8oz) frozen pizza dough, thawed

200g (7oz) goats' cheese

50g (2oz) fresh peas

2 tablespoons honey

100g (4oz) **'Karaka Black'** blackberries

a few fresh oregano leaves and flowers

What To Do:

PREHEAT a baking sheet (essential if you're to get the crispest crust ever).

SPRINKLE the polenta over a chopping board.

ROLL the pizza dough out over the polenta, then turn it over and roll again. You're looking to create a rough disc shape, about dinner-plate size, dusted with polenta on each side.

SCATTER over the goats' cheese and peas and drizzle with the honey.

SLIDE onto the hot baking sheet and bake for 10–15 minutes in a preheated 220°C/425°F/gas mark 7 oven until the crust is crisp and the cheese melted.

SERVE scattered with the blackberries and oregano leaves and flowers.

GROWING BLACKBERRIES, RASPBERRIES & THEIR KIN

As with almost all fruit crops, the more direct sun you can get your plants under, the sweeter and more aromatic their fruit will be. Pick a sheltered spot away from battering winds.

Site & Soil

Hailing from rich woodland soils, most brambles hate having their roots in heavy, waterlogged ground. **For best results, plant them in raised beds with loads of organic matter mixed into the soil.** Follow the instructions for planting shrubs and trees on pages 36-37.

Weeding

Keep the soil under your plants as weed-free as possible to aid the establishment of your little berry patch.

Pruning & Canes

There are technically two different methods of pruning raspberries and blackberries, depending on whether they are summer- or autumn-fruiting forms. This can be confusing to newbies, especially when neighbouring clumps of different varieties inevitably merge together, so you have no idea which is which. Trust me, I have been there more than once.

I prefer to adopt an equal-opportunities approach and treat all of them as if they were summer-fruiting. This has the added benefit of making the autumn-fruiting forms produce a steadier spread of berries over a long period, instead of one massive glut that you have trouble getting rid of come the autumn. The best news is pruning can be done and dusted in just three easy steps.

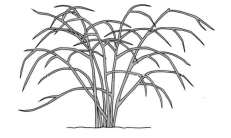

1

WHEN your plants have shed their leaves in the late autumn, carefully cut off any old canes that have finished fruiting right down to ground level with secateurs. Spent canes will be brown or grey with the dried-up remnants of their fruited branches still attached. Young, vigorous canes from the current year's growth will be fresh and green.

2

THIN out the remaining new canes, keeping only the most healthy-looking, evenly spaced ones. Leave just 5-7 canes on raspberries or 3-4 on blackberries.

3

TRIM the lateral branches that spread out from the canes to 30cm (12in) long.

Mulch & Fertiliser

To give the plants a boost each spring, I like to sprinkle a balanced organic fertiliser like blood, fish and bone over the soil, then top it with a generous layer of well-rotted compost to ensure the high fertility these plants enjoy.

BLUEBERRIES

Virtually unknown outside of their native North America just a decade or two ago, blueberries have enjoyed a meteoric rise to popularity thanks to one little word: 'antioxidants'. What supermarkets don't tell you, however, is that while hyping the blueberry's 'superfood' status on packets, behind the scenes they have been actively selecting the lowest antioxidant varieties possible. I kid you not! In the search of ever larger berries (which are quicker to pick), breeders have been selecting for fruit that have a much lower ratio of skin to fruit. They have also been engineering lighter blueberries that shine out on the shelves over blacker-coloured forms. As it is the anthocyanin pigments found only in the skin that are believed to be responsible for the blueberry's purported health benefits, both these actions have – perhaps unknowingly – slashed potential nutritional value.

The good news? By choosing the right variety and following a few growing and cooking tips the foodie grower can get more than triple the anthocyanin content of the supermarkets' standard. Still not convinced? Well, with established bushes yielding up to 5kg (11lb) of fruit each year, at current prices you could be in for a return of up to nine times the cost of the plant every year. Boom!

VARIETY GUIDE

Whether it's pure sweetness, potential health value or just the world's best pie you are after, there is a blueberry variety for you. All of these have been laboriously tried and tasted by me in a massive sampling of varieties at RHS Garden Wisley. Oh, the sacrifices I make for my work.

'Rubel' *Mid-season*

If you are after pure health geek points, this is the one for you. **'Rubel'** is a true superstar that consistently tops the charts as one of the most phytonutrient-packed of all. In one US Department of Agriculture (USDA) study that analysed 107 berry varieties, **'Rubel'** was found to contain more than three times the anthocyanins of supermarket favourite **'Bluecrop'**, which dominates commercial growing worldwide. **'Rubel'** is a clone of one of the first blueberries ever brought into cultivation from the wild way back in 1912, and hasn't therefore had any of its vigour (or flavour) bred out of it. This does mean that its berries are significantly smaller than most blueberries, but they more than make up for this in total yield per bush. **Their small size, concentrated sweet/tart flavour and low water content mean they make the perfect addition to cakes, muffins and pies,** creating knock-out flavour, not slimy blobs of water.

'Legacy' *Mid-season*

A permanent fixture near the top of the taste-test league tables of the USDA, **'Legacy'** is said to be nicknamed Goldbush by growers on account of its heavy production and its large, light blue berries which belie their deep, dark flavour.

'Spartan' AGM *Early*

Rich, sweet and tangy tasting, these are regarded by many as the best flavoured of all. The exceptionally large, light blue fruit start the season off with a bang. The plants are pretty easy on the eye, too, with their leaves erupting into shades of bronze and gold each autumn.

'Patriot' *Early*

Vigorous bushes producing heavy crops of berries with a robust, complex, classic blueberry flavour. **This is a great one for beginners for its tolerance of heavy, damp soils and resistance to root rot and harsh weather.** Lovely autumn colour, too.

'Herbert' *Mid-season*

Another contender for best-ever flavour, with its resinous fragrance and an excellent balance of sugars and acid. There is much debate among Stateside aficionados as to whether this or **'Spartan'** takes the crown. Heavy crops of medium-sized berries follow delicate white flowers and crimson autumn foliage on shorter, 1.5m (5ft) plants.

Darrow's Blueberry *Vaccinium darrowi* (often sold as 'Darrow') *Late*

I find with blueberries that size and flavour seem to be inversely proportional. Not so with Darrow's blueberry which, despite producing some of the largest of all berries, still manages to pack them with a hefty dose of sweetness and aroma. Add to that pretty pink spring blossom followed by fiery red autumn foliage on compact 1.5m (5ft) plants, and you have a real all-year-round winner for small gardens. Intriguingly, this is not a variety as such, but an entirely different blueberry species.

'Pink Lemonade' *Mid-season*

A new, wild-card cultivar bred by the US government that has swapped a high anthocyanin content for candy pink colour and probably the most intense sweetness of all. Admittedly it is a *very* light cropper, but its stunningly complex floral flavour stands out as being almost unrecognizable among blueberries.

☆ 'Rubel' - best for antioxidants

☆ 'Spartan' - best for early summer flavour

'Pink Lemonade'

☆ 'Patriot' - best beginner growers

☆ 'Legacy' - best for knock-out yield

☆ 'Darrow' - best for eating fresh

☆ 'Herbert' - best for pies

LEAGUE TABLE OF ANTIOXIDANTS

Variety	Antioxidant Value Oxygen Radical Absorbance Capacity
'Rubel'	31.1
'Herbert'	19.7
'Bluegold'	14.9
'Darrow'	14.8
'Patriot'	14.4
'Legacy'	13.5
'Spartan'	12.1
'Sunshine Blue'	11.7
'Bluecrop'	10.4

(Source US Department of Agriculture)

WANNA GO ONE BETTER?

Why not try your hand at growing the blueberry's European cousin, the bilberry *Vaccinium myrtillus***, whose modest size belies its mammoth phytonutrient potential?** Stained bright purple to their core, unlike the pale green flesh of North American blueberries, these contain even more of the good stuff – up to 20 percent more antioxidant activity than even **'Rubel'**, according to the US Department of Agriculture's Human Nutrition Research Center on Aging.

BILBERRIES: The messy staining is caused by the natural pigments that give these berries their antioxidant value.

REGULAR BLUEBERRIES: Notice the perfectly clean, stain-free hand by comparison?

TIPS & TRICKS

Go Organic

According to a large, multiple-site study by New Jersey's Rutgers University in 2008, making the switch to organic growing could result in measurably tastier, more nutritious harvests.

The researchers found that, by growing blueberry **'Bluecrop'** (*Vaccinium corymbosum*) organically, doing away with heavy watering and fertiliser use, they could increase the antioxidant capacity of their berries by 50 percent, producing fruit with significantly higher sugars, acids and phenols. These findings have been echoed by other researchers. However, a follow-up study by the same team in 2011 on a different species, the rabbit-eye blueberry (*Vaccinium virgatum*), demonstrated more subtle differences, with not all the organic berries showing significantly higher levels of antioxidants.

To me, on balance, the promise of reducing my workload and being rewarded for my lack of effort with potentially tastier crops has its appeal. Do less work, get better harvests. What an offer!

Have Your Pie & Eat It

Among all this virtuous talk of potential health benefits, it would be remiss of me to neglect to mention one thing. **Blueberry pie just might possess more potent phytonutrient content than fresh, raw berries.** Yes, you read this right.

One study at Oregon's Health Sciences University suggested that cooking blueberries may double their antioxidant capacity. Other studies have found that, while total anthocyanins can be almost halved during cooking, the berries' overall antioxidant activity was paradoxically boosted by 50 percent. **Researchers have suggested that this may be because cooking liberates these water-soluble chemicals from the skin of the fruit, making them easier for the body to absorb.**

While this may not be conclusive proof, I have never needed much of an excuse to eat pie. In the words of one report: 'More research is clearly needed', and this is one greedy botanist who is happy to oblige.

GROWING BLUEBERRIES

Hailing from the Pine Barrens of New Jersey, blueberries are real rugged outdoorsmen, having evolved to thrive in extremely poor soils, bitterly cold winters and total neglect. They don't call them the Pine Barrens for nothing.

Plant
Use The Buddy System
Most blueberries are technically self-fertile, but they will bear far greater crops if hooked up with a partner from **another variety**, and even more if you introduce a third playmate. A nifty trick is to pick an early, mid- and late-fruiting variety, which will greatly extend your harvest season. This works because all blueberries flower at roughly the same time. It is just their ripening season that is staggered.

Site & Soil
Get 'Em On Acid
The blueberry's only diva-like demand is an acidic soil, **ideally with a pH of 4.5–5.5.** If you don't know what kind of soil you have, simple testing kits are available cheaply at all garden centres. However, there is an easier and almost instant way to determine this. Take a look around your neighbourhood: if there are large rhododendrons and camellias growing happily in the ground in gardens all around you, you are likely to have acid soil; if not, you probably don't.

Great Drainage
Although some varieties will tolerate heavier soils, **blueberries generally love light, free-draining plots**, so incorporate plenty of organic matter like composted bark, bracken, leafmould or even sawdust at planting time.

Growing In Pots
Blueberries are perfectly happy growing in pots filled with an ericaceous potting mix. I would go for one that is soil-based, with plenty of composted bark thrown into the mix. Site your mini plantation in a sheltered spot in full sun for berries with the richest flavour, deepest colour and highest anthocyanin content.

Watering & Feeding
Keep Them Moist
Blueberries like to have their roots evenly moist. Chucking a layer of mulch over the soil every other year will help seal in the moisture and keep their roots nice and cool.

During hot, dry weather plants in pots will appreciate a quick moisture top-up. Experts advise using rainwater if you happen to live in a hard-water area; however, in my experience this makes little difference, probably because any alkalinity it contains is soon washed out of the soil by the inevitable rain.

Ditch The Fertiliser
As a general rule you will never need to fertilise blueberry plants growing in the ground if your soil has been well managed. In fact, they are notoriously sensitive to fertiliser, so adding this could do more harm than good. Who likes shovelling manure anyway? Plants in pots should be given only extremely dilute applications of ericaceous feed once a month in the growing season.

Netting
Birds love blueberries as much as people do. In fact, commercial growers in the US employ everything from Japanese robots to trained kite flyers and even radio-controlled drones disguised as birds of prey called 'ornithopters' to defend their harvests. Fortunately for home growers the plants' small size means it is easy to chuck a net over them to keep avian attacks at bay.

Pruning
Blueberries need next to no pruning until they reach full size, meaning you won't have to reach for your secateurs at all for the first five years. On established plants trim out older branches in the winter to encourage new growth to rejuvenate your bushes, as fruit are produced only on two- to three-year-old growth. This is a good opportunity to remove any dead or congested growth as well as any branches brushing the soil.

Picking
Pick fruit when it has turned fully blue and developed a **silvery bloom on the surface** to get it while its sugar and flavour chemicals are reaching their absolute peak.

ANTHOCYANIN-PACKED BLUEBERRY PIE

Serves 6

OK, yes, this is pie. However, with each slice potentially containing as much absorbable anthocyanins as nine packets of some varieties of fresh supermarket blueberries, and only a fraction of the sugar of most desserts, I for one am getting stuck in.

What You Need:

350g (12oz) ready-rolled, all-butter shortcrust pastry

1.5kg (3lb) organic **'Rubel'** blueberries

200g (7oz) sugar (or natural, sugar-free sweetener)

125g (5oz) cornflour

1 large pinch of salt

juice and rind of 1 lemon

2 tablespoons butter

'Pink Lemonade' blueberries for decoration

What To Do:

PREHEAT the oven to 220°C/425°F/gas mark 7.

LINE a greased, 23cm (9in) pie dish with the pastry.

TOSS together the 'Rubel' blueberries, sugar, cornflour, salt, lemon juice and rind.

PILE this into the pastry-lined pie dish, mounding it up toward the middle, and dot with the butter.

BAKE in the oven for 20 minutes, then lower the temperature to 180°C/350°F/gas mark 4 and bake for another 20 minutes.

LEAVE in its pan on a rack until cool. Scatter with the 'Pink Lemonade' blueberries.

SERVE slathered in cream (okay, this is where the health argument begins to break down).

WILD-CARD CROPS

SWEET POTATOES

Despite the sweet potato's exotic Amazonian origins, recent breakthroughs in its breeding have created a new generation of cool-weather-tolerant, fast-maturing varieties that can be grown successfully in some surprisingly chilly parts of the world.

OK, so these may not rival their supermarket siblings for sheer monster size, but they will reward your efforts with a truly massive diversity of unusual flavours and colours in cute, 'one person' portions. From ivory-fleshed beauties with sweet lychee tones and deep purple forms with an intense rose-syrup fragrance, to the more familiar bright orange, pumpkin-flavoured types, these autumnal treats are well worth the extra care it takes to grow them.

VARIETY GUIDE

For some arcane reason seed catalogues tend to insist on pushing the varieties that most closely resemble those sold by supermarkets, despite the fact that they are not always those with the best flavour or even the strongest growers. I feel this is a huge shame, as surely the whole point of making the effort to grow your own is to get something better than, or if not at least different from, what you can buy beautifully shrink-wrapped in the shops? With that in mind, here's my round-up of the best-performing varieties out there.

☆ 'Murasaki 29' *The Best for Fries*

This Japanese-type variety has a very sweet, resinous flavour and waxy texture. Maintaining a delicately crisp bite even when cooked, it is delicious grated raw in salads, fried in rösti or hash browns and turned into super-finely sliced 'skinny' fries.

A relatively new kid on the block, this has proven to have a similar productivity and plant vigour under temperate conditions to the top-selling varieties 'Beauregard', 'Beauregard Improved' and 'Carolina Ruby'.

☆ 'Okinawa' *The Best for Desserts*

The deep, dark burgundy flesh of 'Okinawa' belies its flowery, rosewater-like flavour. Delicately smooth and extremely sweet, it tastes like some kind of fancy, rose-scented cake either baked, boiled or fried and drizzled in honey. Being packed with a hefty dose of anthocyanins, these striking mini spuds are as healthy as they are tasty.

Sadly, although it is available in the US, 'Okinawa' is currently not listed in any of the UK catalogues; however, it does sometimes appear on the shelves of Asian supermarkets (including those online) towards the end of the year. If you find them please do your palate a favour and buy them. A single tuber can make dozens of cuttings, which can be propagated year after year, pretty much indefinitely.

☆ 'T65' *The Best for Soups*

Beneath a bright pink skin lies a creamy white flesh with an intense floral fragrance like a seamless cross between lychees and elderflowers. Its supercharged sweetness is perfectly complemented by its smooth, sticky texture which, unlike most sweet potatoes, is closer to that of a tender parsnip than a starchy spud. For me, this is by far the best choice of all, being delicious in soups and purées or simply baked whole. However, its high water content and lack of starch make it not the best choice for roasting.

'T65' is as much of a star in the garden as it is in the kitchen, being in my experience by far the most productive and cool-tolerant of all varieties, growing vigorously at temperatures that bring other varieties to a shuddering halt. It can be tricky to track down, but is definitely worth an extra five minutes of online rummaging to source.

☆ 'Georgia Jet' *The Best for Mash*

Exceptionally sugary and with a classic sweet-potato flavour, this early-maturing type is known to produce good yields in temperate climates, even outdoors. Its only downside is its relatively watery texture, meaning it makes great soup and mash, but rubbish roasties.

'Beauregard Improved'

This is the most aggressively marketed and certainly the most widely available variety, because it bears a close resemblance to those found in the shops. Hardly the most exciting, though.

'Murasaki 29'

'Georgia Jet'

'Okinawa'

'Beauregard Improved'

'T65'

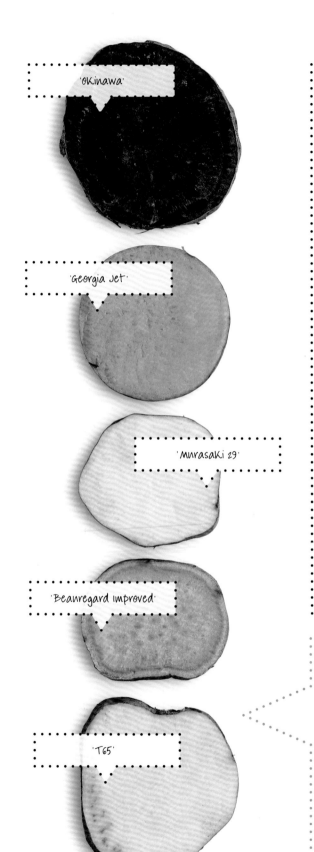

'Okinawa'

'Georgia Jet'

'Murasaki 29'

'Beauregard improved'

'T65'

TIPS & TRICKS

Curing For Flavour

After variety choice, the single most important factor that determines sweet-potato flavour is curing. Never, ever eat sweet potatoes freshly dug from the ground. **As with winter squash, newly harvested tubers will just be mealy blocks of starch and will only reveal their true sugary, fragrant potential when left to 'cure' in a warm, humid environment for a few weeks**. These conditions trigger the spuds to enter 'healing mode', sealing over any cuts and bruises (which also considerably extends their shelf life), while dramatically boosting both their aroma chemicals and their sweetness. **This crucial, but strangely rarely talked about process can in some varieties also increase the level of carotenes** - the orange pigments that give these nutritional powerhouses their characteristic colour and health benefits.

To get curing, dust the soil off your newly harvested sweet potatoes and pop them (unwashed) into a large crate or tub - if possible, arrange them so that they aren't touching each other. Put the container in the warmest place you can find, such as an airing cupboard or warm room near a radiator for two weeks. Lay a damp cloth over the top to raise the humidity, without letting it touch or moisten the surface of the tubers themselves. You are ideally looking to give them an environment of about 25°C (77°F) and 80 percent humidity. Curing can still be done at temperatures closer to 21°C (70°F), which is perhaps more practical for home gardeners, but this will take longer - roughly 3-4 weeks. Apart from this there is very little to do, other than keeping an occasional eye on your curing harvest and removing any that have gone mouldy. **A simple way to check that they are 'done' is to examine any cuts or bruises: these should have healed over with a corky layer and the skin should appear dry and leathery.**

WHAT'S INSIDE THE WRAPPER?

Sweet potatoes come in a surprising diversity of colours from creamy white to intense purple. The pigments responsible for creating their colours not only affect their flavour but also their potential health benefits. Traditional orange sweet potatoes derive their colour from carotenes, which are known antioxidants. Purple sweet potatoes tend to have rosy, berry-like notes and are high in the same phytonutrient pigments found in blueberries and grapes, while white ones have a more floral, lychee-like aroma.

GROWING SWEET POTATOES

Trials have shown that the latest generation of cool-tolerant sweet-potato varieties can and do produce reliable yields outdoors across most of the southern half of the UK given a little protection. But despite their new-found ability to plod on through chilly summers, these little vines still secretly crave warmth, always churning out the largest yields and strongest growth in the cosy confines of a glasshouse. The hotter the better. If growing them outdoors, pick your most sunny, warm, sheltered site.

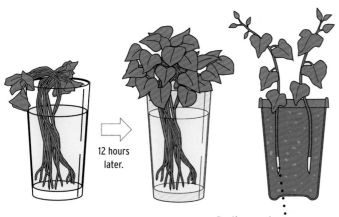

12 hours later.

Rooting powder at the cut tips.

Sow & Grow

Sweet potatoes are normally grown from 'slips' (cuttings made from the young shoots that come out of sprouting sweet potatoes) that are sold through most seed catalogues in the spring. As you can imagine, sending unrooted cuttings through the post means they will arrive extremely dehydrated and in need of some pretty intensive care. **As soon as they arrive, dunk them in a glass of tepid water and leave them in a warm place to soak for at least 12 hours to rehydrate.**

Gently dry off your rehydrated slips with a paper towel or cloth, dip the cut end in rooting hormone and plant them up using a gritty compost in long, deep pots like root trainers. Place them on a sunny windowsill and keep them warm and moist and they will quickly sprout roots to form vigorous young plants.

In The Glasshouse

For best results, **set your little plants out in large tubs or beds of loose, sandy soil.** The light, well-drained texture is essential not only to allow the roots to swell easily, but also to prevent them from rotting in the cooler autumn.

In The Garden

In mild gardens sweet potatoes can make reliable harvests as long as you follow a few simple guidelines to ensure they get maximum warmth (see left).

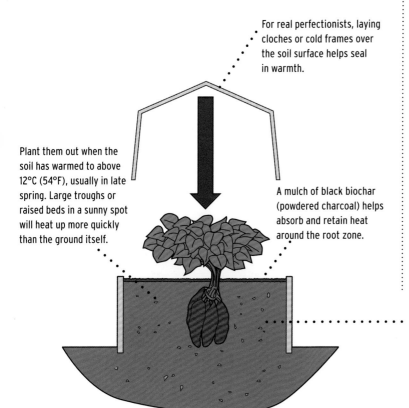

For real perfectionists, laying cloches or cold frames over the soil surface helps seal in warmth.

Plant them out when the soil has warmed to above 12°C (54°F), usually in late spring. Large troughs or raised beds in a sunny spot will heat up more quickly than the ground itself.

A mulch of black biochar (powdered charcoal) helps absorb and retain heat around the root zone.

A light, sandy, well-drained mix will prevent the roots from rotting, as can happen if they are left in cold, damp soil later in the year.

Growing On
Watering & Feeding
Sweet potatoes love lashings of water, which help fuel their rapid growth and give their leaves the humidity they hanker after. However, go easy on the fertilisers, especially those high in nitrogen. The plants are not greedy feeders, and overly generous nutrition will result in vines that are all leaves and no roots. Not good. A monthly douse in molasses tonic (see page 27), which is low in nitrogen, should provide all the extra minerals and trace elements they need.

Pests

Once up and running, sweet potatoes are extremely low-maintenance crops, happy to get on with the job of looking after themselves. **Armies of slugs can, however, be a real menace, so pre-empt their nocturnal raids with a sprinkling of organic slug pellets early in the spring.**

Harvest & Storage
Your harvest will be ready to unearth on a dry day once the first frosts have blackened the leaves. It is critical, however, that harvesting be done incredibly carefully as, despite looking and feeling rock hard, the tubers are surprisingly fragile. **Cracks and bruises from being yanked out of the ground and tumbled into crates will cause the roots to rot quickly in storage. Handle them exactly as you would eggs.**

Once they're harvested, shake off the soil (do not wash them) and cure them according to the instructions in the 'Tips & Tricks' section (page 142).

Fully cured sweet potatoes can be stored for at least six months by putting them in a cool, dark place, spaced evenly in baskets or slatted wooden crates that allow good air circulation around the roots. It is important that the room be cool, but not cold. Around 15°C (59°F) is ideal; at below 10°C (50°F) these tropical tubers experience 'chilling injury', which results in a breakdown of the structure of the spud. This produces 'off' flavours, discoloration, a hard core in the flesh when cooked and a susceptibility to rotting. For this reason never, *ever* store them in the fridge.

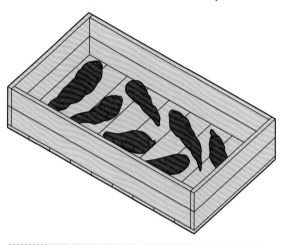

Get Some Freetail Therapy
Sweet potato slips can be quite expensive, sometimes costing the same per cutting as a fully grown supermarket tuber! Fortunately, **there is a super-simple solution that could mean that you never need to buy slips ever again.** All you need to do is save one of your sweet potatoes until the spring (they should keep for several months in a cool, dry place) and then pop it into a pot of damp seed compost on a warm, sunny windowsill. Plant your spud standing upright, one end buried, the other sticking up in the air and keep moist at 18-20°C (64-68°F). In just a few weeks little eyes will start to form on the aerial part, eventually growing into the same spindly 20cm (8in) long slips that catalogues sell. Snip these off when they get long enough (discarding the tuber once you've snipped off the slips) and treat them exactly as you would normal slips.

In the meantime your sweet potato will make a great, quirky-looking houseplant - far more exciting than a boring *Ficus*.

With each spud capable of producing up to 10 slips, and with each one of these being far fresher than anything that will arrive in the post, this little trick could potentially keep you in sweet potatoes for years to come.

HEALTH GEEK FACT
Sweet potatoes contain carbs that are released much more slowly than regular spuds, keeping you fuller for longer and making them a potentially healthy choice. Well, unless you smother them in butter and brown sugar like I do!

FUNGICULTURE

Mushroom-growing can seem an incredibly daunting process, involving elaborate techniques that demand fresh supplies of specific log types, drilling with power tools and even sealing with double boilers full of hot wax. Ouch!

But this simply does not have to be the case. Pick your site and species right and mushrooms can naturalize in any ordinary garden, offering up tasty crops for very little work. These colonies can even help boost the harvests of the crops around them, improving soil fertility, unlocking nutrients, fending off pests and diseases and acting symbiotically to improve their drought-resistance. It's almost too good to be true.

VARIETY GUIDE

From super-easy-to-grow oyster mushrooms to the exotic gamble of summer truffles, here is my express guide to the range of edible fungi you can grow at home.

The Ones That Grow On Tree Roots

This special group of fungi live symbiotically on the roots of trees, where they boost the host plant's access to water and nutrients and in so doing supercharge their growth. **Establishing a colony of these in your garden could therefore provide you with not only healthier trees, but also a tasty crop of gourmet mushrooms to boot**. Not a bad deal.

The best known of these fungi is the undisputed king of mushrooms, the **black truffle** (*Tuber melanospornum*) (see page 176). Selling for extortionate prices, it grows well on hazel, giving you the potential of two crops in the space of one. Similarly, several companies are now selling spawn for rich, meaty-flavoured **French morels** (*Morchella esculenta*), which can be colonized on the roots of apple trees. **Growing this class of mushrooms is not for the impatient as they can take years to bear fruit and their complex relationship with their host plant may never take in the first place**. However, with some luck and the right conditions, they can provide you with years of the highest value harvest around in return for almost zero care and maintenance. A pretty good gamble if I ever heard of one.

The Ones That Grow On Woodchips

If you have a moist, shady spot where nothing else will grow, it is worth trying your hand at **shiitake** mushrooms (*Lentinula edodes*). Smoky, meaty and packed with umami-flavour chemicals, shiitake have been a prized medicinal species in Eastern Asia for thousands of years. They contain lentinan, a complex sugar compound which some studies suggest stimulates the immune system and even triggers certain cells and proteins in the body to attack cancer cells.

Forming cascades of creamy white, coral-like fingers, **lion's mane** mushrooms (*Hericium erinaceus*) have a unique, meaty flavour like lobster cooked in butter. They're pretty much unbuyable in supermarkets, too. Their true flavour potential is brought out through a slow caramelization in butter or oil, until they become crispy along the edges. If you skip this step they can taste mildly bitter, so don't rush them! These fungi contain a range of chemicals that scientists believe may stimulate nerve regeneration, improving memory and even mood. According to a range of studies, they may help to slow anxiety and depression and improve the ability to concentrate.

The Ones That Will Grow Almost Anywhere!

The multicoloured frills of **oyster** mushrooms (*Pleurotus ostreatus*) are well known among fungiculture geeks for being the easiest of all to grow. Give them a damp, shady spot and they will soon get to work, voraciously consuming almost any organic matter from leaves and twigs to straw and even spent coffee grounds, offering up flushes of tasty mushrooms in as little as eight weeks. **Added to a compost heap they speed up the whole process, generating rich, friable compost and an edible treat. Magic!** I like to use some of the brighter coloured forms, particularly the yellow oyster mushroom (which tolerates cooler temperatures than the pink one), as they are easy to tell apart from any other wild mushrooms that may pop up in your heap.

Want a chunkier, meatier texture? Give the **king oyster** (*Pleurotus eryngii*) a go. They are just as easy to grow and amazing sliced and fried until golden.

Morels are known for springing up after forest fires, so adding ashes or charcoal to their growing media may boost their growth.

French Morel

Shiitake

King oyster

Grey oyster

Lion's Mane

GROWING MUSHROOMS

Whether it's a damp spot under some trees, a compost heap or even just a knackered old laundry bin that you have space for, there is a mushroom you can grow. Here are three easy ways to get started.

Despite what many people think, mushrooms are not plants. They belong to a totally different kingdom all of their own: **fungi.** In fact, they are genetically more closely related to animals, meaning that lack of a green thumb is no excuse! Fungi do not trap energy from the sun to make food; instead, like animals, they need to be constantly fed a nutrient source, which they digest through a web of root-like structures called mycelia. This makes them perfect to grow in places that are too dark and dingy to support other crops. **Their favourite food source is dead plants, so mushrooms are a pretty great way to get rid of garden waste.** If you can keep them dark, damp and away from fertilisers and chlorinated tap water then you are good to go.

ON COMPOST HEAPS

1. **MIX** two 50g (2oz) packets of oyster mushroom spawn with a few handfuls of torn-up paper or sawdust in a large mixing bowl (you can buy spawn quite cheaply online and at some garden centres). Pour over a cupful of warm water and ½ teaspoon of sugar and mix together until you have a moist, crumbly consistency. This should be perfect for one average compost heap. Spring is the ideal time to do this.

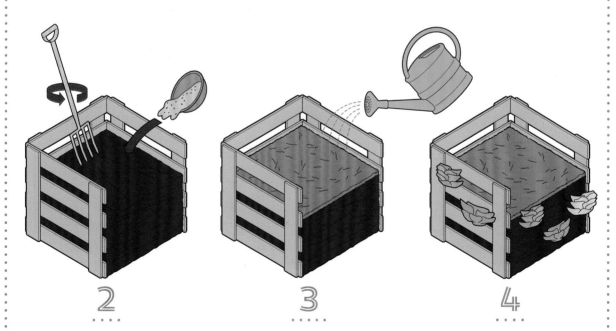

2. **SCATTER** this mix over your compost heap and roughly fork it into the surface of the compost.

3. **COVER** with a 5cm (2in) layer of dead leaves or grass clippings and water in well. It is best to use rainwater from water butts as tap water contains fungi-killing chlorine. At a pinch simply leaving a bucket of water to stand overnight will allow most of the chlorine to evaporate off.

4. **KEEP** the heap damp with an occasional light watering. You should start to see little mushrooms popping up in a matter of months.

UNDER SHRUBS & TREES

With their rich, meaty flavour and beautiful burgundy colour, wine-cap mushrooms (*Stropharia rugosoannulata*) can reach truly staggering sizes. As large as dinner plates and weighing up to 3kg (6½lb) each, it's no wonder they also go by the common names 'garden giants' and even 'Godzilla mushrooms'.

Surprisingly, all you need in order to establish a naturalized colony in your garden is a moist, shady patch beneath shrubs or trees, where they will soon get to work enriching the soil and offering up several flushes of mushrooms each year for decades at a time. Mushrooms have even been recently demonstrated to kill nematodes, worm-like organisms that can harm your plants. A perfect win-win situation!

Wine caps break woodchips down into rich, friable compost, unlocking nutrients, boosting fertility and attracting earthworms.

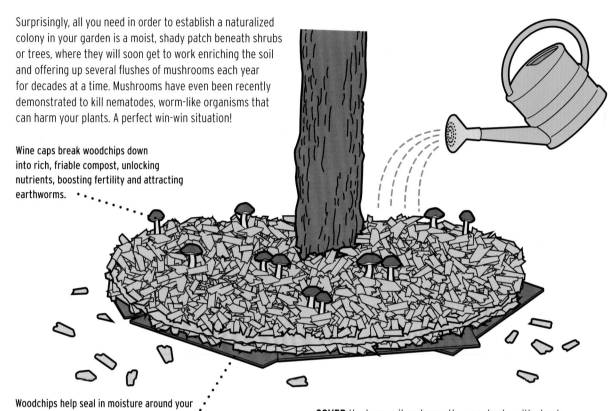

Woodchips help seal in moisture around your tree's roots, suppress competing weeds and reduce the compaction of the soil.

DITCH THE CHEMS

High-intensity fertilisers (particularly those rich in nitrogen or phosphorus) and an array of pesticides will severely hamper the growth of fungi, even to the point of wiping them out altogether. But as these little guys naturally boost the fertility of the soil and can even help plants fight back against a range of pests and diseases, the good news is you may never need to use chemicals in the first place.

COVER the bare soil underneath your shrubs with sheets of newspaper or cardboard.

MIX one 50g (2oz) packet of wine-cap spawn per 4 sq m (45 sq ft) with 2 tablespoons sugar (to provide the infant fungi with a ready supply of food to spark it into action) and sprinkle this over the cardboard. Oyster mushrooms can also be grown this way.

LAYER on a few barrowloads of sustainable hardwood chips (sold under this generic name and available online) to create a layer 5-8cm (2-3½in) deep.

WATER the whole area in well with rainwater and keep moist. Check back regularly, as your first crop of mushrooms will be popping up in as little as three to six months.

Although wine caps can grow to enormous sizes, they are by far at their tastiest and most intensely wine coloured when each little parasol is just 5-15cm (2-6in) across. If kept moist and given a top-up layer of woodchips each spring, your patch can be kept growing almost indefinitely.

IN LAUNDRY BINS

This variation on the basic woodchip technique can also be used for gourmet species like shiitake and lion's mane mushrooms that tend to fruit better when their root-like mycelia encounter a vertical surface.

. . . .

Mushrooms in a Bin

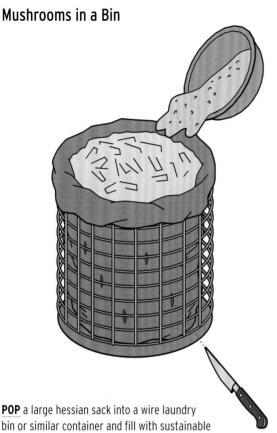

POP a large hessian sack into a wire laundry bin or similar container and fill with sustainable hardwood chips.

STAB a dozen or so holes through the sacking with a sharp knife. These are what the mushrooms will grow out of.

BURY the spores (these are usually sold inoculated into woody dowels) 5–15cm (2–6in) beneath the surface with a sprinkling of 2 tablespoons sugar, then tie the sack shut.

WATER liberally with rainwater and keep moist. Keep topped up with fresh batches of woodchips and your mushroom bin can fruit for several years.

WHY HARDWOOD CHIPS, NOT LOGS?

Although, in the wild, mushrooms usually grow on solid logs, to the home grower this means laborious drilling, stacking and sealing with wax to inoculate the fungi into the wood. Using sustainable woodchips means that not only do you instantly dispense with these chores, but also that the greater surface area means far faster growth and earlier harvests.

Hardwoods contain larger amounts of lignin, the structural carbohydrate that makes up wood. This denser concentration is what makes them harder than softwoods such as pine and spruce, and therefore a richer source of energy for most edible fungi.

The edible fungi that I suggest growing in this section derive their energy from lignin by breaking it down into glucose, which is why, when you are starting off a new colony, adding a little sugar to the mix is a good idea. This quick energy fix kick-starts the mushrooms into growth.

SPECIALITY ONIONS

I used to think growing onions was a total waste of time. After four miserable attempts, battling valiantly against mildew and onion fly, I realized that my crops actually tasted pretty much identical to shop-bought – even when viewed through my 'I grew this therefore it must taste better' goggles.

Then I discovered if you just change the type of onions you grow, ditching plain old *Allium cepa* in favour of its wilder, fancier cousins, you suddenly get virtually unbuyable, exotic veg, from plants that look far better and are a fraction of the work. Fair swap, I would say!

VARIETY GUIDE

Persian Shallots
Allium stipitatum

This exotic, wild species is gathered from the hillsides of Iran as a gourmet delicacy. Tasting like a nutty, aromatic fusion of garlic and shallots, but actually a distinct species from either of the former, these are much prized in Persian cuisine when sliced into salads and chopped into raita-like yogurt dips.

Its culinary charms may remain largely unexplored outside its native land, but surprisingly **gardeners will almost certainly know it via its secret alter ego as a common ornamental flower** - like the mild-mannered Clark Kent to the flavour-packed powerhouse of Superman.

Plant a generous swathe of bulbs in a sunny spot in the autumn to create a spring display that will return for years to come. **Once they're established, you can harvest up to a quarter of the bulbs (they have an intense flavour, so you won't need that many) each year in autumn** to add the exotic warmth of Persia to seasonal dishes.

I love the varieties **'Mount Everest'** for its snowy white spheres of flowers and **'Violet Beauty'** for its reliable colour. Both taste great and are a cinch to grow. Seek them out in the ornamental bulb section.

EAT THEM FROM YOUR GARDEN, NOT YOUR NURSERY!

Do not eat any *Allium* bulbs recently bought from nurseries, as they are likely to contain harmful pesticide residues. After 'detoxing' in your garden for a season they should, however, be ready to make prime eating.

Shallot 'Échalote Grise'
Allium oschaninii

Home-grown shallots will beat onions hands down every time in the flavour stakes, but this little guy goes one better still. Despite normally being lumped together with its commoner kitchen cousins, **'Échalote Grise'** is really not a shallot at all, but a separate species from Central Asia that has been prized for years by fancy French chefs. Described by the Cordon Bleu set as the truffles of the onion world, their richly concentrated, sweet, aromatic flavour easily makes them the best-flavoured of all the family. Sadly, their light yields, short shelf life and lack of cosmetic perfection also mean that you will never see these in the supermarkets. If you only grow one onion crop ever, make this it.

The sets (mini bulbs ready for planting) are easy to track down in the shallot section of almost every catalogue and some good garden centres in winter, although they may go under the pseudonyms **'French Grey'** or **'Griselle'.** The old-school rule of thumb, which works well in my experience, is to plant them at the winter solstice and harvest them at the summer solstice.

Lampascioni
Muscari comosum

Lampascioni are bracingly bitter-sweet with a deep, dark onion flavour. Mysteriously labelled 'wild onions' and sold in posh Italian jars of olive oil, these mini pink bulbs have intrigued me for years. What I didn't expect to discover was that I already had them growing in my garden, disguised as the popular ornamental plant, the tassel hyacinth.

Actually **far more closely related to hyacinths than to onions, this delicacy from Italy's Puglia region have been enjoyed in the Med since the time of the ancient Greeks**. Pungently bitter, but with a rich gutsy nuttiness, it is described by the Italians as reflecting 'the sweet bitterness and bitter sweetness of life itself'. Think the veg equivalent

Shallot 'Échalote Grise'

Persian shallot

onion 'Fireworks Mix' flowers

chinese chive flowers

Lampascioni

of a Campari and soda. Admittedly a potential challenge for 'meat and two veg' tastes, but for the foodie adventurers out there I *implore* you to give them a go.

Lampascioni are delicious as an accompaniment to sugar-glazed roast pork, charcuterie platters and continental takes on a classic ploughman's lunch – helping balance out the rich fats and sweet sauces. Use like a mellow, grown-up take on the pickled onion, just without the two-dimensional, biting acidity.

Flowering Onions
Chinese Chives
Allium tuberosum

The leaves and flowers of Chinese chives exude a rich, sweet garlickyness. Pungent and spicy when raw, they mellow to a buttery nuttiness when cooked, like slow-roasted shallots garnished with fresh chives. Roughly chopped and folded into omelettes, stir-fries and salads, they are effectively a perfect blend of leek, garlic and spring onion, without the fussy prep and peeling.

When sweated down, the leaves and flowers have a slippery, juicy bite that makes them highly prized in high-end Japanese and Chinese cuisine, where the harshness of onions and garlic would be considered brash. Valued for their appearance on the plate as much as for their flavour, the flowers are accordingly sold for over 10 times the price of their more common relatives in Chinatowns all over the world.

The great thing from a lazy gardener's perspective is that these long-lived perennial plants are also far less work. **Plant them once in rich, well-drained soil in a sunny spot and they will return year after year for decades**, creating a clump of virtually zero-maintenance deliciousness.

Pretty much all *Allium* flowers and flower buds can be eaten in a similar way. I love the blossoms of ***A. carinatum* subsp. *pulchellum***, which many ornamental catalogues will sell in a mixed set of colours known as **'Fireworks Mix'**, despite its having once been a popular British herb under the name 'witch's garlic'. There is also the quirky *Allium schoenoprasum* 'Cha Cha', a relatively newly introduced strain of the regular European chive that churns out leafy green pompoms instead of flowers throughout the summer.

LAMPASCIONI ONIONS IN OIL

The bulbs must first be prepared to make them edible as they are really bitter and slimy. A bout of peeling and simmering will make short work of this, unveiling the lampascioni's true nutty potential.

PEEL, top and tail the bulbs as you would an onion and leave them to soak in cold water for a day or 2, changing the water halfway through to remove some of the bitter sap.

ONCE they're soaked, bring 1 part vinegar and 2 parts water to the boil in a saucepan and tip in the bulbs along with 2 tablespoons sugar and 1 teaspoon salt.

SIMMER for 30 minutes or until tender. Strain.

FRY the cooked bulbs in olive oil and serve them immediately or pop them still warm into jam jars, top with hot olive oil, seal and store for months in the fridge.

'HIMALAYAN GIANT' GARLIC

The enormous cloves of this rare garlic are touted as being far less fiddly to peel and with an altogether more complex fragrance.

Want to grow these beauties for yourself? Great, just take regular garlic and ignore the rule books, planting it out in early spring instead of late autumn. That's all there is to it.

Exposure to weeks of winter cold is what causes garlic to divide up into the loads of little bulblets we know as cloves. Plant them in the spring and they make one massive, easy-to-peel clove. Always go for **'hardneck' varieties,** as these are not only hardier but tastier and higher in the phytonutrient allicin than the larger but relatively bland 'softneck' types favoured by supermarkets. They also have the wonderful fringe benefit of producing delicious **'scapes',** edible flowers buds that to me are far more delicious than the bulbs themselves (see page 159).

TIPS & TRICKS

Whichever type of onion you decide to grow, there are a few tricks that can either jack up their sweetness and quell their pungency or render them eye-wateringly fiery. This is done by manipulating their levels of pyruvic acid, the chemical that gives onions their characteristic sharp tang, causing them to slide up (or down) what onion growers call the 'pyruvic scale' of sweetness.

Sugary Sweet
Great for sandwiches, salads and burgers
Lower in phytonutrients

Variety
For me, the sweetest of all is **'Walla Walla',** from the valley of the same name in America's Washington State. Its extremely low levels of pyruvic acid send its natural sugars rushing to the forefront of your palate, often making them taste as mild and sweet as an apple. So sweet are 'Walla Walla' onions that sugar-glazed bulbs are sold on a stick like toffee apples at an annual Stateside festival in their honour. Yes, totally weird, I know.

Climate
Cold, wet weather and overcast conditions send pyruvic acid levels crashing, causing onions to taste milder and sweeter meaning (finally) cool-climate growers like me have a real home advantage. To maximize this effect **wherever you live, plant in semi-shade and keep these onions well watered.**

Soils
Onion plants use sulphur extracted from the soil by their roots as the key chemical building block to create pyruvic acid. **Soils that are low in sulphur (like those that cover most of the UK) will naturally produce sweeter-tasting onions.** In fact, as the sulphur emissions from industrial pollution (ironically once the key source of this nutrient in many soils) have crashed across the developed world since the 1980s, it is likely that for many of us onions will get even sweeter as the years go by.

onion 'Walla Walla'

Tear-jerker
A richer flavour for soups, stews and sauces
Higher in phytonutrients

Variety
I love **'White Ebenezer'** for its take-no-prisoners pungency. When cooked down, this pungent onion creates a far more complex, multifaceted richness than the mild crunch of the sweet types. However, biting into a raw slice can be a serious challenge to most palates, like fire and brimstone on your tongue.

Climate
Pyruvic acid is a defence compound produced by onion plants under stress from water shortage in full sun and searing heat. **Plant on the sunniest site you have going and be remorselessly mean with the hose.** Harvesting as late as possible and storing these onions for long periods of time will help further spike their spice.

Soils
Supplementing your soil with sulphur gives your plants the raw material they need to build pyruvate, which is particularly important if your soil is deficient in this nutrient. To do this, sprinkle a teaspoon of Epsom salts (magnesium sulphate) over each square metre (10 sq ft) of your beds every spring just before planting out.

onion 'White Ebenezer'

WINTER RADISHES & MOOLI

Pick up any article on getting kids into 'growing your own' and I'll be willing to wager that summer radishes will come in the top three crops to grow. The logic behind picking a vegetable that is at best blandly bitter and at worst pungently fiery is more than a little curious given the sensitive palates of little sugar monsters. Talk about setting them up for disappointment!

Make the switch to the summer radish's exotic Asian cousin, the mooli or winter radish, however, and things suddenly start to look up. Coming in an array of pick 'n' mix colours, the crisp flesh of some varieties can easily rival watermelons or apples for pure, sweet fruitiness. Mooli and winter radishes are hardy, easy to grow and perfectly adapted to a temperate but damp climate, so it really is a mystery to me why they are not more widely grown away from their native land.

VARIETY GUIDE

'Green Meat'

This variety is extremely sweet and refreshing with zero hint of spiciness. It genuinely tastes far more like watermelon, green apples or crisp Asian pears than a root vegetable. In fact, **in a blindfold test you would be hard pressed to identify it as anything but a fruit, with its lingering sweetness staying with you for a good few minutes after eating it.**

A triumph in salads, salsas and home-made pickles or cut wafer-thin between buttered sliced bread, **'Green Meat' is easily one of my favourite vegetables for both its flavour and its surprising versatility**. Its fruity taste and total lack of earthiness mean that, when chopped into cubes to disguise its vegetable identity, it works amazingly in a winter fruit salad with pomegranates, lychees and fragrant home-grown pears. To me, it's definitely the most flavourful, yet the easiest to grow of the lot. Seed for these can sadly be very tricky to find in garden centres; an online auction site is the place to track it down.

'China Rose'

Starting with a crisp, cool freshness, these glossy, candy-coloured radishes lull you into a false sense of security before unleashing an almighty fiery kick. This is the closest of the group to a standard European summer radish, albeit with a brighter, more intense flavour and no dusty aftertaste. **For spice lovers like me it is the perfect balance of fire and ice, with surprisingly juicy texture**. With most of the spicy chemicals concentrated in the skin, simply peeling them will knock their heat for six for those with more sensitive palates.

'Minowase Summer Cross No.3'

An ice-white variety with a classic, mild radish flavour. It is crisp and clean, balanced with the faintest hint of earthiness when eaten raw and succulent and rich when simmered in soups, stews or curries. Use it in all the ways you would a turnip.

'Black Spanish Long'

Not an exotic eastern cousin at all, but a European variety dating back to the 15th century. **This has a sweet, pleasantly earthy flavour and a more starchy, foam-like texture (in a good way).** Delicious sautéed in butter till softened, with a touch of nutmeg and cream, or used as a succulent, slippery replacement for leeks in a twist on the classic leek and potato soup.

'Mantanghong'

The ivory and emerald skins of this variety belie their vibrant pink centres, which we Chinese refer to as 'beauty within' radishes. **'Mantanghong' is much-prized as a seasonal delicacy and is carved into the shapes of roses, peonies and chrysanthemums and sold from stalls at the autumn harvest festival** - like toffee apples on Guy Fawkes Night.

Crisp and mild, they have a classic radish flavour, although with a touch more sugar. Their unique balance of sweetness with just the right level of mustardy spice means that they are traditionally eaten in Asia both as a veg, grated in salads or pickled in vinegar, and like a fruit, dipped in chilli-plum sugar.

While this variety is arguably the prettiest of them all, it is also highly variable in colour, with only one in three roots having a perfect pink core.

Mooli 'Green Meat'

Mooli 'Minowase Summer Cross No.3'

Winter radish 'Mantanghong'

winter radish 'China Rose'

winter radish 'Black Spanish Long'

HOW TO GROW WINTER RADISHES

Sowing & Growing

Winter radishes can essentially be grown in the same way as regular radishes or indeed carrots, apart from one fussy request. **They need to be sown during the warmth of summer or they will bolt at the first opportunity, skipping straight to flowering mode without ever producing the succulent, swollen roots you are after.** Follow my tried-and-tested methods and you should have bolt-free radishes, with the sweetest, freshest roots.

Sow seed indoors from late spring to late summer, in modules on a sunny windowsill. This may sound a little unorthodox for a radish, but supplemental warmth during this crucial period will slash the risk of your plants bolting later in the year.

When your little plants have grown five leaves, transplant them outdoors into a large trough of well-drained soil exactly as you would for carrots (see page 74).

Winter radishes are one of the very few root crops that don't mind being transplanted,

as long as this is done early enough in their lives and you are careful not to damage their roots.

Growing On

Keeping plants evenly moist but not wet throughout the season is key. If too dry, the roots will become woody and overly pungent; if waterlogged, they can start to rot in the cold, wet soil.

Despite being generally easy to grow, winter radishes are also martyrs to cabbage root fly. Draping your patch in a veil of fine mesh netting is a cheap and effective way to keep the marauding bugs at bay. This netting can be picked up at good garden centres and online.

Harvest

The roots of winter radishes can be brittle, so loosen the soil around each one with a hand fork before gently pulling them up. Most varieties are more pungent when newly harvested, becoming distinctly sweeter and less peppery within a few days of being picked.

CONTROL THEIR FIRE

The pungent pepperiness of radish is produced by sulphur-based compounds created by the plant, which serve as a natural chemical defence against attack from pests and diseases. The more stress the plants are under (think drought, heat and insect attack), the more pungent they will be. However, the plant's ability to produce these compounds in the first place is directly related to the availability of sulphur in the soil, which they use as building blocks to create their fiery flavour.

Want more spice? Sprinkle a teaspoon of Epsom salts (magnesium sulphate) over each square metre (10 sq ft) of your beds to boost the level of sulphur in the soil, particularly if you are growing on sand or chalk, where this essential mineral can be deficient. This could be a healthy choice, as these pungent chemicals, also found in broccoli and Brussels sprouts, are thought to have anticancer effects.

Want them milder? Generous waterings will not only plump up radish roots, diluting their potential fieriness, but can also to a lesser extent even help leach excess sulphur from your beds. Simply peeling radishes will dramatically reduce any potential spicy or bitter flavours as the vast majority of these chemicals are concentrated in their skin. They are defence chemicals, after all.

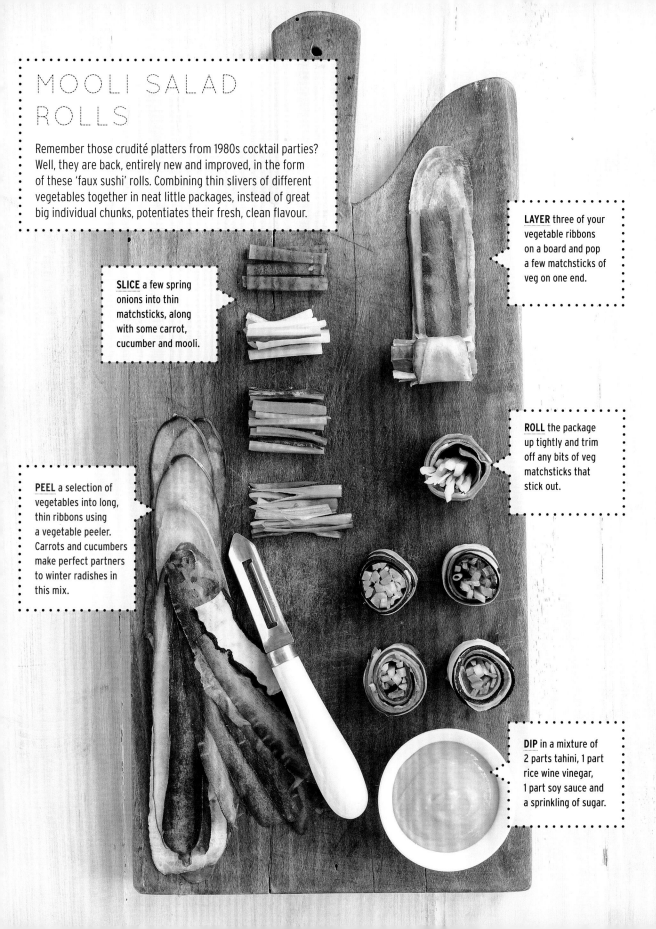

MOOLI SALAD ROLLS

Remember those crudité platters from 1980s cocktail parties? Well, they are back, entirely new and improved, in the form of these 'faux sushi' rolls. Combining thin slivers of different vegetables together in neat little packages, instead of great big individual chunks, potentiates their fresh, clean flavour.

LAYER three of your vegetable ribbons on a board and pop a few matchsticks of veg on one end.

SLICE a few spring onions into thin matchsticks, along with some carrot, cucumber and mooli.

ROLL the package up tightly and trim off any bits of veg matchsticks that stick out.

PEEL a selection of vegetables into long, thin ribbons using a vegetable peeler. Carrots and cucumbers make perfect partners to winter radishes in this mix.

DIP in a mixture of 2 parts tahini, 1 part rice wine vinegar, 1 part soy sauce and a sprinkling of sugar.

UNDERCOVER EDIBLES

Want to know a simple trick that will allow almost any veg grower instantly to double their harvest with little or no extra effort? Well, hiding in plain sight there are a whole range of fantastically flavourful crops that we walk past unawares, borne on the very same plants we tend to every day.

You see, many fruit and veg plants produce more than one edible part, yet we scandalously often eat the least flavourful, high-value bits and chuck the tastiest morsels on the compost heap. It's like throwing away the cereal and eating the box!

In this section, I reveal the secret bounty of overlooked harvests that are just as edible, if not downright more delicious, than the parts we know and love. Introducing my ultimate edible multitaskers…

SQUASH FLOWERS

The beautiful, butter-yellow male flowers of squash plants may never turn into fruit like their female counterparts, but that does not mean they have no merits to the greedy grower. They have an irresistible egg-like flavour much like that of yellow courgettes. The great news is that by harvesting just the male flowers you can gather as many as you want without denting your harvest of the fruits, as courgettes are borne only on the female flowers. (For details of how to cook and eat courgette flowers, check out Edible Flowers on page 166.)

BLACK CURRANT LEAVES *Ribes nigrum*

Packed with up to five times the aroma compounds that give the berries their unique herby fragrance, black currant leaves have been used for centuries in all sorts of recipes to amp up the flavour of their fruit.

When infused into hot syrups or cream, either teamed up with black currants or on their own, the leaves form the basis of some of the best sorbets, ice creams and custards imaginable. Picked young and shredded into fine confetti, the leaves also impart their incredible blackberry-meets-bay leaf aroma to fruit salads, salsas and marinades for fish and chicken.

Want to know the best bit? The ideal time to prune black currant bushes is just after harvesting the fruit, meaning that you will have plenty of leaves on hand just as you need them the most.

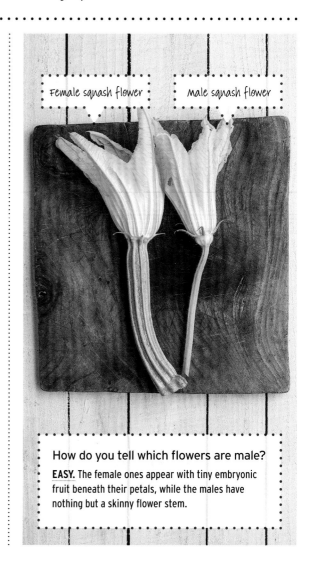

Female squash flower   Male squash flower

How do you tell which flowers are male?

EASY. The female ones appear with tiny embryonic fruit beneath their petals, while the males have nothing but a skinny flower stem.

TURNIP & BEET TOPS

If you have ever wondered what those fancy-looking cima di rapa in little, beautifully designed jars of oil in Italian delis are - well, I have news for you. They are simply chopped, fried turnip leaves. These pleasantly bitter, slightly peppery leaves are cut off young turnips that are harvested as trendy 'baby' veg and used like an ultra-refined cabbage. Fulfilling the continental love of bitter flavours, they are prized in Spain, Italy, France and Greece, where they are wilted and served with pasta, fried and served with polenta and sliced sausage, stirred into egg dishes and stuffed into sandwiches. I love them tossed into orecchiette pasta, with orange rind, crumbly Wensleydale cheese, olive oil and a squirt of lemon juice to balance out their earthy bitterness. Radish leaves can be used in a very similar way.

Although barely heard of nowadays, beetroot leaves were the first part of the plant to be eaten, centuries before anyone thought of breeding the new-fangled varieties with swollen, sweet, 'superfood' roots. Packed with even more phytonutrients than the roots themselves, the leaves taste much like their close relative the chard and can be used in all the same ways. They are particularly delicious chopped into creamy coconut vegetable curries or stirred into clear chicken broths. I love the variety **'Bull's Blood'**, which kicks out plenty of lush, intensely red leafy greens atop sugary-sweet, non-earthy tasting roots.

PUMPKIN LEAVES

Across Latin America, Asia, Africa and the Mediterranean the young tendrilly tips of all pumpkins (as well as trailing courgettes and winter squashes) are harvested and eaten as a much-loved green vegetable. In fact, it seems the only people who haven't cottoned onto their charms are we in the West! With a pleasant nutty flavour, like a hybrid between spinach, asparagus and stem broccoli, the young leaves have a satisfying juicy crunch with no hint of bitterness.

A world away from murky brown spinach, **these leaves keep their vibrant colour and firm texture when cooked, with their cute whorls of whip-like tendrils tasting as good on the palate as they look on the plate**. In Korea and Japan they are usually stir-fried or gently steamed and topped with spiced chilli oil, shards of slivered ginger and a splash of rice wine. In West Africa they are chopped and stirred through rich coconut-cream sauces or in a béchamel flavoured with a touch of ground peanuts, while in the Mediterranean they are blanched and added to salads and omelettes. Snipping back the tips of the rampant sprawling plants even helps keep them from devouring your garden in mid-summer, so it is win-win all round!

GARLIC SCAPES

Hardneck varieties of garlic (*Allium sativum* var. *ophioscorodon*) not only produce much more flavourful, nutrient-rich (not to mention expensive!) bulbs than the softneck types (*Allium sativum*) so beloved of supermarkets, but as a nifty bonus they also throw out garlic scapes. To me, **these deliciously nutty, edible flower buds make for far more interesting eating than the bulbs themselves**.

Harvested as an early summer treat before the buds burst, these edible flowers are one of the truly elegant garden veg, up there with artichokes, spring peas and asparagus - but with a more complex flavour than any of those. The stem portion has the meaty crunch of asparagus and a similar irony, 'green' flavour, but with an added chive-like sweetness. The tightly closed flowers at the tips, on the other hand, have the texture of broccoli and a similar nutty bite, making this vegetable a real all-rounder.

I like to cook and serve the scapes just like asparagus, steamed and dressed with fresh hollandaise. **They are popular grilled, sautéed and served with pasta, but are probably at their very best sliced, flash-fried in butter and added to creamy scrambled eggs**. It is important to remember, however, that most scapes are produced by hardneck varieties of garlic, not softneck types. These will be clearly marked next to the variety name in all good catalogues, nurseries and garden centres.

BROAD BEAN TOPS

If you are an avid grower of broad beans you will know that all gardening books tell you to pinch off the top 7cm (2½in) of the plants once the beans begin to form. The removal of these uppermost leaves hastens the development of the pods, making for an earlier harvest, while also greatly reducing the risk of a pest called blackfly that can infest the young, tender growth later in the season. However, no-one ever seems to mention that these soft, succulent leaves make great eating and are in fact a delicacy in northern Spain.

With a sweet, fresh broad bean flavour and delicious fleshy crunch, they are wonderful either raw in leafy green salads or cooked as a green. **Having the added virtue of being one of the earliest leaf crops each spring, they are lovely flash-fried in garlic and unfiltered olive oil, stirred into wild mushroom risottos and even scattered over pizza with black olives and lardons just before popping them in the oven.** Try them wilted in a salad with toasted pecans, chicory and blood oranges for an early spring treat.

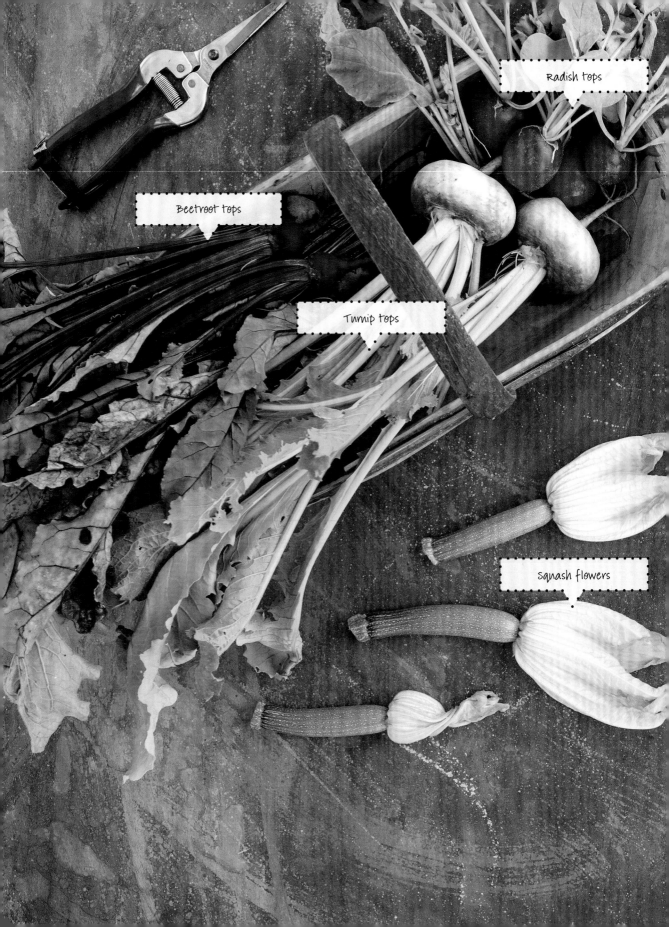

Radish tops

Beetroot tops

Turnip tops

Squash flowers

Yellowflower onion blossoms

Elephant garlic scapes

Hardneck garlic scapes

Broad bean tops

Black currant leaves

EAT YOUR WEEDS

Fighting off barrages of weeds can seem like a never-ending battle for the foodie grower. Yet ironically many of the worst offenders are prized 'wild food' delicacies in fancy cuisines all over the world. So why deploy an army of chemical herbicides, when you can turn weeding into an instant gourmet harvest of no-work crops? Here's my guide to the ultimate tasty veg that literally plant themselves.

GROUND ELDER

Aegopodium podagraria

This spring delicacy has a delicate lemony flavour and fresh parsley-like aroma. **Ground elder has a somewhat cult following throughout Scandinavia and Eastern Europe and it even features on the menu of Denmark's renowned 'world's best' restaurant Noma**, sold at truly scandalous prices.

Ground elder is a perfect partner for fish in an elegant white wine sauce. Alternatively, it can be stirred into a rustic herb omelette or chopped over a steaming mountain of potatoes with a dousing of olive oil. Just remember one thing: this traditional spring treat develops a bitter flavour (and mild laxative effects!) if harvested after it flowers in summer. My solution? Trick the plants into believing it's perpetual spring by picking the leaves on a regular basis. This prevents flowering and results in fresh leaves (with no unexpected consequences) all summer long.

NETTLES *Urtica dioica*

With a rich, 'green' flavour and sky-high mineral content, this wild vegetable is enjoying something of a resurgence on fancy restaurant menus and is even sometimes sold at posh farmers' markets, with prices to match.

As soon as nettles are cooked the sting completely disappears, leaving only a broccoli/watercress-like flavour without a hint of the bitterness of either. They're wonderful blitzed into soups, stirred into quiches or steamed, then used in pesto instead of basil. Harvest great handfuls of the fresh green growth (wearing gloves) in early spring as mature plants quickly become full of stringy fibres. Free five-star food with a minimum of effort.

SHEPHERD'S PURSE

Capsella bursapastoris

There can't be an allotment anywhere in Britain that doesn't harbour a hidden harvest of this rampant weed, which leads a secret double life as a dainty, miniature relative of watercress, coming complete with the same health-giving glucosinolate compounds.

In Japan the shepherd's purse leaves are served just like rocket or watercress in spring salads and stirred into risotto-like rice dishes, while in the regional cuisine of Shanghai they are stir-fried and stuffed into dumplings, with a virtually identical peppery, mustard-like flavour.

DANDELION *Taraxacum officinale*

A major vegetable in the regional cuisines of Italy, France and Greece, the humble dandelion is essentially a wild chicory, just without any of the work. I dig up any seedlings that appear and plant them in my salad beds, where judicious waterings create lush leafy greens with a pleasant bitter-sweet flavour. The leaves also contain seven times the antioxidants of the so-called 'superfood' spinach, making them a resoundingly healthy choice.

Dandelion leaves are lovely in salads with croutons, lardons and slivers of fried garlic. **In France, gardeners often cover live plants with a large plate or bucket roughly 10 days before harvesting to exclude light from the growing plant, magically turning the long leaves butter yellow and giving them an altogether more delicate flavour.**

WILD ROCKET

Diplotaxis tenuifolia

The trendy salad green that plants itself. Yes, indeed, **this common weed of drought-stricken waste ground is one and the same as the fancy bistro salad green**. Positively thriving in the driest of conditions, these fiery filigree leaves frequently pop up in the gravel paths between my raised beds, providing more harvests of free salad than I ever get round to eating for a full 12 months of the year. Away from the massive soakings commercial growers lavish upon them they develop an altogether more pungent oomph, not to mention the fact that you won't have to clear out those sad, half-eaten bags of the supermarket stuff languishing at the back of your fridge, ever again.

Shepherd's purse

Wild rocket

Ground elder

Dandelion

Nettles

DEATH
& TAXES

Like death and taxes, weeds – those under-appreciated plants we're always trying to get rid of – are an unavoidable part of life. Turn them into crops, however, and you'll virtually never need to weed again!

NETTLE, LEMON & CASHEW PESTO

Serves 4

Blitzed together in less than five minutes, this cheat's pesto uses cashews instead of pine nuts as a cheaper, easier-to-get-hold-of substitute. I promise no-one will know the difference.

WILT 150g (5oz) young nettle tops in a saucepan with 1 tablespoon water, stirring occasionally for about 5 minutes.

BLITZ the wilted nettle tops in a food processor with 50g (2oz) grated Parmesan, 2 garlic cloves, 50g (2oz) cashew nuts, the rind of 1 lemon and 150ml (¼ pint) unfiltered extra virgin olive oil and a generous grating of nutmeg.

TASTE your emerald blend and add any extra oil, salt or pepper you think it needs.

SLATHER the pesto over slices of crusty white bread, top with cooked chicken pieces, add Parmesan shavings and drizzle with extra virgin olive oil for the ultimate spring treat.

EDIBLE FLOWERS
ACTUALLY WORTH EATING

With flavours spanning everything from intensely aromatic to fizzy and sherbet-like and even rich and meaty, edible flowers can be much more than pretty garnishes. After all, some of our best-loved crops, such as artichokes, broccoli and cauliflowers, are nothing more than blossoms bred for the table.

This handful of examples is just a tiny remnant of a huge range of edible flowers that featured heavily in Western cuisine for centuries, right up until the Victorian period. Sadly, however, after a gap of a century or more, the latest flowery additions to our culinary repertoire have usually taken the form of species that look great, but taste of almost nothing. I'm looking at you, violas, cornflowers and carnations!

But to dismiss all flowering veg as edible gimmicks would be to miss out on a whole world of unusual flavours. Behold the amazing range of common garden flowers that live secret double lives as esteemed ingredients in cuisines all over the world.

THE SAVOURY ONES

They might look almost too pretty to eat, but I promise you these flavour heavyweights are grown on a truly massive scale as everyday supermarket vegetables in cities from Shanghai to San José. Ladies and gentlemen, let me present the gourmet crops that lie hidden in your beds and borders.

Courgette Flowers

A central ingredient in the rustic peasant cuisines of Italy and Mexico for centuries, male courgette flowers are now popping up on the menus of fine-dining restaurants and fancy farmers' markets everywhere. Now **sold at prices up to 50 times those of the courgettes themselves gram for gram, their wonderful creamy, eggy flavour is sadly missed out on by all too many gardeners** who have no idea they are edible.

To cook, snip off their bases and toast them sandwiched between flour tortillas with fried onions, roasted red peppers and mountains of cheese, as they do in Mexican street markets, for a deliciously slippery crunch. In Italy whole open flowers are stuffed with herby ricotta, tied tightly closed with a chive leaf, then battered and deep-fried in hot oil. Alternatively, fry French beans in garlic and olive oil and toss the courgette flowers in at the last minute before serving, or stir great sliced handfuls into summery vegetable broths. **Flowers appear in profusion throughout the summer, but be careful to leave one or two male flowers on each plant so that they can pollinate the female ones and ensure a steady supply of fruit.**

Onion Blossoms & Garlic Scapes

Both the flower buds and delicate unfurled petals of onion plants make excellent eating, containing all the classic pungent flavour of this well-loved vegetable, albeit in a much prettier package. This is true of the flowers of the whole allium family, including garlic, shallots, leeks, chives and even the wide variety of ornamental cultivars out there. **For an extra splash of colour both in the garden and on your plate, you can't beat yellowflower onion** *Allium coryi*. This highly ornamental plant from the southwestern USA is perfect for a dry, sunny border, producing masses of delicate, chive flavoured flowers in mid summer.

Chinese Chives
Allium tuberosum

These elegant, white flowers have been a popular vegetable in the Orient for centuries, with an altogether more complex, nutty sweetness than the caustic tang of regular onions. These chives are cooked and eaten more like a fresh green than an onion: chopped and scattered into a hot wok for the last two minutes of a stir-fry, or sautéed with prawns and added to an Asian take on Spanish omelettes. The best bit is that they grow on perennial, self-seeding plants that can live for decades with almost no care or attention. And if you've ever seen the price these sell for in Asian supermarkets, you too will soon be growing your own.

Allium 'Fireworks Mix'

Being delicate and tangy, these multicoloured sprays add mini fireworks of oniony flavour to summer salads, dressings and canapés, making a beautiful garnish in almost any savoury dish.

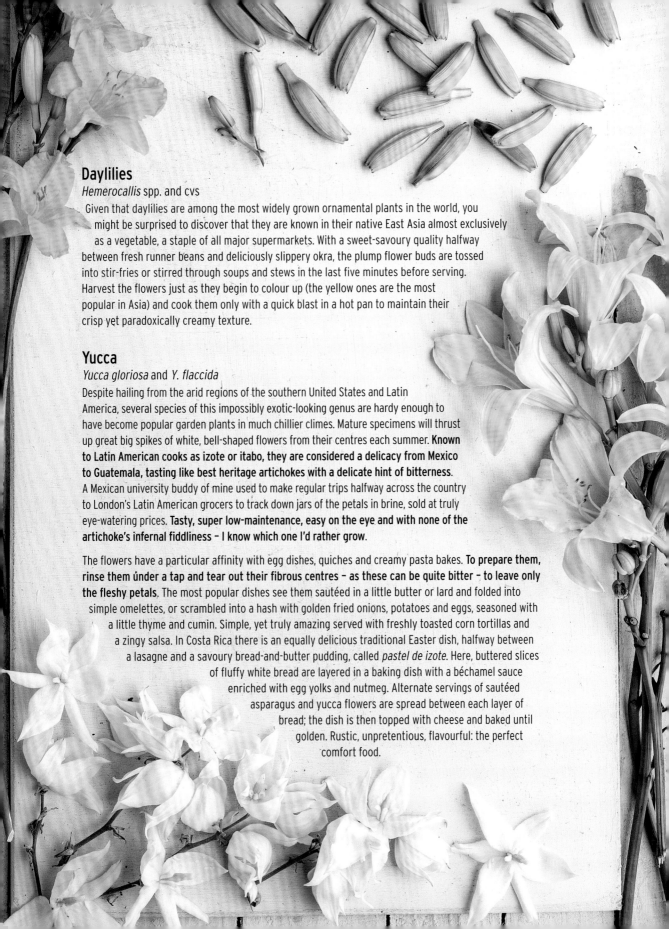

Daylilies

Hemerocallis spp. and cvs

Given that daylilies are among the most widely grown ornamental plants in the world, you might be surprised to discover that they are known in their native East Asia almost exclusively as a vegetable, a staple of all major supermarkets. With a sweet-savoury quality halfway between fresh runner beans and deliciously slippery okra, the plump flower buds are tossed into stir-fries or stirred through soups and stews in the last five minutes before serving. Harvest the flowers just as they begin to colour up (the yellow ones are the most popular in Asia) and cook them only with a quick blast in a hot pan to maintain their crisp yet paradoxically creamy texture.

Yucca

Yucca gloriosa and *Y. flaccida*

Despite hailing from the arid regions of the southern United States and Latin America, several species of this impossibly exotic-looking genus are hardy enough to have become popular garden plants in much chillier climes. Mature specimens will thrust up great big spikes of white, bell-shaped flowers from their centres each summer. **Known to Latin American cooks as izote or itabo, they are considered a delicacy from Mexico to Guatemala, tasting like best heritage artichokes with a delicate hint of bitterness.** A Mexican university buddy of mine used to make regular trips halfway across the country to London's Latin American grocers to track down jars of the petals in brine, sold at truly eye-watering prices. **Tasty, super low-maintenance, easy on the eye and with none of the artichoke's infernal fiddliness – I know which one I'd rather grow.**

The flowers have a particular affinity with egg dishes, quiches and creamy pasta bakes. **To prepare them, rinse them under a tap and tear out their fibrous centres – as these can be quite bitter – to leave only the fleshy petals.** The most popular dishes see them sautéed in a little butter or lard and folded into simple omelettes, or scrambled into a hash with golden fried onions, potatoes and eggs, seasoned with a little thyme and cumin. Simple, yet truly amazing served with freshly toasted corn tortillas and a zingy salsa. In Costa Rica there is an equally delicious traditional Easter dish, halfway between a lasagne and a savoury bread-and-butter pudding, called *pastel de izote*. Here, buttered slices of fluffy white bread are layered in a baking dish with a béchamel sauce enriched with egg yolks and nutmeg. Alternate servings of sautéed asparagus and yucca flowers are spread between each layer of bread; the dish is then topped with cheese and baked until golden. Rustic, unpretentious, flavourful: the perfect comfort food.

Nasturtium

Lavender

Dill

Fennel

Camomile

THE HERBY ONES

It isn't just the leaves of herbs that make good eating. In fact, many of their flowers are packed with way more of the essential oils that give the leaves their characteristic flavour. What's not to like?

Nasturtium
Tropaeolum majus
A distant relative of watercress, **this common garden flower was first grown by the Incas in Peru and Ecuador for its wonderfully peppery flowers and leaves**. It is fantastic used just like rocket or watercress to add spice to salads. Thinly sliced petals give potato salad an incredible colour and flavour boost. The plants will even self-seed through your beds, meaning that once you've sown them you will almost certainly never be without them again.

Lavender
Lavandula angustifolia
Once one of the most popular culinary herbs, lavender now enjoys the somewhat dubious honour of being simultaneously one of the best-known floral ingredients and one of the most despised. This reputation is no doubt due to its recent trendiness, with chefs sprinkling great handfuls of the stuff into pretty much anything they can think of. When used overzealously it has a pungent soapiness, far more 'granny's knicker drawer' than 'delicate heritage herb'. However, when used very sparingly in sweet and savoury dishes, just as you would thyme or rosemary, it adds all the wonderful resinous aroma of the former, but with an uplifting light floral note.

The easiest way to capture lavender's flavour is to combine it with sugar (see page 170) to make scented cakes, biscuits and scones, or to swap the fresh flowers for mint in traditional jellies served with roast meats such as lamb or beef. Chucking half a torn-up flowerhead and a sprinkling of black pepper into the oil used to fry a steak elevates an everyday meal to a whole new level.

Camomile
Anthemis nobilis
Although mostly known in its dry form for use in tea, camomile tastes remarkably different when fresh. **Cut straight from the garden, the fresh flowers have a honey-like flavour that is fleetingly similar to the dried version, but with a surprisingly pronounced pineapple aroma**. I love them chopped into a honey-mustard glaze for grilled chicken or blended into butter with citrus peel, either to spread on hot toast or to use in fragrant cakes and biscuits.

The best bit? **Propagating camomile is as simple as ripping open an unused camomile tea bag (these contain hundreds of seeds) and sprinkling the contents over any bare patch of earth in spring** for a batch of fresh flowers by summer. They'll even grow in gravel paths. It doesn't get easier than that!

Dill & Fennel
Anethum graveolens & *Foeniculum vulgare*
The dainty flowers of fennel have recently achieved notoriety as the uber trendy (and crazily expensive) spice known as wild fennel pollen (see page 184). Just like those of its close relative, dill, these flowers have the classic aroma of the seeds, only magnified and made sweeter. Picking them off extends your harvest of the fresh leaves, too.

THE HOLY TRINITY OF EXTRACTING FLORAL FLAVOURS

Compared to most other ingredients, the flavour compounds in flowers are notorious for their ability to evade attempts to extract them. Follow these three basic rules, however, and you will be cooking up floral concoctions with the best of them.

1) Get 'Em Early: For most species the best results are obtained by picking flowers in the mid-morning on a cool, dry day. This may sound overly fussy, but this is when concentrations of the aroma compounds are generally at their highest. Any earlier and the petals have yet to ramp up their production of these compounds; any later and the heat of the day will have evaporated most of them into the air. Harvested flowers should be used as quickly as possible and should also be perfectly dry to prevent loss of flavour.

2) Don't Overheat Them: Rapid boiling will quickly evaporate the delicate aroma compounds of flowers, leaving you with a kitchen that smells incredible but food that tastes of little more than cabbage water.

3) Use Only Highly Scented Species and Cultivars: Flowers vary enormously in their content of aroma chemicals, even within the same species. Unsurprisingly, therefore, if you pick a barely scented rose such as 'St Patrick', you are not going to get anywhere near the flavour of a true fragrance bomb like 'Champagne Cocktail'. Remember, however, that not all fragrant flowers are safe to eat, so stick to the species mentioned in the following pages.

THE DESSERT ONES

Capturing the delicate fragrance of a summer garden and infusing it through all sorts of sweet treats is far easier than you might think. With just a few simple tips and tricks, anyone can savour the scent of summer even in the depths of winter.

FLOWERS THAT TASTE LIKE FRUIT

There are two particular blooms I have discovered that taste (astonishingly) almost identical to fruit straight from the plant, without any need for kitchen alchemy.

Begonia

Pineapple guava

Pineapple Guava

Acca sellowiana

The fleshy petals of this popular garden shrub from southern Brazil, also known as feijoas, have evolved as a sweet, sugary reward to lure potential pollinators such as mammals and birds to fertilise their flowers. **Thick, succulent and with the flavour of minty marshmallows (no, really), these are like nature's pick 'n' mix eaten straight off the plant or tossed over fruit salads.** Yum!

Begonia

Begonias might grace windowboxes and hanging baskets all over the world, but their edible wonders have remained a well-kept secret. With a bright, zingy acidity and jelly-like texture these flowers taste just like the sour green apple sweets I loved as a kid, minus the E numbers. **Enterprising growers of high-end chefs' ingredients have sold these to top restaurants under the glossy brand name 'apple blossoms'.** Try the new generation of scented versions, which come in peach and apricot hues for edible cake decorations that look as good they taste.

FLOWER-SCENTED SUGARS

One of the best ways of extracting the scent of flowers in edible form is to entomb them in an avalanche of sugar. This sucks in all the moisture and, along with it, the aromatic compounds, trapping them in the sugar crystals and preserving them for months. It also gives you a wonderfully versatile vehicle to add to all manner of recipes.

TOSS the flowers into 10 times their weight of sugar in a mixing bowl, then pour into a sealed preserving jar.

LEAVE for at least a month for the sugar to get to work. Bear in mind that, as flowers are far lighter than sugar, this will look like an awful lot of flowers!

AFTER the month is up, sieve the spent flowers out and store the scented sugar in an airtight jar. Great choices for this treatment include violets, honeysuckle, jasmine, lavender, elderflower and roses.

CRYSTALLIZED FLOWERS

Crystallizing uses a similar approach to floral sugars, except that here the sugar is 'glued' directly onto the individual flowers. This requires a little more patience, but the stunning results are worth the extra little bit of fiddliness.

LAY your freshly picked flowers face down on a sheet of baking paper and paint one side of each flower with a little egg white. A clean, dry paintbrush is perfect for this. The aim is just to moisten each one, not douse it in big dollops of egg white.

SPRINKLE the whole sheet with pinches of caster sugar, holding your hands up high to ensure a steady, even coating of every petal. You will see that the sugar sticks to the moistened petals and coats them evenly in a fine crust. Leave them to dry for 30 minutes.

TURN your petals over and repeat the painting and sprinkling processes on the reverse side. Once they are evenly covered leave to dry for another 30 minutes.

PUT a sheet of folded kitchen paper in the bottom of an airtight container to absorb any moisture and keep your crystallized flowers fresher for longer. They should last in the fridge for two weeks.

FLOWER WATERS & SYRUPS

The aroma chemicals in flowers are highly soluble, meaning that a simple overnight soaking in a jug in the fridge is all it takes to transform plain old tap water into a surprisingly intense floral elixir by morning.

This infused water makes a refreshing, calorie-free drink in the summer and is an ideal base for a zingy floral lemonade with a squirt of citrus and a swirl of sugar syrup. You can soak a few pieces of sliced fruit with the flowers to double the flavour. I love the bright, clean flavours of Honeysuckle, Peony & Cucumber, Elderflower & Strawberry and Gardenia & Jasmine White Tea. Cold-infusion techniques have long been used in China and Japan with high-end teas to ensure the delicate flavours are retained in the brewing process.

If you are feeling less virtuous, adding an equal quantity of sugar to the strained infusion in a saucepan and heating it very gently over a low flame, just until the sugars have dissolved, will turn the infused water into a knock-out cordial. Covering with a tight-fitting glass lid during this process and swirling (not stirring) the pan occasionally will trap the aromatics in the liquid, preventing them from wafting away. Ideal candidates for this treatment include honeysuckle, jasmine, robinia and meadowsweet.

Peony & Cucumber

Honeysuckle

Elderflower & Strawberry

Gardenia & Jasmine White Tea

FLORAL JAMS

Makes 1kg (2lbs)

Floral jams, unlike the more familiar fruit-based ones, involve recipes that have been rejigged to cut down cooking time and restrict heating temperatures to a bare minimum: just enough to thicken the mix without the prolonged simmering that would obliterate delicate floral flavours. The same basic recipe will work with honeysuckle, violets, jasmine or almost any other edible scented flower, but my favourite is the classic rose.

This traditional Lebanese speciality is delicious over ice cream, slathered over scones or used as the base for fragrant summer cocktails. Don't panic that cooking with roses will result in the cloying 'cheap-perfume' flavour. In fact, roses come in an enormous variety of scents, some of which are almost completely unrecognizable from the Barbie-pink stereotypical 'rose' fragrance that many people dislike (me included).

I am positively in love with the tropical fruit-like aroma of **'Lady Emma Hamilton'**, which is like a blend of lychees and mango, and the rich, clove-infused spiciness of **'Wild Edric'**. There is the woodland berry flavour of **'Sharifa Asma'** and, if you really must, **'Harlow Carr'** delivers up the classic rose flavour and an overwhelming fragrance of Turkish Delight.

TOSS 200g (7oz) fragrant rose petals and 400g (14oz) sugar together in a bowl until evenly coated. Cover, and let stand at room temperature overnight.

SIMMER 750ml (1¼ pints) water over a low heat and stir in the flower and sugar mixture, plus 1 x 13g/½oz sachet of pectin and the juice of 1 lemon. Stir until the sugar has dissolved.

WHACK up the heat, cover and bring to a rolling boil for 3–5 minutes until the jam has thickened.

POUR into warm, sterilized jars and screw on the lids.

EVERLASTING BOUQUETS

Wish you could make that special bunch of Valentine's flowers last forever? Well, with a bit of home cloning you can do exactly that, turning them into plants for decades of flowers in just four surprisingly simple steps. This is also a great way to get hold of rarer varieties not often sold in garden centres, or simply to secure your own plant of that rose in your mum's back garden that no-one knows the name of.

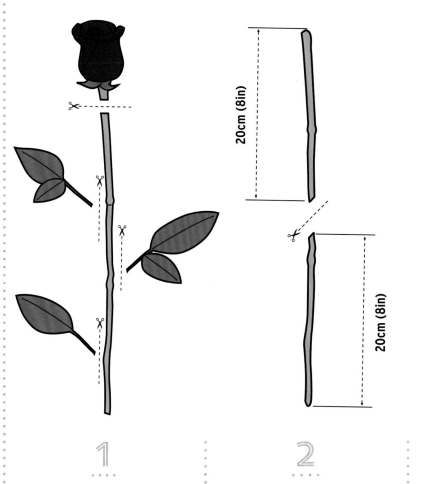

1

TAKE one of your rose stems and snip off the flowerhead and the lowest 1cm (½in) of the stem, then remove all the leaves.

2

SNIP the remaining stem into 20cm (8in) lengths (long-stem roses will give you several cuttings). Trim the lower end at an angle to ensure you remember which end is up.

3 + 4

DIP the base of your cuttings in rooting hormone and insert them around the edge of a pot of gritty compost.

WATER in well, then cover and place the pot on a shady windowsill. Check back every few days to ensure the compost is just moist but not wet. Once your plants are in active growth, sending out fresh flushes of new leaves, they can be planted up in individual pots or out in the garden.

TRUFFLES

Think you need a Tuscan hillside or at the very least a specially trained dog to hunt out your truffles? Allow me to let you in on a well-kept secret. Even in soggy, temperate climates, truffles will thrive, with chilly old Britain having at least three native species, including the sought-after summer truffle *Tuber aestivum* var. *uncinatum* that sells for hundreds of pounds per kilo.

In fact, in cool, damp climates summer truffles will obligingly grow at far shallower depths than in warmer ones, lurking just below the surface of the soil. This means that they can often be found – easily and without the need for canine detection – as far north as southern Scotland. With truffle plantations popping up everywhere from New Zealand to the western United States, if you have a plot with chalky soil and a little patience, home-grown truffles are now a genuine possibility for even the most novice plant geek.

HOW TO GROW TRUFFLES

Check Your Soil

Truffles grow best on thin, alkaline soils over a bedrock of chalk or limestone, making some of the worst ground for growing fruit and vegetables the best for truffles. Bonus! In gardening there is always a silver lining. **The perfect truffle-growing soil has a pH of roughly 8 and is characteristically poor in nutrients.** Not sure what pH your soil is? Testing kits can be picked up very cheaply in any good garden centre.

Pick Your Host

Truffles are fungi that live on tree roots in a symbiotic (mutually beneficial) relationship. They provide the tree with access to key nutrients or increase the uptake of water; in exchange, the tree guarantees a supply of sugars, which the fungus uses to fuel its growth. Several mail order companies sell tree saplings that come pre-inoculated with truffle spawn, including certificates of DNA testing to guarantee this has taken place.

Although there are several truffle species to choose from, **in cooler climates your chances of success are likely to be highest with the summer truffle** *Tuber aestivum* var. *uncinatum.* They will happily grow on a range of tree species, including oak, beech and hazel. For me, however, by far the best choice is hazel, as not only are the trees much smaller (and thus more practical for small gardens), but they also offer up a tasty crop of nuts while you are waiting for your truffles to mature.

Being also the fastest growing of those three suggested species, hazel trees will be the first to establish themselves, potentially giving you the quickest route to a bumper truffle harvest.

Planting
When Your Saplings Arrive

When your little saplings arrive, stand them up in a bowl of water for 12 hours to rehydrate after their long journey.

ONE DELICIOUS GAMBLE

Despite being to all intents and purposes a trouble-free, low-maintenance crop, truffles are notoriously temperamental about establishing themselves, with the full range of factors that influence their growth only beginning to be understood. Following the tips on this and the following page should give you the best possible chance of abundant harvests, but as with all crops the results will vary greatly from site to site. If you are expecting an instant, reliable return, truffles are not a crop for you. But for experimental gardeners, the potential pay-off for your gamble does not come any more delicious than this.

Site & Spacing

Pick a site well away from established trees, especially oak, beech and hazel, which may harbour competing fungi on their roots. **Studies have shown that interspersing inoculated plants with normal saplings can be a cost-effective way of establishing a new plantation, as the spores in established plants can infect the surrounding trees.** You are looking for one regular plant for every two inoculated ones.

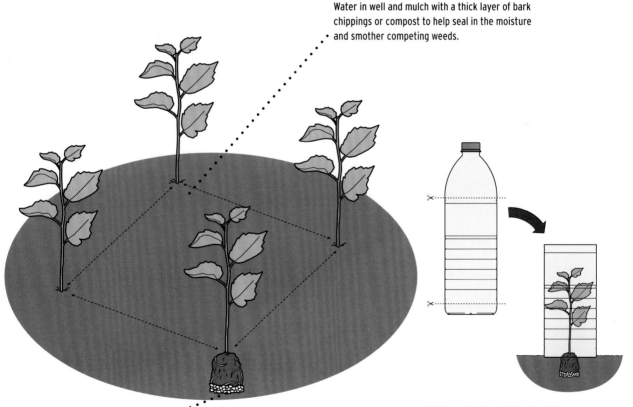

Water in well and mulch with a thick layer of bark chippings or compost to help seal in the moisture and smother competing weeds.

Some plantation owners believe that placing a handful of limestone chippings (available at all garden centres) at the bottom of each planting hole can provide the ideal conditions for establishment.

Sitting a plastic cylinder (made from a water bottle with the top and bottom sliced off) over the saplings will help protect them from the elements for their first year or so of growth.

Maintenance

Keep your new plants constantly moist, preferably with rainwater, while they are establishing. After that, they will barely need any further coddling. Both hazel and summer truffles are, after all, resilient wild species, perfectly adapted to thriving without any human intervention.

A monthly dose of molasses tonic (see page 27) may help further boost the establishment of both the hazel plants and the truffles growing on their roots by providing them with a source of sugars and trace minerals.

Do not apply any other fertiliser. Be particularly careful to avoid those high in phosphorus, as this has been shown to impede the union between the fungi and their host plant, and eventually to be capable of killing off your little truffles altogether. High nutrient levels can also make the host plant too vigorous, producing excessive growth that is difficult to manage.

Harvesting
(Really) Good Things Come To Those Who Wait

You can start to expect your first harvest of both hazelnuts and truffles 4–7 years after planting. OK, this is a bit of a wait, but in the meantime the saplings will require very little care and attention, providing you with one heck of a potential return for minimal effort.

TRUFFLE HUNTING

Three Hunting Tip-Offs

Cracked Earth: Summer truffles grow just beneath the surface of the soil – so close that they often announce their presence by breaking through the surface. Look for bulges or cracks in the earth under your trees, or even partially unearthed truffles when they are in season (between late spring and early autumn).

Scorched Grass: The aromatic compounds that give truffles their flavour (and make them detectable to the noses of man's best friend) are also potent herbicides. These cause the vegetation growing directly over fruiting truffles to become scorched, forming rings of dead grass, which the French call *brules*, around the trees. *Brules* generally start as a small ring around the trunk, expanding outwards each year.

Animal Digging: The scent of truffles is appealing not just to dogs, pigs and humans, but also to a large range of mammals including squirrels and badgers. Evidence of little paws digging or scratching the surface of the soil during summer truffle season is a telltale sign that yours may be ready to harvest.

Digging Them Up

Summer truffles are so shallow-growing that they are easy to unearth. Simply scratch the soil lightly with a spring-tine rake to a depth of just a few centimetres (an inch or so), where the leaf litter joins the mineral soil.

NO DOG? NO PROBLEM!

We have been conditioned to think that a specially trained dog (or even pig) is necessary for truffle gathering, but this is simply not true. Animal detection is only one of many methods traditionally used to hunt down these subterranean delicacies. Others include raking (mainly in North America), hoeing (China) and tapping (North Africa) around potential host trees.

Of course, in home plantations, zeroing in on the approximate location of your potential hoard is made easier by the fact that you are the one who planted the truffle spores in the first place. Hours of detecting likely locations with a canine companion are largely unnecessary.

TRUFFLE & HAZELNUT CIABATTA
Serves 4 as a starter

Truffles and hazelnuts are not just a perfect partnership in the garden, but a match made in heaven in the kitchen too. This simple recipe fuses them together in a late-summer treat that takes just minutes to make.

MASH together 125g (5oz) mascarpone, 1 soft boiled egg, ¼ teaspoon brown sugar and a generous grating of nutmeg. Season well.

SPREAD the mix over thin slices of cooled toasted ciabatta (or shop-bought crostini).

GARNISH with 1 teaspoon chopped chives, 2 tablespoons chopped hazelnuts and the fine shavings of 1 truffle.

HERBS, SPICES & NUTS

EXPERIMENTAL HERBS

For growers after true knock-out flavour, it doesn't get any better than herbs. Not only can relatively tiny amounts transform whole meals (great if you suffer from time or space restrictions), but most of them also originally evolved the compounds that give them their flavour to help fight off extreme conditions and pest attacks, making them some of the easiest of all edibles to grow.

As most of the flavour of herbs is derived from delicate essential oils that can quickly degrade once harvested, they are one of the top crops on the 'home-grown really does taste measurably better' list. Coriander, for example, experiences a precipitous loss of its aroma chemicals after about 10 days, even if it is stored under industrially controlled conditions of precise chilling and modified atmospheres. However, as its leaves can *appear* fresh to the naked eye for a good three weeks, supermarkets will happily continue to stock it – meaning that at any given time as much as half of the coriander on their shelves will have lost much of its flavour!

TURNING UP THE FLAVOUR VOLUME

The flavour compounds in herbs evolved largely as defence chemicals, allowing them to adapt to threats like drought, sweltering heat, searing UV rays and the attack of pests and diseases in some truly tough environments. Triggered to escalate by exposure to harsh conditions, these very same chemicals also give many herbs not only their flavour but also their antimicrobial and medicinal values. Quite literally, the more aromatic your herbs are, the more potent their health benefits are likely to be.

When spoiled with lashings of water and cossetted conditions, however, as herbs grown for supermarkets are, they often lack the necessary triggers to provoke the development of these chemicals. The plants respond by throwing up great mounds of lush, leafy growth with only a fraction of the flavour: great for supermarket bank balances, not so great for your pesto.

With that in mind, here's my guide to treating 'em mean to keep 'em keen…

Low Fertiliser

Generous doses of high-nitrogen fertiliser are sometimes recommended for growing herbs. There are even specialist 'herb fertilisers' out there. In most cases this will create gigantic, luxurious-looking plants that sadly taste of very little. In fact, as most domestic garden soils are naturally relatively fertile, digging large amounts of grit or sand into your bed (up to 60 percent or more on heavy soils) can be useful for *lowering* their fertility. This keeps the plant's roots on the dry side, which not only helps prevent disease but can also work to boost flavour by stressing it out. **Growing herbs in soils with poor fertility creates a noticeable spike in the flavour of crops as diverse as basil, camomile, edible marigolds, caraway and rosemary.**

Aspirin Spray

Aspirin mimics the naturally occurring hormone that can jump-start the production of aromatic compounds in a wide range of herbs.

Studies have shown that even a single drenching in a spray containing the equivalent of one 300mg soluble aspirin tablet dissolved in 1 litre (1¾ pints) of water can up to double the essential oil content (and thus flavour) of herbs from sage and basil to mint and marjoram in as little as one week. This works by effectively 'fooling' the plants into believing they are under attack – they respond by churning out more tasty flavour chemicals.

Conveniently, **this spray also had the effect of making the plants bigger, leafier and more resistant to cold,** which may prove a lifeline for foodies keen on growing more tender crops such as basil or lemon verbena in a chilly climate.

Apply a good drench of this spray once every month, ideally on a cool, dry morning, throughout the summer. Just 1 litre (1¾ pints) of the stuff should be more than enough for even the largest bed of home-grown herbs.

Full Sun

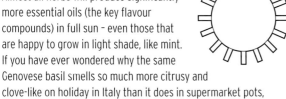

Almost all herbs will produce significantly more essential oils (the key flavour compounds) in full sun – even those that are happy to grow in light shade, like mint. If you have ever wondered why the same Genovese basil smells so much more citrusy and clove-like on holiday in Italy than it does in supermarket pots, it's because the aroma chemicals linalool (lemon-scented) and eugenol (clove-scented) are sent sky-high with maximum light levels and water scarcity. To mimic this, **treat your plants to the sunniest spot in the glasshouse, preferably high up on the staging, where they will enjoy more light and heat.** Studies show that basil grown at 25°C (77°F) contains up to three times the aroma compounds of those grown at 15°C (59°F).

Close Spacing

It may seem totally counterintuitive, but **planting your crops closer together has been demonstrated significantly to increase the essential oil concentration of a range of herbs from mint to cumin.** Although at closer spacing each plant receives less light, it is believed that the competition of close neighbours provides just enough stress for the plant to start producing more defence chemicals.

In one US Department of Agriculture trial, basil plants produced significantly more flavour compounds when grown through a sheet of green plastic mulch. These plants not only grew more strongly but were also significantly more aromatic than those grown through the same plastic in shades of red, white or blue. The researchers concluded that the light that reflected off the green plastic mulch was of a similar spectrum to that which would have bounced off neighbouring plants, effectively 'tricking' the basil into producing more defence compounds as a reaction to potential competition. Weird, but true.

To take advantage of this phenomenon, **space herbs an average of 30cm (12in) apart (found to be ideal in several studies) and mulch the surface of the soil with black or other dark-coloured material.** If you don't fancy the idea of a garden covered in sheets of coloured plastic, try scattering a 1cm (½in) layer of black biochar (ground-up charcoal) over the surface. Much like dark plastic, it will help keep down weeds and significantly increase the warmth of the soil, helping plants grow even faster.

Low Water/No Water

Drought stress has been demonstrated dramatically to boost the content of aromatic compounds in a wide variety of herbs, from thyme and camomile to lemongrass and catmint. Just as well most herbs hail from semi-arid regions of the world, making them ideally adapted to cope with this.

In most climates this means that, once established, herbs grown in the ground should almost never need watering. **If your soil is on the heavy side or you live in a high-rainfall climate, incorporating large amounts of sand and grit into it can be really useful at ensuring the herbs' roots stay fairly dry.** In fact, trials have shown that herbs such as thyme can produce *double* the essential oil if grown on sandy rather than clay, loam or chalky soils, even under desert conditions.

Note that the **one notable exception to this low-water rule is mint.** Several trials have shown that this herb bucks the trend, showing increasing concentrations of flavour chemicals and essential oils when well watered. In a temperate climate this would mean a generous watering once every week to 10 days during the summer. Don't get too carried away, though, as the same trials suggest that overzealous watering also reduced total aroma concentration.

NEW HERBS FOR FOODIE ADVENTURERS

Want to explore growing some of the more weird and wonderful herbs that are still almost impossible to track down in even the fanciest supermarkets? With these maverick choices anyone with space for a couple of pots can access flavours that are truly unbuyable.

WILD FENNEL POLLEN

Foeniculum vulgare

What Is It?

'If angels sprinkled a spice from their wings, this would be it,' raved *Saveur* magazine. 'A natural flavour enhancer', 'a rare luxury' and 'saffron's stiffest competition' have trumpeted others. **Nothing in the culinary world seems to have had such lavish praise heaped upon it as the de rigueur spice known as wild fennel pollen** - with each teaspoon selling for astonishing amounts of money in specialist food retailers. Just as well, then, that it is also incredibly easy to grow, being little more than the dried flowers of fennel with a new brand name.

Although oomphing up foods with fennel flowers is an age-old tradition in Italy's Calabria region, their culinary value was little known outside their native land until they were introduced recently to California by enterprising Italian migrants, who encountered massive wild stands of the plants that had escaped from gardens. Unlike so many trendy new ingredients, however, this one really does live up to the hype. **Its tiny golden grains are infused with rich, honey-aniseed fragrance that is infinitely sweeter and more uplifting than fennel seeds or leaves**. With a mere pinch or two noticeably intensifying the flavour of a wide range of foods, **I like to think of it as edible pixie dust that grows like a weed**.

How To Grow It

Growing fennel couldn't be easier: **just take a shaker of supermarket fennel seed out into the garden and scatter it over a patch of well-drained soil in the sunniest site you have**. Coming from the dry Mediterranean, these plants will self-seed freely, popping up on gravel driveways, piles of rubble and railways lines where little else will grow, meaning you will almost certainly only have to do this once.

How To Gather It

Get out into the garden on a warm, sunny day and gather up big bunches of the flowers when they are fully open and the yellow pollen is showing. Stick them head first into a paper bag and tie it shut, leaving the stems poking out at the top. String the bunch up upside down and leave in a cool, dry place like a garage for a week or two, to dry. Then give it a really good shake to dislodge the pollen, which will fall into the bottom of the bag. The flavour-packed grains will keep for up to a year in an airtight container. Like saffron, each individual flower yields very little, under ¼ teaspoon each, but as a tiny sprinkling goes a very long way and the plants are notoriously free-flowering, you will hardly be left in short supply.

How To Eat It

Traditionally, the grains are sprinkled over fresh egg pasta along with garlic and chopped walnuts; mixed with olive oil and brushed onto grilled bread; or tossed through great steaming bowlfuls of broccoli, artichokes or tomatoes. Fennel also has a dramatic effect on roast chicken and braised pork belly - dust the 'pollen' over the meat minutes before serving to keep its heavenly (and I don't use that word often) flavour intact. Happy to bestow its magic on both sweet and savoury dishes, this versatile herb is equally delicious scattered over sliced Comice pears as it is rubbed on chargrilled salmon.

DOUGLAS FIR

Pseudotsuga menziesii

What Is It?

Contrary to what you might imagine, cooking with fir needles won't leave you with food that tastes like a car deodorizer or a thorny mouthful of prickles. In fact, **the young, soft shoots of Douglas firs have an altogether more subtle woodsiness, containing similar flavour compounds to rosemary and thyme, only far more delicate and refreshing.** They are an elegant alternative to many of the classic woody Mediterranean herbs, without the domineering, turpentine-like flavour that these can kick out. Imagine citrus, rosemary and mint fused together with a wild-foresty twist.

How To Gather It

In the tree's native North America the tender spring shoots have been used by the First Nations peoples for centuries to make a lemony, fresh-tasting tea. I find their bright resinous flavour makes the perfect base for a sensationally smooth hot toddy with a heavy-handed shot of whisky. After all, who am I to question ancient wisdom?

For the very best flavour, be sure to harvest Douglas fir while their bright green shoots are still soft to the touch and no more than 5cm (2in) long; soon after this they turn into a mass of tough, spiky needles with a duller, more bitter note.

Three Ways To Eat It

1

Adding a handful of the soft tips to a bottle of white wine vinegar creates an incredible dressing for rich roast meats and game, while experimental chefs infuse the shoots through meat juices to create foresty, herbal gravies.

2

I love drowning fistfuls in gin in the early summer, to concoct a festive Christmas tree-scented martini for when the nights draw in (check out page 215 for the recipe).

3

When added to a preserving jar of sugar Douglas fir tips soon surrender their unique balsamic scent (see Flower-scented Sugars on page 170), creating a base for delicately fragrant icing for mince pies or spiced Christmas biscuits.

CORIANDER ROOT
Coriandrum sativum

What Is It?

Let's get one thing out of the way from the very start. I *hate* coriander leaves. I know it probably makes me a rubbish foodie, but I do have a pretty good excuse. **Along with roughly a fifth of the population, I possess a copy of a gene that makes coriander taste not fragrant and citrusy, but soapy and bleach-like**. Hence the strong love or hate response the herb elicits.

However, even if you are one of the same unfortunate minority, please do not let it put you off coriander roots. **Surprisingly, these contain a totally different combination of flavour chemicals, giving them a floral, sweet carrotiness much like coriander seeds** - a key flavouring ingredient in Belgian white beer and even Coca-Cola. If you like either of the former, you will love the fresh, spicy aroma these skinny, parsnip-like roots exude.

The great irony for Western chefs looking to capture authentic Southeast Asian flavours is that coriander *leaves* are used much less in Thailand, Malaysia and Vietnam than the fragrant *roots*, which most Europeans toss straight in the bin. Sacrilege!

How To Grow It

For the fattest, most fragrant roots, plant coriander seeds 5cm (2in) apart, directly into beds of rich, well-drained soil in light shade. Transplanting, drought and searing sunlight stress plants out, causing them to direct their energies into producing seeds at any expense, which results in tough, woody roots - not to mention runty, stunted leaves. **This is one plant worth spoiling!**

How To Eat It

When peeled and minced up fine, coriander roots form the base for countless curries, giving the blended spice pastes a smooth, floral lift to offset the brashness of fiery chillies and pungent shrimp pastes. They are also peeled and sliced into stir-fries to add a rich depth of flavour. The Thais will even combine all three parts of the plant, adding coriander seeds, roots and leaves at different stages of the cooking process.

LEMON VERBENA
Aloysia citrodora

What Is It?

Love the flavour of lemongrass but curse how tricky it can be to grow? Then consider its far easier and more intensely citrusy competition: lemon verbena.

How To Grow It

Lemon verbena is **native** to the Mediterranean-like climate zones of South America, so **trick your plants into thinking they are in Buenos Aires by planting them in a sheltered spot on a sunny wall in well-drained soil**. If you have a sheltered garden in a mild area large specimens should be happy outdoors all year round. If not, grow them in a pot that can be whipped indoors to a sunny porch or windowsill when frosts strike. Frequent bouts of baking should keep the plants' size in check. In milder areas they may well reappear every year, but **in colder climates I'd advise planting them in pots that can be brought under cover in the winter**.

How To Eat It

The leaves can be used as a direct replacement for lemongrass in teas, **cocktails, curries and stews, giving a wonderfully mellow lemon-drop tang**. When infused into sugar, the leaves make a good glaze for a lemon drizzle cake, with the young leaves easily crystallized to make tasty cake decorations. The older leaves are more strongly flavoured, but as these can be a little fibrous it is a good idea either to slice them finely before cooking, or to pick them out before serving.

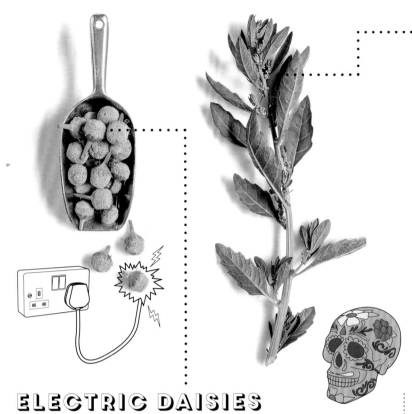

EPAZOTE
Dysphania ambrosioides

What Is It?

A staple of authentic Mexican street food, epazote is a food writer's nightmare because of its almost impossible-to-describe flavour. **Pungent, resinous and a bit like the smell of diesel (albeit in a good way) it is something that you really must taste to believe**. It has a broad similarity to flavours like oregano, mint and pine, but is at the same time totally, deliciously different.

How To Grow It

Seeds can be tricky to track down in mainstream garden centres, but are easily picked up online and through specialist nurseries. Although it's a common weed in its native land, **the seeds can take up to a month to germinate, but this is quickly remedied by an overnight soak in a glass of water before planting**. Once they are up and growing treat them in the garden exactly as you would tender herbs such as basil (see page 188), although in milder areas they will often pop back up from the roots the following spring.

How To Eat It

I first discovered the magic of epazote while researching for my master's in a remote region of northern Ecuador, where it grows as a roadside weed amongst the nettles and dandelions. When added to egg dishes, chopped over grilled chicken and scattered over beans, epazote's robust flavour was a godsend to my bland field-work diet. In Mexico it is an essential ingredient for salsas, soups, salads, and bean and lentil dishes, and even comes with the supposed ability to increase intelligence to genius-like proportions. Clearly, I am living proof that that last bit was just made up so kids would eat their greens.

ELECTRIC DAISIES
Acmella oleracea

What Are They?

A favourite of experimental chefs, these pretty button-like flowers are undeniably one of the most unusual edible experiences out there. **As their name suggests, biting into one almost immediately sparks off an electric shock-like sensation on the tip of the tongue, which quickly morphs into a remarkable 'fizziness' that moves over the surface of the palate like popping candy**. This is swiftly followed by a tingly numbness akin to that produced by Szechuan peppers, giving the plant a truly Willy Wonka-like three-part flavour that comes in successive waves.

How To Grow Them

While in their native Brazil electric daisies are a much-loved herb, in more temperate climes they live a double life as a bedding plant. They are easy to grow from both seeds and cuttings, treated in exactly the same way as you would basil (see page 188).

How To Eat Them

In the kitchen, use them sparingly in all the same ways you would other pungent spices such as mustard powder, wasabi, chillies or horseradish. The flowers can be chopped up with fiery chillies and used to add zip to fried chicken and grilled fish. Some adventurous chefs even sprinkle them over desserts, where their 'effervescent' sensation acts as a natural popping candy. When flaked on the rim of a cocktail glass, like salt on a margarita, the flowers have the magical ability to make non-carbonated drinks taste fizzy. Be forewarned, however, that **these little guys have an extremely intense flavour, so approach with caution!**

BASIL

Ocimum spp. and cvs

Basil is one of the world's best-loved herbs, with a massive number of varieties that span arguably a more diverse range of flavours than any other. Here are my top picks for the weirdest, most wonderful varieties, all of which have been trialled by the RHS to perform well outdoors in temperate regions, even in the most miserable of summers.

'Mrs Burns' Lemon' AGM

A compact form that releases a burst of sherbet lemon zestiness as soon as the leaves are rubbed, with flushes of pretty white flowers that bees love.

'Thai Sita'

To my mind the best Thai-style basil for growing outdoors, with that characteristic liquorice and clove warmth. It is only trumped by 'Christmas', an East-meets-West hybrid that fuses Thai and Italian forms to create plants with masses of mulled-wine-flavoured leaves.

'Emerald' AGM

This classic Genovese type is considered to be the best for making pesto. It boasts extra large leaves which look great folded between slices of tomato and mozzarella in a classic Caprese salad. I also love basil **'Chilly'** AGM with all the classic basil aroma, only amplified to lofty heights.

'Dark Opal' AGM

Being much milder in intensity than the familiar Genovese types, 'Dark Opal' has an altogether more complex flavour with hints of clove, liquorice, cinnamon and mint.

KEEPING SUPERMARKET BASIL ALIVE

The No.1 edible plant that timid first-time growers tend to turn to is pot-grown supermarket basil. But, quite frankly, if you can keep one alive for any length of time, you are more green-fingered than I am.

The problem is not that basil is difficult to grow, nor that you are the grim reaper of culinary herbs; it lies in the way these plants are grown for supermarkets. Each tiny pot contains not just one super-healthy basil plant, as you might expect, but sometimes up to 20 seedlings that have been crammed together and then often shocked into growth under powerful artificial lights to give the impression of a lush, adult plant quickly and cheaply. When you get them home, these mini basils start jostling with each other for light and space, leading to weak, stunted plants that soon die.

To get over this, simply ease a newly purchased plant out of its pot and gently split the rootball into four pieces with your fingers. Pot each of these quarters up individually. Give your newly divided plants a thorough drench of water and sit them on a bright windowsill away from direct sun for a week or two. They will quickly recover from this ordeal to make great houseplants for a sunny spot and can be planted outdoors during the frost-free months of the year.

For the very best flavour in chillier climes, however, treat your little basil plant to pride of place on the top shelf of a glasshouse or failing that a sunny windowsill in a warm room. Researchers at the University of Nottingham found that basil grown at 25°C (77°F) contained three times the aroma of that grown at 15°C (59°F), suggesting that while basil can and will grow outdoors in cool summers, it will never be quite as tasty.

'Emerald'

'Dark Opal'

'Christmas'

CHILLIES

Chillies attract a level of all-consuming devotion enjoyed by few other ingredients and they have risen from obscure exotic to cult phenomenon in little over two decades.

Yet despite the masses of chilli-growing advice out there, the 'experts' somehow seem to ignore the single piece of info we chilli heads crave most: how to get our little beauties really packing the fire power. This is my heat-seeker's guide to kicking out maximum spice.

VARIETY GUIDE

Ladies and Gentlemen, Choose Your Weapons

The spice level of chillies is determined mainly by their genes, which dictate the approximate range of capsaicin - the chemical responsible for their fiery kick - that the fruit are capable of producing. There are literally hundreds of varieties to choose from, which can be neatly ranked along the infamous Scoville scale (the Richter scale of spiciness).

VEGETABLE TYPES

These super-mild types are used much more like a vegetable than a spice. Coming in a dazzling flavour range from sweet and fruity to nutty and asparagus-like, they are delicious stuffed, roasted or fried, like spice-enhanced bell peppers. These vegetable types are the perfect chillies for people who think they don't like chillies.

'Padrón' *0-500 Scoville*

A northern Spanish delicacy and tapas bar staple. These little, bullet-shaped chillies are picked immature and green and seared in olive oil and sea salt. **While they are generally mild, with a great green-pepper flavour, one in every 10 or so has a pronounced kick, making eating them a sort of culinary Spanish roulette.**

'Trinidad Perfume' *500 Scoville*

If you love the tangy, fruitiness of habanero (Scotch bonnet) peppers but can't handle the heat, I have some good news for you. **'Trinidad Perfume'**'s golden fruits have traded gut-wrenching fire for an incredibly flavourful, aromatic citrusiness. Being sweet and with barely any capsaicin, this is the ultimate chilli-hater's chilli.

'Santa Fe Grande' *500-700 Scoville*

Ripening from a pale yellow through to fiery red, **these little gems have such a delicious flavour that you can forgive**

them their chronic identity crisis – torn between vegetable and spice. Their medium heat ranking and sweet tang make them great stuffed with cheese and grilled, pickled in sugary brine or chopped in salsas.

'Poblano' *1,000-1,500 Scoville*

A giant green pepper with a rich, undercurrent of heat and an altogether deeper, richer flavour. This muchacho is a culinary staple in Mexico, battered and fried or stuffed with anything from cheese to rice or meat and slow-baked. **Want more heat? Let them ripen to a ruby red and their spice level soars.** Drying and smoking these turns them into anchos, with a dramatically sweeter, stickier kick.

'Chilaca' *1,500-2,500 Scoville*

The dark brown, almost black flesh of this Mexican type is sometimes used fresh to spike enchiladas, chilli sauce and stews, but it is when it is dried and smoked that it really comes into its own. It then becomes known as a pasilla, meaning 'little raisin', because of its sweet, berry-like flavour with distinct hints of chocolate. Essential for an authentic Mexican mole sauce: see my recipe for Endorphin-rush Mole Sauce on page 197.

NOT ALL CHILLIES ARE CREATED EQUAL

The Scoville scale ranks chillies according to how many times they would need to be diluted for their spiciness to become unnoticeable, meaning fiery **'Tabasco'** (maximum 50,000 units) can be up to a hundred times spicier than a mild **'Padrón'** (maximum 500 units).

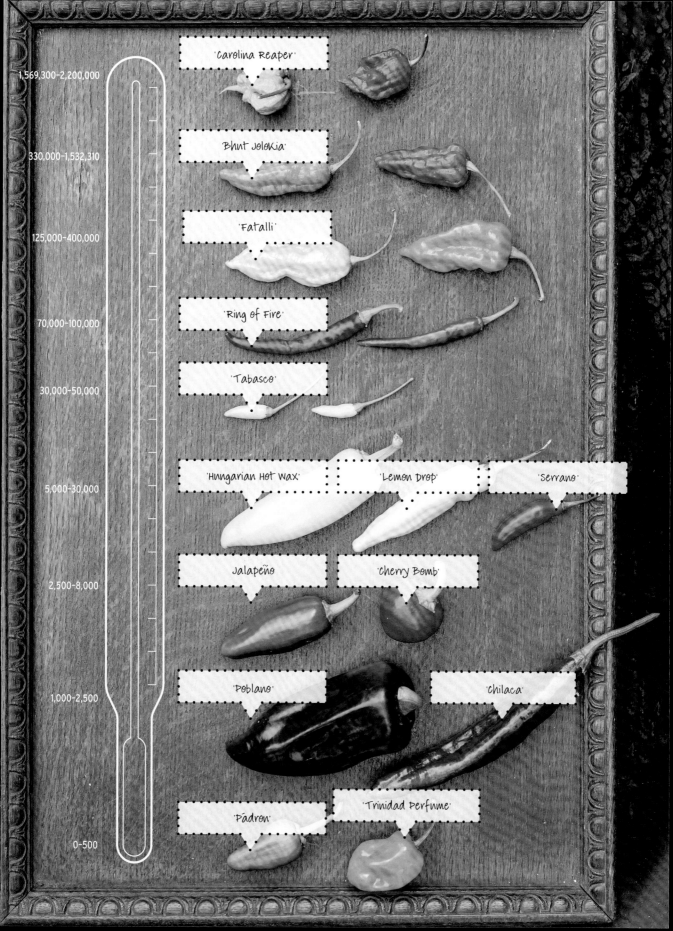

'Carolina Reaper'

1,569,300–2,200,000

'Bhut Jolokia'

330,000–1,532,310

'Fatalli'

125,000–400,000

'Ring of Fire'

70,000–100,000

'Tabasco'

30,000–50,000

'Hungarian Hot Wax' 'Lemon Drop' 'Serrano'

5,000–30,000

'Jalapeño' 'Cherry Bomb'

2,500–8,000

'Poblano' 'Chilaca'

1,000–2,500

'Padron' 'Trinidad Perfume'

0–500

SPICE TYPES

These intensely spicy, richly flavoured types contain the highest concentrations of capsaicin and are used in tiny amounts, like mustard or black pepper, to flavour dishes.

'Cherry Bomb' *2,500-5,000 Scoville*

One of the best chillies for outdoor growing, outperforming almost all others in my garden trials. Thin skins coupled with rich warmth (not searing heat) make 'em fantastic raw, pan-fried or simmered up in jams and salsas.

Jalapeño *2,500-8,000 Scoville*

Straddling the delicious culinary boundary between vegetable and spice, fresh jalapeños are wonderful roasted, pickled or stuffed with cheese and wrapped in bacon and baked. Ripened to deep red, dried and smoked, these become chipotles, fusing sweetness, umami and spice into one glorious combination. 'Summer Heat' is a reliable, early cultivar proven to perform well in temperate climates.

'Hungarian Hot Wax' AGM *5,000-15,000 Scoville*

A great performer outdoors, kicking out loads of mild, yellow, banana-shaped fruit. When 'Hungarian Hot Wax' chillies are grilled, roasted or chucked on the barbecue the sugars within them concentrate and caramelize, giving them an incredible roasted sweet corn flavour. This is one of the easiest of all chillies to grow and is tolerant of cool summers.

'Serrano' *10,000-25,000 Scoville*

Jalapeño's badass little brother, this guy gives a similar bright, biting flavour but with a ton more heat. Usually eaten raw, its thick, crisp flesh adds an amazing crunch to guacamole and salsas.

'Lemon Drop' *15,000-30,000 Scoville*

With a bright citrusy flavour and gutsy kick, this staple of the newly trendy Peruvian cuisine is traditionally added towards the end of cooking time to light dishes like fish or chicken. Pairs fabulously well with coriander and lemon peel, when finely diced and sprinkled over like a fragrant confetti before serving.

'Tabasco' *30,000-50,000 Scoville*

A key ingredient in the world-renowned hot sauce of Creole cooking that bears their name, 'Tabasco' chillies balance a supercharged spice with an intense fruity flavour. They are the only chilli variety I know whose flesh is more thick and juicy than dry and crisp.

'Ring of Fire' *70,000-80,000 Scoville*

This Cayenne-type chilli is the perfect candidate for early-season heat, kicking out little fire crackers from as early as mid-summer. Eat green or red, sliced into curries or Thai dishes.

'Fatalii' *125,000-400,000 Scoville*

This chilli hails from central and southern Africa. Its initial sweet fruitiness belies the spike of searing habanero-like heat that follows swiftly after. Being the world's seventh hottest pepper, this is not one to be treated lightly.

'Bhut Jolokia' *330,000-1,532,310 Scoville*

Up until December 2012 this traditional hybrid from northern India was officially the world's hottest pepper, with its dried fruit astonishingly ranking more than 400 times as spicy as Tabasco sauce. So intense it really teeters on the boundary between barely edible and full-on caustic.

'Carolina Reaper' *1,569,300-2,200,000 Scoville*

The constant battle among breeders to create the world's spiciest pepper never seems to be won for more than a few short years. The reigning champion as of 2012 is 'Carolina Reaper'. Bred by the ominously named PuckerButt Pepper Company in South Carolina, at their peak these fruit are significantly spicier than US Grade Pepper spray. As it is quite literally 'weapons grade', I calculate that a single gram of the flesh would be detectable in half a metric ton of curry. Grow this nuclear-strength chilli as a novelty and approach with *great* care, wearing gloves.

CHILLI OR PEPPER?

One of the fruit I am holding is an ordinary sweet pepper with no spice at all, the other is the spiciest chilli known to man, capable of kicking out more heat than US-grade pepper spray. They are both roughly the same size, shape and colour, so which is which? Well, sweet peppers are actually just a variety of chilli which have undergone a mutation to contain a single recessive gene that blocks their production of capsaicin, making them botanically one and the same. In fact, they are just one of dozens of varieties of capsaicin-free chillies that until recently have been entirely unknown to foodies outside of Latin America.

Sadly, without being familiar with the variety though, there is only one way to tell how spicy it is likely to be. So read the seed catalogue description carefully!

TIPS & TRICKS

Trick 'Em Into It

Capsaicin, the magic ingredient responsible for the glorious spiciness of chillies, evolved as a chemical defence to protect their seeds from being eaten by mammals. **Plants stressed by blazing sun, drought and poor soil have an increased incentive to protect themselves from the perceived threat and will react by ramping up their capsaicin levels.** Armed with this bit of geekery, crafty chilli heads can 'trick' their plants into turning up the heat by faking these conditions.

Fake A Drought

After the fruit have set, let plants dry out a little between waterings, just until the leaves begin to wilt ever so slightly. Don't let them go into full wilt, though, as this can trigger them to abort their flowers and fruit. Conversely, it has been shown that **doubling the watering of peppers can double their yield – to a point – resulting in far less pungent fruits, but more of them.**

Treat 'Em Mean, Keep 'Em Keen

Fertilisers, especially those rich in nitrogen, have been demonstrated in some studies to reduce the capsaicin content of chillies, which generally produce the hottest fruit in poorer soils. So go easy on the plant food.

THE SPICY SEED MYTH

It's not the chilli seeds themselves that have the most fiery kick, but the placenta – this white spongy protective tissue that surrounds them. It contains a higher concentration of capsaicin than any other part of the fruit, which helps the plant protect its precious seeds from being eaten.

Why go to so much effort to protect your seeds, only to then encase them in colourful, sugar-rich fruit? Well, it turns out that plants produce capsaicin as a selective deterrent that only effects mammals, whose digestive system destroys chillies seeds. Birds on the other hand are immune to their heat, and their droppings are the plant's key way to disperse its seeds in the wild.

Add Salt To Up Their Flavour

According to research at Arizona State University, treating plants to a drench of salt solution similar to that recommended on page 52 resulted in chillies with a 20 percent higher capsaicin content. The same study also reported that (in stark contract to tomatoes) **salt water could double the fruit production of chilli plants.** Not a bad deal, hey?

PICK YOUR HEAT LEVEL

This same jalapeño chilli can be made as hot as a **'Lemon Drop'** or mild as a **'Chilaca'** by simply tinkering with its growing conditions.

'Chilaca' 2,500 Scoville   Jalapeño average 5,000 Scoville   'Lemon Drop' 15,000 Scoville

Turn Up The Thermostat

Treat your plants to pride of place in the glasshouse (if you have one) or pick the most sheltered area of your plot and let them bask in full sun. **Containers warm up more quickly than open ground and the darker the pot the more efficient it will be at absorbing heat**. Go for dark-coloured clay pots, rather than the standard black plastic, as the ceramic traps and retains the precious warmth for longer.

Siting pots along a sunny wall is ideal, as the brickwork acts like a storage heater on chilly nights, radiating out warmth soaked up during the day.

In a glasshouse, place pots high on the staging: as hot air rises, this is prime real estate for charging your plants with spice and comes with the bonus of having the most direct access to sunlight.

HOW TO GROW CHILLIES

Sow & Grow

Start your chilli seeds into growth from late winter to early spring by planting two seeds per 10cm (4in) pot of good-quality compost. Place on a warm, sunny windowsill indoors.

If grown at 18-21°C (64-70°F), seedlings should emerge within 1-2 weeks. At this point, remove the weaker one.

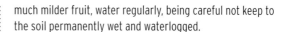

When your young plants reach 10cm (4in) tall, transfer them to 30-40cm (12-16in) pots of soil-based compost, give them a good spritz with my aspirin booster spray (see page 28).

Place the pot in the sunniest, warmest spot you have, ideally the top shelving of a glasshouse or failing that a conservatory or sunny porch. **Some varieties of peppers will grow well outdoors in temperate summers, but all will be more vigorous and flavourful indoors, in warmer temperatures.**

Growing On
Site
Colour Therapy: Line your glasshouse shelves with kitchen foil to produce a massive increase of fruit with significantly less aphid damage (see page 23).

Watering
Water To Taste: For maximum spice, once your plants are established give them only a very light watering when they start to show signs of wilting. However, for bumper crops of much milder fruit, water regularly, being careful not keep to the soil permanently wet and waterlogged.

Protect Them with Mist: Spraying your plants regularly with plain old H_2O will not only keep infestations of red spider mite (the glasshouse grower's nemesis) in check by maintaining the humidity they hate. It can also, rather handily, up your harvest by encouraging good fruit set.

Feed
Dose 'Em Up
Aspirin spray has been shown to improve the sugar levels in capsicums by as much as 50 percent, while also boosting their total phytonutrient content, including vitamin C. **Soakings of molasses tonic (see page 27) once a month throughout the summer will provide your chillies with a rich source of potassium, which has been demonstrated to improve fruit quality and yield.**

Soak with Seawater
When the small, green fruit have begun to swell to the size of a pea, drench the plants in a sea salt solution just as you would tomatoes (see page 52) and then drench them again two weeks later.

WHERE THERE'S SMOKE, THERE'S FIRE

While chillies are eminently edible fresh, in the cradle of chilli culture that is Mexico, drying and smoking them is considered to elevate them to an altogether more exalted state. Intensifying their flavour and infusing them with smoke also causes chemical reactions within the fruit that can dramatically change the way they taste – with some varieties rendered almost unrecognizable after this treatment (think the difference between pork chops and crispy, maple-cured bacon). Turning a humble vegetable into a game-changing spice is easier than you might think, requiring no special kit or laborious techniques apart from an old wok with a tight-fitting glass lid and a wire rack.

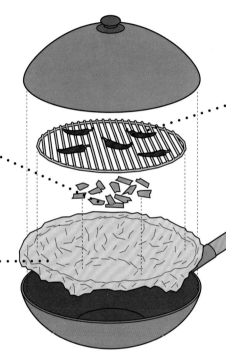

PLACE 1 tablespoon oak, apple or hickory woodchips (you can find these in the charcoal section of garden centres, larger supermarkets or online) in the centre of the foil and put a wire rack on top. There should be gap of at least 1cm (½in) between the rack and the woodchips.

LINE the wok or large saucepan with a double sheet of kitchen foil, leaving plenty of excess around the edges.

COVER the rack in chillies, sliced in half with their cut sides facing down. Pop the lid onto the wok and fold the edges of the foil over it to make a tight seal. Whack your extractor fan up to high, open the windows and place the wok on a low heat for 20 minutes, until the peppers begin to soften. Turn off the heat, wait for the smoke to settle, then remove the chillies. Alternatively, just toss them on the grill of the barbecue as the embers are dying, jam a lid on and leave until cool.

USE straight away or dry on a baking sheet in a low oven – 4 hours at 110°C/210°F/gas mark ¼. Once dried, either use the chillies ground up into flakes or rehydrate them by soaking for 10 minutes in hot water. They can then be sliced and added to stews, salsas and sauces or blitzed into pastes.

A MAGICAL TRANSFORMATION

The flavour change that arises from this smoking and drying process is often so dramatic that the same varieties of chilli bear entirely different names (and culinary uses) depending on whether they are fresh or smoked. Here is my guide to steer you through this minefield of ever-changing names.

JALAPEÑO TO CHIPOTLE

The chipotle is smoky-sweet and packs a fiery punch with an almost chocolaty hint.

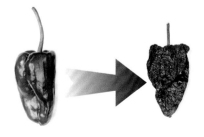

POBLANO TO ANCHO

Deep and dark with a slightly sharp tang reminiscent of tobacco, the ancho has a low spice level.

CHILACA TO PASILLA

Translating as 'little raisin' because of its intense fruitiness, the pasilla has a liquorice-like flavour.

ENDORPHIN-RUSH MOLE SAUCE

Serves 4

I have my Mexican uni buddy Ruth to thank for introducing me to this wonder of Latin American cuisine. An improbable mix of exotic spices, smoked chillies, dried fruit, nuts and – wait for it – dark chocolate, that somehow just works . And boy how it does. I have tinkered with Ruth's original family recipe by adding saffron, which contains mood-enhancing chemicals, to create a snigger-triggering trifecta between the endorphin kick of chillies and the slight psychoactive effect found naturally in dark chocolate. Eat with your mates, slumped on the sofa, and see who's the first to crack a silly smile.

What You Need:

2 tablespoons olive oil

1 small onion

4 garlic cloves

½ cinnamon stick

1 teaspoon coriander seeds

2 large pinches of saffron

2 tablespoons raisins

4 tablespoons flaked almonds

rind of 1 orange

475ml (⅘ pint) chicken stock

1 pasilla chilli

1 chipotle chilli

2 chopped plum tomatoes

50g (2oz) dark chocolate (70 percent cocoa solids minimum)

1 tablespoons peanut butter

What To Do:

FRY the onion, garlic, spices, raisins, almonds and orange rind in the olive oil over a very low heat, until the onions are soft and caramelized (about 10 minutes).

POUR in the chicken stock, chillies and tomatoes, bring to a gentle simmer for 20 minutes, then turn off the heat.

BLITZ the whole lot together with a hand blender until the sauce is smooth.

MELT the chocolate and peanut butter into the still warm sauce, stirring until totally incorporated.

SERVE over grilled, poached or roast chicken with fluffy white rice and a green salad.

HOME-GROWN SPICE RACK

Think the idea of home-grown spices is an impossible dream? Well, think again. All these exotic spices were grown outdoors in temperate climates, harvested from common garden plants that most people don't even know are edible. No, really.

LOVE-IN-A-MIST SEEDS

Nigella damascena

An old-time cottage-garden favourite, these dainty flowers are followed by wisp-encircled seed pods, packed full of fragrant black seeds that are a popular spice in their native Syria.

Do not confuse these with *Nigella sativa*, which is the source of the 'Kalonji' or 'Black Onion' seeds that feature in classic Indian dishes from Peshwari naan to mango chutney. In contrast to the cumin-like earthiness of its close relative, *N. damascena* releases an unexpected fruitiness, virtually identical to purple grape sweets when bitten into. This E-numberless flavour treat works culinary magic on everything from fruit salads and ice cream to cheesecakes and salsas.

To harvest, cut the plants off at the ground in the autumn when the seed pods have become dry and brittle. Pop them head first into a paper bag, holding the bunch upside down to allow the little seeds to tumble out into the bag. They will keep for a year or more in a sealed jar in a cool, dry spot.

CAROLINA ALLSPICE

Calycanthus floridus

The name of this glossy-leaved garden shrub, which is flecked with deep red, magnolia-like flowers in the summer, proudly advertises its delicious product: a richly scented bark that miraculously combines the flavours of cinnamon, cloves and nutmeg. Yet despite being a beautiful, low-maintenance, widely grown ornamental, for some reason it has yet to register on the foodie grower's radar. Once established, the only real care it needs is a light pruning each autumn to remove congested, dead or crossing branches. It will then give a ready supply of an exotic, food-mile-free spice, almost all of which is sadly normally consigned to the compost heap.

To get at the good stuff, pick the largest branches with the most bark and gently scrape this off with a sharp knife. Laying these shavings between two sheets of kitchen paper on a windowsill should dry the fragrant shards out in a week or two. These can be used just as they are or ground into a fine powder with a few bashes of a pestle and mortar. Use in all the ways you would cinnamon. Incredible mixed with sugar and sprinkled atop hot buttered toast.

BAY

Laurus nobilis

Good old bay really does have it all. Shiny evergreen leaves, rich clove-like scent, not to mention being virtually bomb-proof in the easy-to-grow stakes, as long as you give it an occasional watering if the weather's extremely dry. Think twice about planting one in the ground, though, as it can quickly form a large, vigorous tree if left unchecked. Go for a roomy pot on a patio instead, the closer to the kitchen the better.

SMOKED CHILLIES

Capsicum spp.

Chillies are incredibly versatile crops, as tasty as they are ornamental. But you don't just have to enjoy them fresh; drying and even smoking them can transform their flavour into a totally different animal – or should that be vegetable? For instructions on how to do this check out page 196.

TASMANIAN PEPPER

Tasmannia lanceolata

With its bewildering cocktail of flavours that somehow fuses the searing spiciness of horseradish with the headiness of black pepper and the clovey warmth of bay leaves, this plant can be forgiven its rather confusing common name. Although it's not

Szechuan pepper

Bay leaves

Nigella seeds

Smoked chillies

Saffron

Carolina allspice

Tasmanian pepper berries

Tasmanian pepper leaves

actually a pepper at all, the deep green leaves and claret red stems of this stunningly exotic evergreen shrub are suffused with the same unique flavour. **Fast becoming a sought-after ingredient in its native Australia, its leaves are dried and ground into a peppery, herb powder or added to the pot whole and fished out just before serving like a bay leaf.** Culinarily, you can use them as you would use thyme or rosemary, while remembering they have a far more intense kick.

If you have the space, growing a hedge or clump of these will result in small, black berries in late summer that at first taste of blueberry jam and then unexpectedly hit you with a Taser jolt of horseradishy fieriness. These were once even grown in Cornwall as a commercial crop, giving this Antipodean plant its other (even more confusing) common name of Cornish pepper. Once dried, the berries look much like large pepper grains and can be used in exactly the same way, imparting a burst of fruity spiciness to steaks, barbecued meats and game. Along with their dried leaves these are now a major crop in certain parts of Australia thanks to the growing popularity of local Aboriginal cuisine.

Unfortunately, **the plants need both a male and female to produce fruit** and there is no way of telling which is which until they reach flowering size. I have yet to find a nursery that sells plants of labelled sex, so you need to have the space to grow quite a few and cross your fingers that you get at least one male and one female. If you've ever tried a sirloin steak seared with a pepper sauce made from these berries, however, you'll know that this is *definitely* worth the gamble.

SZECHUAN PEPPER

Zanthoxylum simulans

A handsome ornamental shrub or small tree in the *Citrus* family, this plant is increasingly popular for its enormous garden value. With glossy, pinnate leaves and bunches of pink and orange fruit in the autumn, combined with a scent that reminds me of a gloriously spicy Thai green curry, Szechuan peppers seem to be popping up everywhere these days. **One fact that is often overlooked is that the ornamental berries are also eminently edible** - being the self-same, tongue-tingling spice that is sold in most supermarkets thanks to the exploding interest in the West in regional Chinese cuisine. Like a cross between orange peel, pepper and fiery chillies, they are an essential ingredient in classic five-spice powder and have the power to transform any simple stew or stir-fry into a fragrant explosion of exotic spiciness.

There are several species to choose from, but I would go for the self-fertile *Zanthoxylum simulans* unless you have space

for a selection of trees. To harvest the berries, pick them off just as they begin to burst, revealing the small black seeds within. Scatter them over a baking sheet in a warm spot indoors and leave to dry for a few days. Once dry they will stay fresh in an airtight jar for a year or more.

SAFFRON

Crocus sativus

As the world's most expensive spice, worth literally its weight in gold, **the exotic threads of saffron, you might be surprised to learn, are not just possible to grow in the Northern Hemisphere, but were for centuries an iconic British crop**.

Saffron Hill, Saffron Walden and even my home town of Croydon are all named after large saffron plantations - 'Croydon' coming from the Anglo-Saxon words for 'saffron valley'. Who knew? The spice was in fact grown in Britain for thousands of years, from the time of the Romans right up until the late Victorian period, and considering this coincided with a mini ice age that is pretty good going!

Nowadays, the only place you are likely to see saffron growing in temperate climates is in rock gardens and alpine houses, where its dainty, scented, purple flowers flush into growth each autumn, cheering up the darker months of the year. They are delicious added to all manner of cakes, rice dishes and (my personal favourite) rum or gin, to make bright amber-coloured cocktails. The alcohol leaches out the antioxidant chemicals, which give saffron its vivid hue and its wonderfully rich, eggy flavour. These same health-boosting phytonutrients also have mildly mood-enhancing effects that can induce giggliness for up to 30 minutes. Don't believe me? Well, there's only one way to find out.

Actually a species of crocus very closely related to the common 'municipal' variety, these little plants are surprisingly easy to grow and a 2 x 1m (6½ x 3ft) bed planted with them will provide more than the average family is likely to eat in a year. Fantastic!

3cm (1in)

How To Grow Saffron

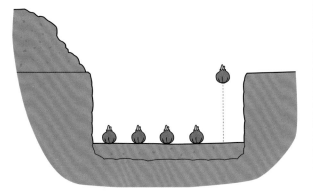

As soon as they arrive, plant the corms (on sale from late summer) in a bed filled with a well-drained potting mix (i.e. one rich in sand or grit), in the sunniest spot you have. Choosing a supplier carefully is important, as the corms don't bloom until they measure about 3cm (1in) across.

If your corms are smaller than this, you may have to wait a few years before you see a harvest. The best suppliers will state on the package whether their corms are ready to flower in the first year.

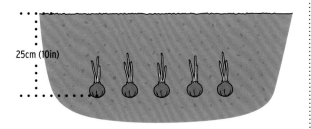

25cm (10in)

I picked up a further tip during a recent filming trip to a family-run saffron plantation in Greece, which left me astounded. Instead of planting according to the standard recommendation of about 10cm (4in) deep, these farmers were burying their corms with their bases as low as 25cm (10in) below the soil's surface, backfilling the hole with gravel. According to their trials – and despite looking ridiculous to someone brought up on a diet of horticultural rule books – this deep-planting technique results in as many as twice the number of flowers, and resultantly abundant harvests. It also all but eliminates the losses from the plant's only major pest: squirrels that love to dine on freshly planted corms. As with most autumn-flowering bulbs and corms, the leaves of saffron emerge only in the winter months. It is important not to damage or cut these off, as this will weaken the plants.

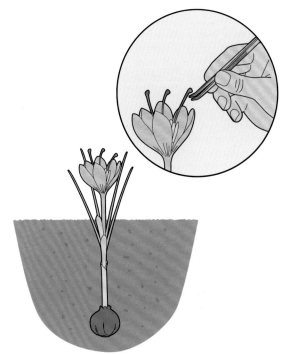

In late summer, saffron requires a six-week period of soil temperatures consistently above 20°C (68°F). At this time of year the corms lie dormant underground, so it is easy to forget them and if the bed has become smothered with weeds the resultant shade may make conditions too cool. Planting them in a Mediterranean-style gravel garden is a great way around this problem, as the stones and pebbles serve not only to suppress weeds but also to trap extra heat. There is currently a commercial plantation in the mountains of chilly North Wales, however, so don't think they are a crop just for those in milder and sunnier areas. **I pick the bright red threads at the centre of each flower out with tweezers, so as not to ruin their display, and dry them on paper towels indoors.**

BEWARE DOPPELGANGERS

Make absolutely sure that the corms you are buying are from the edible saffron crocus *Crocus sativus*, and not similar-looking or similarly named plants such as meadow saffron or autumn crocus. **Some of these doppelgangers are extremely toxic.** All reputable suppliers will make the edible nature of their genuine saffron crocus clear on the label. If in doubt, do not purchase!

GREEN ALMONDS

One of the best-kept secrets of Middle Eastern cuisine, green almonds – as you might expect – are simply the fresh, young pods of almonds picked before their fuzzy shells harden. But this is where their similarity to the familiar store-cupboard staple ends.

GROWING THEM

Almond trees are hardy in all but the very coldest climates, proving very low-maintenance and extremely attractive once established. Coaxing them into fruit, however, has often been quite a different story, with almonds sadly having a reputation for poor fruit set and succumbing to fungal diseases like peach leaf curl in regions with short soggy summers. Fortunately, a new generation of varieties and grafting methods now means that, with just three crafty horti-tricks, home-grown green almonds are becoming a real possibility.

1) *Either* Get A Late-Flowering Variety

Almond trees have a habit of flowering early in the spring, which can often mean that there are simply not enough pollinators buzzing around. This flush of delicate blossoms at the very beginning of the season can also be extremely vulnerable to damage from late frosts. Either one of these problems will cause the flowers to fall without setting fruit. Not good.

The new, late-flowering French cultivar **'Mandaline'** gets around both these problems in one fell swoop by not producing its pretty pink blossoms until mid-spring – incredibly late for an almond. The Dutch variety **'Robijn'**, which is actually a cross between an almond and a peach, is also a comparatively late flowerer. Coming with the bonus of being all but immune to leaf curl, it is also one of the highest-yielding and sweetest-tasting types. However, perhaps the most reliable variety for growing outdoors in temperate climates is the Scandinavian variety **'Ingrid'**, which has traded in huge yields in favour of dependability, producing light crops of tasty nuts on trees that are partially resistant to leaf curl.

Or (The Best Option) Bring 'Em Under Cover

If you have a porch, glasshouse or conservatory you can opt for the variety **'Princesse'**, a deliciously sweet-tasting form that is commonly grafted onto a super-dwarfing rootstock. This limits the tree's size and spread to that of a 1.2m (4ft) bush that is perfectly happy growing in a pot, which means if late frosts are forecast the plant can be easily lifted and popped indoors. **'Robijn'** is now also sold on a dwarfing rootstock, meaning that with the right pruning it can be kept no taller than 1.8–2.5m (6–8ft) and thus easily grown in a pot.

Bringing your plant under cover has the convenient side effect of keeping its buds dry, helping to prevent them becoming infected with the airborne spores of the leaf curl fungus, which is also carried by raindrops. This, coupled with the natural genetic resistance of all these varieties, virtually eliminates the risk of an outbreak.

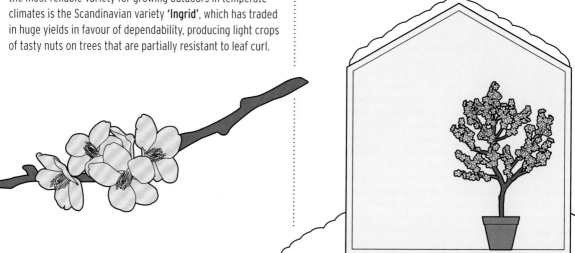

Early in the season the whole of a green almond is soft and sweet; as it develops, the skin becomes progressively more fibrous and the nut needs to be peeled.

2) Pretend To Be A Bee

Hand-pollination carried out by tickling the centre of each flower with a soft paintbrush is a simple cheat.

It does the bees' work for them if they aren't around, transferring pollen from flower to flower and thus triggering fruit formation and bumper crops. This is essential if you have brought your trees under cover, as bees cannot access the flowers, but it's worth the 10 minutes of effort it takes even if the plants are outdoors. All the varieties mentioned here are also self-fertile - they can produce viable seed from their own pollen - so there is no need to dash between numerous trees of different varieties to get good fruit set.

3) Pick Your Warmest Spot

Planting your little almond in the warmest, sunniest spot your garden has available will further up your chances of optimal harvests. Against a brick wall is ideal, as the brickwork acts like a storage heater, absorbing the warmth of the sun each day and emitting it each night to keep frosts off.

QUICK TIPS

• With their stunning spring blossom, I would give almonds pride of place in the most used part of the garden, ideally within view of the kitchen window to brighten up your day when doing the washing up during a soggy spring.

• Whether you're growing them indoors or out, make sure you opt for a plant grafted onto a dwarfing rootstock to keep the size of your trees in check. 'St Julian A' and 'VVA1' are good choices. At the other extreme, plants grafted onto a 'Myran' rootstock will turn into a monster tree, with nuts far out of reach. Stay well away, unless you have plenty of space - and a sturdy ladder!

• Do not plant almonds near peach trees, as they are closely related and may cross-pollinate, which can result in unpleasantly bitter harvests.

• Almond trees produce flowers and fruit on two-year-old wood, so do try to keep any scissor-happy pruning urges under control. I would recommend removing only dead, crossing or congested growth or any wayward shoots popping out in strange directions that could cause the tree to loose its shape just after harvesting.

EATING THEM

Soft and crisp enough to devour whole, green almonds are not rich and nutty, but refreshing and mildly tart, with a flavour that reminds me of the smell of newly mown lawn - green and spring-like. Often described as tasting like something between green apples and green grapes, they have an outer hull covered in downy fuzz with a crunchy-yet-watery texture. The infant seed within complements this perfectly with its soft-yet-firm, jelly-like consistency and delicate marzipan flavour. The result is an interesting 'two-tone' taste and texture.

Across the Middle East, from Iran to Israel, these spring-time treats are dipped in oil and salt and eaten as snacks. In Lebanon the fruit are more often pickled in a sugary brine with chillies and coriander seeds and eaten as an accompaniment to roast chicken. I love them sliced into thin slivers and tossed into a hot frying pan with the season's first broad beans. Pure magic with a crumbling of goats' cheese and crispy fried lardons.

Green almonds also work well in a pasta primavera with a great mountain of Parmesan shavings and lemon oil. But perhaps the best and simplest way to eat them is in spring herb salads, where their fresh acidity really shines through.

CHEATING THE SEASONS

To me, the best bit about eating almonds 'in the green', however, is the simple fact that in temperate climates summers are not always long enough for regular almonds to ripen to the normal supermarket stage. Eating them unripe and green is a cunning trick that allows you to cheat the seasons, rewarding you with a far more unusual, hard-to-find and expensive-to-buy product, instead of the heartbreak of seeing your harvest hopes dashed by a lacklustre summer.

GREEN ALMOND
SPRING SALAD Serves 4

Green almonds are key to probably the most refreshing raw
spring salad ever created. Feel free to customise this basic
recipe with anything you have at hand in the garden. Here I
have chucked in borage flowers and some wild asparagus.

What You Need:

100g (3½oz) green almonds

100g (3½oz) fresh spring peas

100g (3½oz) sliced cucumber

200g (7oz) radishes

200g (7oz) asparagus

a drizzle of unfiltered olive oil
and sherry vinegar

What To Do:

TOSS all the ingredients
together and serve. Simple!

CAPTURING FLAVOUR

VINEGARS, BALSAMICS & PICKLES

Arguably, the simplest way to capture the flavour of your harvest is dunking it in vinegar, to create all manner of wonderful pickles and vinaigrettes, even home-made balsamics.

QUINCE *ACETO BALSAMICO*

Italy's original *Aceto Balsamico* is in reality not a vinegar at all, but the juice of tart Trebbiano grapes that has been slowly simmered down to a thick caramel and aged in oak barrels.

Anyone with a glut of overly tart fruit like quince can adopt this idea. It also works with Bramley apples and, of course, grapes. To make a truly marvellous home-grown version of balsamic, run the fruit through an electric juicer and simmer the resultant juice down in a wide-brimmed saucepan. Amazingly, 2 litres (3½ pints) juice will reduce to just 250ml (less than ½ pint) after a gentle simmering of an hour or so, so it is a really efficient way to use up masses of excess harvests. This reduction will keep in the fridge for at least a month.

PICKLED CHERRIES   Makes 1.5kg (3lb)

Pickling fruit is not only far simpler than pickling vegetables (no need to worry about keeping them firm and crisp), but pickled fruits are far harder to buy outside of luxurious food halls. Here's my basic recipe that can be tweaked to almost any fruit that takes your fancy.

SIMMER 350g (11½ oz) sugar with 175ml (6fl oz) vinegar in a large saucepan for 5 minutes, until all the sugar has dissolved.

ADD 1kg (2¼ lb) cherries into this mix with any herbs or spices you like and simmer gently for an extra 5 minutes or until soft.

PACK the simmered fruit into a warm, sterilized jar. Sieve the rest of the syrup through a sieve lined with a coffee filter or cheesecloth.

REDUCE the syrup by popping it back on a medium heat for 5–10 minutes until it has reduced by one third. Pour this boiling liquid over the fruit and seal your jars.

STORE the mix in a cool, dark place. Your pickles will be ready after steeping for about a month, but will keep for at least a year.

RASPBERRY & BAY VINEGAR   Makes 500ml (17fl oz)

It's time to flashback to 1989 with this retro concoction. Fresh, fragrant and ultra-versatile, it is hard to find a food it doesn't work well with.

CRUSH 500g (generous 1lb) raspberries in a mixing bowl and pour over 500ml (17fl oz) cider vinegar. Add a bay leaf or 2, cover and leave to soak in the fridge for a week.

STRAIN the mix through a sieve into a saucepan and stir in 100g (4oz) sugar.

SIMMER the sweetened vinegar until the sugar has dissolved. Pour into sterilized bottles while still piping hot and store in a cool, dark place – it will keep for well over a year.

BALSAMIC FIG REDUCTION

Soft fruit like figs, berries and plums add an incredible fruity richness and silky texture to home-made balsamic reductions which, despite sounding super-fancy, couldn't be simpler to make. My favourite version contains figs and a dash of vanilla extract, truly amazing on a salad or drizzled over fresh strawberries.

BLITZ up equal volumes of fig pulp and balsamic vinegar in a blender and strain through a sieve to remove the seeds.

POUR into a wide, shallow pan and simmer on a very low heat until it is reduced by half, stirring occasionally (about 30–40 minutes).

BOTTLE UP and serve. If you don't want to use it straight away, it will keep in the fridge for at least a month.

Raspberry & Bay Vinegar

A spoonful works shockingly well drizzled over vanilla ice cream. Don't knock it 'til you've tried it!

Pickled Cherries with Bay in Red Wine Vinegar

Incredible scattered over a pizza with a generous crumbling of Stilton.

Quince Aceto Balsamico

A nifty way to condense giant fruit gluts into super-special Christmas presents.

Pickled Apricots in White Wine Vinegar

Heavenly over herby grilled chicken in the summer.

Balsamic Fig Reduction

Turns a regular cheese toastie into the food of the gods.

Pickled Figs with Chilli in Cider Vinegar

Cheddar will never be the same again.

CUT & DRY

Drying is probably the quickest and easiest way to preserve a range of fruit, vegetables and herbs naturally. When strung up in great garlands by a warm windowsill, they look great as quirky home decor as the nights draw in.

Chillies & Mushrooms: These can simply be threaded on a length of kitchen string or cotton using a large needle. Hang them up by a window and, within a few weeks, they will be dry and ready to use. Store them in large preserving jars with a thin layer of uncooked rice on the bottom: this will help absorb any excess moisture.

Herbs: Tough-leaved Mediterranean herbs such as rosemary, sage, thyme and bay will dry out in as little as a week or so, hung upside down on a length of string.

PRESERVING IN OIL

Bathing in oil is an excellent way to preserve all manner of fruit and veg, transforming your gluts into super-fancy jars of deli-style goodies. Here are four great recipes for preserving tomatoes, chillies, lampascioni and herbs.

DRIED 'SAN MARZANO' TOMATOES WITH BASIL

Makes 1kg (2lb)

DRY 3kg (6½lb) tomatoes by slicing them in half, scattering them cut side up on 2 baking sheets. Season well and drizzle with 2 tablespoons garlic oil, then pop them in the oven at 110°C/210°F/gas mark ¼ for 4 hours or until they are soft and sticky.

MIX with a handful of basil leaves and pack lightly into a sterilized jar while still warm. Pour over roughly 200ml (⅓ pint) extra virgin olive oil.

SEAL and leave to soak in the oil for at least a day before using. In a cool, dry place they should keep for up to a month.

SMOKED CHIPOTLE CHILLIES   Makes 500g (1lb)

PACK freshly smoked chipotle or jalapeño peppers (see page 196) into a sterilized jar, and drizzle over 2 teaspoons sherry vinegar.

TOP up with extra virgin olive oil.

LEAVE to soak for a day or 2, store in a cool, dark place and use within a month.

LAMPASCIONI ONIONS IN OIL

Mellow and tender with an addictive hint of bitterness, check out my recipe for these on page 152.

FROZEN HERBS IN OIL

Chopped herbs frozen in suspended animation in ice-cube trays filled with olive oil provide a quick flavour hit ready to go straight in the pan: as a bonus, they come in perfectly measured-out portions. Adding chopped garlic or pre-fried shallots is a great way to deal with home-grown gluts and get your meals off to a flying start.

WE'RE JAMMING

It's amazing how a little heat and sugar can magically turn the volume up on certain flavours, transforming them into something altogether different from the fresh product. There is even some evidence that a light simmering can raise the available phytonutrient content in the fruit. So what are you waiting for?

In a cool, dark environment most jams and jellies will keep for up to a year in a sealed jar. Once opened, store in the fridge and use within two weeks. All recipes make four medium-sized jars.

CARAMELIZED SHALLOT & BACON JAM

Makes 500g (1lb)

Smoky, sticky-sweet and intensely rich, there is no better condiment in a home-made cheeseburger at your summer barbecue. Use the best-quality bacon you can afford.

GRILL 8 rashers (about 300g/11oz) smoked bacon under a medium grill until done.

RESERVE the bacon fat and heat 2 tablespoons of it in a frying pan. Fry 400g (14oz) thickly sliced shallots very gently for about 20 minutes until they are fully caramelized and just beginning to char. Season the mixture well with salt and pepper.

CRUMBLE the cooked bacon rashers into the shallots and stir in half a grated cooking apple (unpeeled), ¼ teaspoon each of mustard powder and cinnamon, 200g (7oz) Demerara sugar and finally 3 tablespoons sherry vinegar. Bring to the boil and simmer for 10 minutes on a low heat, stirring occasionally.

SPOON into warm, sterilized jars and screw on the lids.

SPICED PUMPKIN & CARROT JAM

Makes 1kg (2lb)

This is a popular breakfast treat in southern France and Italy. Sacrilegiously good on a hot, buttered croissant.

GRATE 400g (14oz) each of pumpkins and carrots into a large saucepan.

SAUTÉ the grated veg, together with 1 tablespoon butter and the juice and rind of 2 oranges, for 20 minutes until softened.

STIR in 600g (1¼lb) sugar, ½ teaspoon mixed spice, 2 cardamom pods and a large pinch of salt.

SIMMER on a medium heat for a further 1 hour or until the jam thickens. It is ready when a wooden spoon drawn across the bottom of the pan shows the base clearly.

SPOON into warm, sterilized jars and screw on the lids.

Like the sound of pumpkin jam? There is even an heirloom Italian variety bred specifically for the purpose: 'Zucca da Marmellata', which has an incredible gel-like slipperiness and rich 'golden' pumpkin flavour. An autumnal treat I look forward to all year.

Worried about the sugar? Freezer jams contain 80 percent less of the sweet stuff, but taste just as good. Substitute a natural stevia-based sweetener and you can stop worrying altogether.

BLACK RASPBERRY FREEZER JAM

Makes 625g (1¹/₄ lb)

Freezer jams are a simple, no-fuss way to make all sorts of fruit spreads with a fraction of the time and sugar. Fresh-tasting and super low-calorie, these jams rely on icy temperatures rather than sky-high sugar contents to preserve them.

CRUSH 500g (1lb) black raspberries in a large mixing bowl with the back of a fork to create a chunky pulp. Add the grated rind and juice of half a lemon.

SPRINKLE 1 tablespoon agar flakes (available from health-food shops or in the baking section of supermarkets) over 400ml (²/₃ pint) cold water in a small saucepan and give it a quick swirl. Without stirring, put the pan on the heat and bring it slowly to a simmer until all the agar has dissolved.

STIR 100g (4oz) sugar into the agar mix and simmer lightly for a further 5 minutes until the sugar is fully dissolved.

POUR the hot agar syrup over the crushed fruit and stir well to combine. Then spoon into small freezer-proof plastic containers and leave to cool.

CHILL in the fridge overnight for the mix to finish setting.

This super-easy, guilt-free jam will keep in the fridge for 2 weeks or in the freezer for up to a year. Defrost the little batches as needed.

QUINCE, CHILLI & GINGER JAM

Makes 1kg (2lb)

Transforms a humble Cheddar toastie into something altogether more special.

GRATE 2 cored quinces, a thumb-sized piece of ginger and the zest of 1 lemon.

PUT the gratings and half their volume of pomegranate juice (about 500ml/17fl oz) into a saucepan. Add the juice of half the lemon and half a sliced red chilli, bring to the boil and simmer for 30 minutes, until the fruit has softened.

STIR in 500g (1lb) sugar and let the mixture simmer on a medium heat for a further 60 minutes, until it turns pink and starts to thicken.

Want guaranteed crimson jam? Cheat! The magical transformation that happens as raw yellow quince simmers down to a rich red is dependent on the amount of tannins in the fruit. This can vary between batches, so add pomegranate juice for crimson every time.

BOTANICAL BOOZE CUPBOARD

Alcohol is by far the best solvent with which to extract and concentrate the aromatic flavour chemicals deep within your harvest, with its potent antimicrobial properties also giving it the amazing ability to preserve this for years to come. Its silly-behaviour side effects are just a pleasant bonus! Here's my guide to making home-grown tipples from the contents of your beds and borders.

PEAR IN A BOTTLE

How on earth did you do that?! Hands down the easiest way to win snob food points at your next dinner party. See how to make it on pages 106–107.

SPICED SAFFRON RUM   Makes 350ml (12fl oz)

Harnessing saffron's mood-enhancing, mildly psychoactive chemicals, this concoction is guaranteed to make the most giggle-inducing martini known to man. Pour 350ml (12fl oz) white rum into a jar with 1 teaspoon saffron, 4 cloves, half a cinnamon stick, 1 vanilla pod and 2 cardamom pods, then leave in a cool, dark place for one month. Strain through a sieve and you are ready to get mixing. The strained mix will, however, noticeably improve in flavour if you store it for an extra 2–3 months. Believe me, it's worth the wait!

FRAGOLA
Makes 600ml (1 pint)

A traditional Italian liqueur that captures the intense aromatics of wild strawberries and deploys them to devastating effect. To get started just pop 200g (7oz) wild strawberries in a bottle and cover with 300ml (½ pint) vodka and 200ml (7fl oz) sugar syrup. Leave to age for at least 3 months in a cool, dark place. Perfect for bringing the flavour of summer into the depths of winter.

MARASCHINO CHERRIES

No, these aren't the ghastly, chemically dyed fruit of '80s children's parties, but my take on the original booze-soaked Marasca cherries (*Prunus cerasus* var. *marasca*) that are still made on Croatia's Dalmatian coast. Make just as you would fragola but swap the strawbs with 'Morello' cherries.

ELECTRIC DAISY, MINT & PINEAPPLE VODKA
Makes 750ml (1¼ pints)

Being tingly, fragrant and fruity, this tipple is ideal for spiking a tropical fruit salad or giving added zip to a fiery ginger beer. To make, pop 750ml (1¼ pints) vodka, 50g (2oz) electric daisies, 3 large mint sprigs and 200g (7oz) chopped pineapple into a jar and leave to infuse for 2 weeks. Strain and pour into bottles.

DOUGLAS FIR GIN
Makes 750ml (1¼ pints)

This gin is fresh, bright and infinitely fragrant: pure extract of Christmas tree. You can drink this straight away, but it tastes better if you make it in advance and store it for three months.

750ml (1¼ pints) gin
75g (3oz) Douglas fir needles
Peel of 1 lemon

BLITZ everything in a blender.

CHILL in a sealed jar in the fridge for a week.

STRAIN through a coffee filter or cheesecloth.

BOTTLE up and pop in a sprig of spruce or fir needles.

MIXIN' IT UP

SAFFRON BUTTERED RUM

Makes 300ml (½ pint)

COMBINE 1 tablespoon brown sugar, 2 shots Spiced Saffron Rum (see page 214) and a cinnamon stick in a glass mug.

TOP with hot tea and a small slice of salted butter and serve.

'EARTH MOTHER' WHITE SANGRIA
Makes 1 litre (1³/4 pints)

POUR 300g (11oz) each sliced strawberries and white peaches into a large jug and add the juice of ½ lemon, 100ml (⅙ pint) elderflower cordial, a handful of fresh basil and 1 tablespoon finely sliced stem ginger. Leave to soak for 1 hour.

TUMBLE over loads of ice, pour over 1 bottle of white wine, give it a quick stir and serve.

O TANNENBAUM
Serves 1

SHAKE 1 shot each of Douglas Fir Gin (see page 215)and Martini Bianco together in a cocktail shaker with 1 teaspoon icing sugar, a squeeze of lemon and loads of ice.

LEAVE to stand until the shaker is frosted.

STRAIN into a martini glass with a fresh sprig of young spruce.

ROSEJITO
Serves 1

MUDDLE 2 large sprigs Moroccan mint (*Mentha spicata* var. *crispa* 'Moroccan'), 1 shot white rum, 2 tablespoons rose jam (see page 174) and half a sliced lime in a glass with loads of ice.

TOP with soda water, garnish with a rose bud and serve.

ICE, ICE BABY

Freezing is an excellent way to preserve the taste of summer right into the depths of winter. Turn your harvest into botanical icicles and you can chill your drinks without ever diluting them.

PIMPED-UP PIMM'S

Makes 4 lollies

BLITZ 1 peeled cucumber with the juice and zest of 2 limes, 100g (4oz) sugar and 250ml (²/₅ pint) flat ginger beer.

PLACE a few thin slices of Bramley apple in each of 4 ice-lolly moulds and pour the liquid over them.

FREEZE the lollies for 6 hours and pop into a traditional Pimm's and lemonade drink.

ELDERFLOWER & CUCAMELON G&T

Cucamelons are a dinky, grape-sized relative of the cucumber that look like watermelons shrunk by a ray gun. They taste just like cucumber with a bright acidity of twist of lime and can be eaten in the exact same way – plus they are far easier to grow!

DILUTE 100ml (⅙ pint) elderflower cordial with 600ml (1 pint) boiled, cooled water and pour into ice cube trays filled with sliced cucamelons, borage flowers and sprigs of Moroccan mint.

FREEZE for 6 hours and pop a few of the ice cubes into a traditional G&T.

FROSTED BERRIES

A perfect garnish or chilling stick for sparkling white wine.

THREAD summer berries onto a bamboo skewer or toothpick.

LAY on a baking sheet, leaving a gap between each skewer so they don't stick together.

FREEZE for at least 3 hours.

2 shots of Pimm's, plus slices of strawberries, orange and cucumber, topped with lemonade.

MEET THE DEALERS

The internet has opened up enormous possibilities for greedy growers, from some truly wonderful specialist UK nurseries whose wares you will never find at your local DIY superstore to uber-innovative Stateside seed suppliers who will happily post anywhere in the world. Here are my tried-and-trusted favourites.

Baker Creek Heirloom Seeds

An amazing collection of rare and unusual heirloom seeds. US-based but they deliver internationally.
www.rareseeds.com

Blackmoor Nurseries

From mini kiwis to mouthwateringly tart apples that are crimson to the core, these guys are what it is all about. Fantastic quality and knowledgeable service.
www.blackmoor.co.uk

Brogdale Collections

Home to the UK's National Collection of Fruit, including literally thousands of varieties from sour cherries to Asian pears, this charity does some truly vital work to help conserve the diversity of fruit crops. Pick any one of their thousands of varieties and get it grafted onto the rootstock of your choice. As far as I know, no-one else in the world can offer a fully customizable tree grown exactly to your order. Astounding!
www.brogdalecollections.co.uk

Johnny's Selected Seeds

A massive choice of quirky fruit, veg and flowers, many of which are otherwise not available outside North America. Hallelujah for internet shopping!
www.johnnyseeds.com

Lubera

Founded by Markus Kobelt, one of Europe's greatest hort geeks, this Swiss breeding company has to be one of the most innovative out there, churning out an ever-increasing range of unique fruit crops. They sell Europe-wide.
www.lubera.co.uk

Orange Pippin Fruit Trees

A huge choice of fruit trees, not just in terms of varieties themselves, but also how they are trained and the rootstocks they are grafted onto. Every catalogue sells doughnut peaches, but if you want 'em trained as a perfect fan instead of a twiggy sapling, this is the company to go for.
www.orangepippintrees.co.uk

Plant World Seeds

With a catalogue as thick as a telephone phone book, including literally hundreds of tomato varieties alone, basically if these guys don't sell it then no-one will.
www.plant-world-seeds.com

Pomona Fruits

One of the UK's top suppliers of fruit trees and plants, including an excellent range of strawberries. Good value, great choice. What's not to like?
www.pomonafruits.co.uk

Reads Nursery

Run by my Twitter buddy Stephen Read, who is the UK's guru on fig growing, the holder of the National Collection and an all-round nice guy. It has a choice of figs that is second to none and that's before we even start talking about apricots, plums and peaches.
www.readsnursery.co.uk

Real Seeds

One of just a handful of seed companies that actually grows all of its own seeds, including loads of exclusive varieties they've bred themselves, this Welsh indie is model for how things should be.
www.realseeds.co.uk

South Devon Chilli Farm

Two dudes that jacked in their jobs in the City to grow awesome chillies in South Devon. Fantastic choice of old-school Mexican varieties, both in seeds, plants and fruit.
www.southdevonchillifarm.co.uk

Sunnybank Vine Nursery

Some 450 grape vine varieties all in one place, probably half of which are not sold by any other company in the UK. The lovely Sarah at this National Collection knows more about vines than anyone else I know. Browse their catalogue and drool at the possibilities.
www.sunnybankvines.co.uk

Suttons Seeds

One of the oldest and largest seed and plant companies in the UK, with a range of edibles personally trialled and tested by yours truly in their massive Devon trial grounds.
www.suttons.co.uk

Trade Winds Fruit

Probably my favourite source of the truly weird and wonderful, this Californian supplier specializes in edibles from around the world. Want a wild tomato from the Galapagos islands? A corn variety once grown by Hopi Indians? They can do that.
www.tradewindsfruit.com

INDEX

aspirin and seaweed soak 34
seed composts 34
stroking seedlings 34-5
shallots
'Échalote Grise' 150, 151
'French Grey' 150
'Griselle' 150
Caramelized Shallot & Bacon
Jam 212
Persian 150, 151
Persian 'Mount Everest' 150
Persian 'Violet Beauty' 150
shepherd's purse 162, 163
shrub planting 36-7
Sium sisarum 60
skirret 60, 61
slugs 144
Smoked Chipotle Chillies 211
soil 26
liquid feeds 27
soup
Spiced Pumpkin, Tarragon &
Marshmallow Soup 90-1
sour cherries *see* cherries
Spiced Pumpkin & Carrot Jam 212
Spiced Pumpkin, Tarragon &
Marshmallow Soup 90-1
Spiced Saffron Rum 214
spices 198-201
spinach 'Amazon' 55
squashes 82
Cucurbita maxima 86, 88, 90
Cucurbita moschaya 86, 90
Cucurbita pepo 86, 89, 90
curing 90
flesh colour 89
growing 85
harvesting 89
side-stepping bitterness 82
squash flowers 158, 160, 166
summer squashes 82, 83
SuperSquash tonic spray 85
winter squashes 33, 86, 87
'Costata Romanesco' 82, 83
'Early Golden Crookneck' 82, 83
'Parador' AGM 82, 83
'Peter Pan' AGM 82, 83
'Sunburst' AGM 82, 83
'Trombomcino' 82, 83
storing produce 33, 52, 74, 144
strawberries 16, 18, 23, 33
Earth Mother White Sangria 216

enhancing flavour 96
feeding and watering 97
Fragola 215
Frosted Berries 217
growing 95-7
netting 97
organic cultivation 96
picking 96
planting 95, 97
post-harvest care 97
'Albion' 94
'Aromel' 94
'Baron Solemacher' 94
'Buddy' 94
'Cambridge Favourite' 94
'Candy Floss' 93, 94
'Elsanta' 12
'Frau Mieze Schindler' 92-4
'Gariguette' 92, 93
'Honeyoye' 92, 93
'Korona' 92
'Malwina' 94
'Manille' 92, 93
'Mara des Bois' 18, 93, 94
'Marshmello' 92
'Mignonette' 94
'Snow White' 12, 93, 94
'White Soul' 94
'White Surprise' 93, 94
sugar 10, 12, 13
fruit and vegetable varieties 14
sugar beet 77
sweet potatoes 140
carbohydrates 144
colour 142
curing 142
growing conditions 143-4
growing from slips 143, 144
harvesting and storage 144
slugs 144
'Beauregard Improved' 140,
141, 142
'Georgia Jet' 140, 141, 142
'Murasaki' 140, 141, 142
'Okinawa' 140, 141, 142
'T65' 140, 141, 142
sweetcorn 18, 62
eating 64
growing supersweet varieties 65
harvesting 64
mutant strains 64
'Earlibird' AGM 64

'Illini Extra Sweet' 62-4
'Indian Summer' AGM 64
'Mirai White' AGM 64
'Ruby Queen' 62, 63
'Sugar Baby' 62, 63
'Swift' 62
sweetness 10
Swiss chard 'Ruby Red' 55
Szechuan pepper 199, 200

T

Taraxacum officinale 162
Tasmania lanceolata 198-200
Tasmanian pepper 198-200
taste 10-11
thinning 31, 74, 105, 112, 123, 127
three-in-one tree planting 112
tomatoes 15, 16, 17, 18, 23
beefsteak tomatoes 43
cherry tomatoes 43
cooking varieties 46-7
defoliating 49
Dried San Marzano Tomatoes
with Basil 211
feeding 48, 52
glasshouses 48
grow bags 48
harvesting 52
One-Pot Tomato-Leaf Pasta 53
propagating from cuttings 51
salad varieties 44-5
salt water 49, 52
single-truss training 50, 52
sowing and growing 51
spraying 48-9
storing 52
tomato leaves 52-3
varieties available 20
watering 52
'Artisan Sunrise Bumble Bee'
42, 46
'Belriccio' 41, 47
'Clackamas Blueberry' 42, 46
'Corazon' 41, 46
'Flamingo' 40, 44
'Gardener's Delight' AGM
40, 44
'Green Envy' 42, 45
'Green Zebra' 42, 44
'Ildi' 41, 44
'Indigo Cherry Drops' 42
'Indigo Pear Drops' 42

'Indigo Rose' 42
'Orange Paruche' 42, 45
'Pink Brandywine' 41, 47
'Rosella' 40, 45
'Russian Rose' 41, 45
'San Marzano' 40, 46
'Sungold' 18, 41, 45
'Tangerine' 41, 47
'Tomaccio' 40, 46
'Yellow Pear' 41
toxins 10, 15
tree planting 36-7
Tropaeolum majus 57, 169
Truffle & Hazelnut Ciabatta 178-9
truffle, black 145
truffle, summer 176
cultivating 176-8
harvesting 178
truffle hunting 178
Tuber aestivum var. *uncinatum* 176
T. melanosporum 145
turnip tops 159, 160

U

Urtica dioica 162

V

Vaccinium darrowi 134
V. myrtillus 135
vinegars 208-9
Vodka, Electric Daisy, Mint &
Pineapple 215

W

watering 24-5
weeds, edible 162-3
wild rocket 55, 57, 162, 163
wine grapes *see* grapes
wineberries, Japanese 129, 130
winter radish 154
controlling fieriness 156
growing 156
harvesting 156
'Black Spanish Long' 155
'China Rose' 154, 155
'Mantanghong' 154, 155

Y

yucca 167

Z

Zanthoxylum sinensis 200

MEET THE GEEKS

You might see pictures of only one guy as you flip through the pages of this book, but here's the bit where I fess up to the dozens of superstars behind the scenes who have collaborated to make all of this possible.

The RHS

I would like to start by giving a huge shout out to all the uber-geeks at the RHS. Firstly, I have to mention Rae Spencer-Jones and Chris Young from their publishing team for having the foresight and vision to commission what is in many ways a little left of field for the traditional gardening text.

Of course, none of this could be done without the hort geniuses at RHS Garden Wisley. Oliver Wilkins, Mario De Pace and Matthew Pottage helped me grow the hundreds of varieties I needed to munch through and photograph for the book. Their science gurus Alistair Griffiths and Guy Barter kept me on the straight and narrow, vetting my claims and the hundreds of academic papers connecting me with the latest research.

The Growers & Foodies

With both my garden and RHS Garden Wisley filled chock-a-block, I needed to find willing victims to help me trial the rest of my crops. Alfie Jackson at Suttons Seeds really stepped up to the plate with my corn varieties, over 200 tomatoes and 150 summer squash. The ever-patient Sarah Bell at the National Collection of Vines offered up dozens of grape cultivars to test and Stephen Read at the National Collection of Figs grew some of the best I have ever tasted. Steve Waters at the South Devon Chilli Farm helped out with a mind-boggling array of chillies and Kimberly Campion at Brogdale Collections let me munch through their hundreds of cherry and plum varieties. Plant geeks are so generous, it is amazing what happens when you just ask! Miracle worker David Swain at the fancy fruit and veg sourcing company Mash Purveyors has been a godsend when scrambling for crops for photo shoots, talks and tastings.

The Publishers

These poor, long-suffering people put up with my bossy ideas and picky changes with a super-positive, can-do attitude. Yasia Williams-Leedham, Leanne Bryan, Alison Starling, Geoff Fennell and Clare Churly have been real stars, helping me to create what I hope will be a totally different take on standard gardening books that looks and feels as stupendously cool as the geeky facts it contains.

Thanks also to photographic geniuses Jason Ingram and Antony Potts who worked more than 16-hour days throughout the summer, sometimes right into the night with the exposure whacked up and mobile phones as lights to create the stunning images that are crucial to making this book work. Their professionalism and patience might just have helped me get over my phobia of having my photo taken.

The Scientists

Last but absolutely not least, this book would not have been possible without the amazing, cutting-edge research carried out by horticultural scientists all over the world. Based on a massive review of more than 2,000 academic papers, I have uploaded the highlights of some of the 'best of the best' to my website. I hope you find them useful!

www.jameswong.co.uk
@botanygeek

An Hachette UK Company
www.hachette.co.uk

First published in Great Britain in 2015 by Mitchell Beazley, an imprint of Octopus Publishing Group Ltd, Carmelite House, 50 Victoria Embankment, London EC4Y 0DZ

www.octopusbooks.co.uk

Published in association with the Royal Horticultural Society, London

Design, photography and layout copyright © Octopus Publishing Group Ltd 2015
Text copyright © James Wong 2015
Illustration copyright © Toby Leigh 2015

ISBN: 978-1-84533-936-4

A CIP record for this book is available from the British Library.

Printed and bound in China.

Publisher: Alison Starling
Senior Editor: Leanne Bryan
Copy-editor: Caroline Taggart
Art Director: Jonathan Christie
Deputy Art Director: Yasia Williams-Leedham
Designer: Geoff Fennell
Photographer: Jason Ingram
Food Stylist: Nico Ghirlando
Illustrator: Toby Leigh
Senior Production Manager: Katherine Hockley

RHS Publisher: Rae Spencer-Jones
RHS Consultant Editor: Simon Maughan

The Royal Horticultural Society is the UK's leading gardening charity dedicated to advancing horticulture and promoting good gardening. Its charitable work includes providing expert advice and information, training the next generation of gardeners, creating hands-on opportunities for children to grow plants, and conducting research into plants, pests and environmental issues affecting gardeners. For more information, visit: www.rhs.org.uk or call 0845 130 4646.

NOTE When making jams, chutneys, pickles, preserves and alcoholic drinks, it is crucial to sterilize all jars, screw-top lids and bottles after washing and just before filling. Rinse them well with hot water to remove any soapy residues, drain and then stand in a roasting tin. Warm in a preheated oven set to 160°C (325°F), Gas Mark 3, for 10 minutes. Alternatively, wash in a dishwasher and use as soon as the programme has finished while still warm, but make sure they are perfectly dry before filling.

JAMES WONG

James Wong is a Kew-trained botanist, writer and broadcaster based in London. Graduating with a master of science degree in Ethnobotany in 2006, he has pursued his key research interests of under-utilised crop species and traditional food systems through field work in rural Ecuador, Java and southern China.

He is the author of the best-selling books *Grow Your Own Drugs* and *Homegrown Revolution* as well as a presenter of programmes including BBC2's award-winning *Grow Your Own Drugs* and *Countryfile* and Radio 4's *Gardeners' Question Time*.

Becoming an RHS Ambassador in 2014, James is passionate about communicating plant science to new audiences in relevant and accessible ways. With his obsession for food almost eclipsing his love of plants, James's small London garden serves as a testing station for all manner of crops and horticultural ideas from around the world.

THE RHS

The Royal Horticultural Society (RHS) is the UK's largest gardening charity, dedicated to advancing horticulture and promoting good gardening. Its charitable work includes providing expert advice and information, training the next generation of gardeners and promoting the ecological, aesthetic and psychological benefits of gardening in an urban environment.